FINE HAITIAN CUISINE

Mona Cassion Ménager

Fine Haitian Cuisine
Author: Mona Cassion Ménager
Page layout and cover design : Peterson Joseph

For information, please contact
Educa Vision Inc.,
2725 NW 19th Street,
Pompano Beach, FL 33069
Telephone: 954 725-0701.
E-mail: educa@aol.com.
web: www.educavision.com

DEDICATION

To my mother Herta Lubin-Cassion, who taught me everything I know about cooking.

To my children Jean Bernard, Rachel, and David to whom I wanted to hand down a slice of Haitian culture when I started this project.

To the Haitian People who, over the centuries, have developed such a wonderful cuisine.

THANKS

To my mother Herta Lubin-Cassion, who helped me assiduously in my research.

To my husband Henri, my children Jean Bernard, Rachel, and David, my brothers and sisters, Henry Cassion, Léon Cassion, Michelle C. M'Bida, and Rachel C. Alerte for their constructive criticism, and their unfailing support which gave me the strength to complete my project.

To my publisher Féquière Vilsaint and his staff at Educa Vision for their patience and understanding.

To Carol Hollander for her tremendous work of editing.

Special thanks to my children for their poems, drawings, and illustrations that add a unique touch to *Fine Haitian Cuisine.*

To all my friends for their words of support and encouragement.

To Peterson Joseph, graphic designer at Educa Vision, for his hard work and patience while working with me on the second edition of Fine Haitian Cuisine.

Table of Contents

INTRODUCTION

Fine Haitian Cooking is an effort to preserve and share a great tradition of fine cooking which has evolved over more than five centuries in the picturesque country of Haiti. Haitian cuisine is mostly the product of tightly intertwined African, French, and Native Indian cooking traditions, taking advantage of all the richness of the Caribbean fauna and flora to the fullest. Haitian cuisine is highly praised by many Creole cuisine connoisseurs. However, most of the recipes are still transmitted orally, and few cookbooks have been published so far. It is my great honor to contribute to the preservation of this fabulous, tradition-rich, and exotic cuisine with this book.

Fine Haitian Cooking contains something for each occasion and each taste. It is designed to provide the reader with one of the best cooking experiences and a greater appreciation of Caribbean delicacies.

In this book, you will find a selection of the most delicious and mouth-watering Haitian recipes, more than thirty traditional menus, a comprehensive glossary, and, in addition to its very detailed table of contents, an index which will help locate the variations of certain recipes and other perks. It is worth a try. I guarantee it!

Mona Cassion Ménager

Haitian Beach

BACKGROUND ON HAITI

The Haitian flag

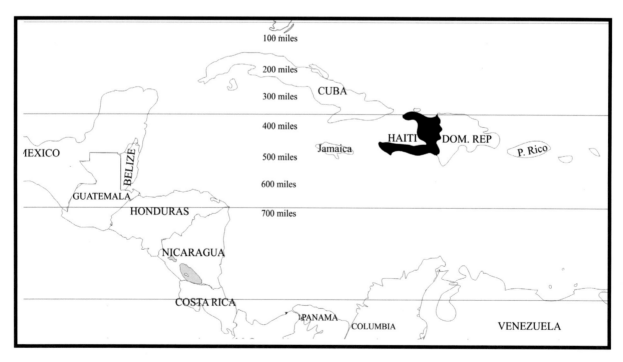

Map of the Caribbean Basin

The Republic of Haiti shares with the Dominican Republic the Island of Hispaniola located in the Caribbean Sea, between Cuba and Puerto-Rico. It is a mountainous country with an area of 27,550 square kilometers, and its population is estimated at 7, 500,000 inhabitants. It is a tropical country with an average temperature of 80 degrees Fahrenheit. The capital of Haiti is Port-au-Prince and its official languages are French and Creole.

A former French colony, Haiti was the first Caribbean state to declare its independence. It was also briefly occupied by Spain. For a short period of time also, Great Britain was politically involved in Haiti.

Haiti was populated by peaceful Arawak tribes when Christopher Colombus, sent by Spain in search of Asia, reached in 1492 what Europeans later called "The New World," opening the way for Spanish soldiers, colonists, and missionaries. The indigenous population, named Indian by Colombus who thought he had reached India, was quickly decimated by hard labor imposed by the Spanish and by diseases imported from the East. By the early 1500s, the remaining Indian population was insignificant. The first group of Africans was brought to Hispaniola in 1520, and was intended for forced labor, filling the gap left by the decimated Indian population.

After an early Spanish colony, in the north of Hispaniola, was destroyed by the natives, the Spanish established their settlement in the eastern part of the island. French pirates progressively overran the west neglected by Spain. In 1697, with the Peace of Ryswick, Spain gave up to France the occidental third of the island which was subsequently named Saint-Domingue. About 500,000 slaves provided labor for the plantations. Saint-Domingue shortly became France's richest colony in the Western Hemisphere, thus its surname *La Perle des Antilles*, which means *The Pearl of the Antilles*.

In 1791, the slaves rebelled against France. It was the beginning of a war that would last more than a decade. By 1794, the slaves led by Toussaint Louverture freed Saint-Domingue of its French and British presence. A few years later, Toussaint was captured and incarcerated in France. On January 1, 1804, led by Jean-Jacques Dessalines, the slaves declared the independence of Saint-Domingue and reinstated its Indian name of Haiti. A nation was born.

With the interaction of different cultures in this fertile land endowed with a rich exotic fauna and flora was also born a new way of cooking that takes different cuisines into account. So Haitian cuisine developed, exploiting to the fullest the edible goods abundantly available on the island.

A HAITIAN FOLKTALE

TEZEN IN THE WATER

TEZEN LAN DLO
LA LEGENDE DE TEZIN

Tim-Tim! Bwa!

Once upon a time, in a small village nestled in the woods, lived a sweet and beautiful young girl, named Noemi. She lived in a cozy hut with her father, her mother, and her young brother, Ti-Frè. Life was serene and pleasant as the children were growing up. Mother was the one taking care of the family and the house, and sometimes Noemi would help her. That was a way for the young girl to learn how to be a good wife and a good mother later. Father was the one taking care of their vegetable garden, and sometimes Ti-Frè would help him. They had a few neighbors with whom they maintained excellent relationships. Life was beautiful.

In those days there was no running water. So everybody in the village had to fetch water from a small river nearby. People were used to the fact. However, there was a hitch; the water was always unpleasantly muddy and everyone had to decant it before using it. They had no other choice, since there was no other source of water several miles around.

Noemi grew up to be a beautiful young lady, and with that came the time when she could go to the river by herself. Everyone in the family was surprised to see how crystalline was the water she brought home. Her mother noticed also that she spent a lot more time than needed to come back from the river. But she did not think much of it. Nobody knew Noemi was the good friend of a fish living in the river. This fish had taught her a beautiful song she had to sing before taking the water in her container. There was one condition: no one else should know that song.

One day, dying of curiosity, her brother sneaked behind her on her way to the river. To Ti-Frè's surprise, when she arrived at the river bank, she sang a melodious song.

"Tezen, Tezen, bon zanmi mwen, Tezen lan dlo, bon zanmi mwen Tezen, O Zen!"

Tezen, Tezen, my good friend, Tezen in the water, my good friend Tezen, O Zen!

Immediately, Tezen came out. They talked, and talked, and talked for a very long time. Then Noemi dipped her container in the water to fill it up. The water was as clear as crystal. Then she left.

"Thank you, Tezen, my good friend. See you tomorrow," she said.

Ti-Frè was astonished. He memorized the song on his way back home. As soon as he got home, he reported what he had seen to his mother. Later, when Father returned from the garden, Mother discussed the matter with him. Both concluded that the fish was surely what they believed to be the supernatural guardian of the river, a *loa*. They were scared for Noemi's life. So they decided to take matters into their own hands. The next day, they sent the young lady to the market to sell vegetables harvested from their garden. There were so many vegetables that Noemi had   to take a mule to transport them. On her way to the market, Noemi went to the river to visit with   Tezen. She sang and Tezen came up. The fish was sad.

"What is the matter? Why are you so sad? Talk to me, my good friend", Noemi asked.

The fish became sadder and said: "Take this white handkerchief with you. When the sun is high in the sky, inspect it. If you see a red spot, that means bad news, and our present talk will be our last one at this shore. Don't be sad, we will see each other again."

Noemi started crying. Tezen consoled her. They talked for a very long time, then Noemi rode to the market as she was told to do.

Meanwhile, Mother, Father, and Ti-Frè rushed to the river. Each of them sang but it was the young voice of Ti-Frè, very similar to Noemi's, that succeeded in attracting Tezen out. Without wasting time, Father scooped the fish out of the water with a large wicker basket. Then they rushed back home. As soon as they got there, they cooked the fish, ate, left some for Noemi, then   went to the garden.

When the sun was high in the sky, and Noemi looked in her handkerchief. There was a small bright red spot on the fabric. Immediately she threw the harness on her mule, and hurried   back home as fast as she could, even though she still had lots of vegetables to sell. When she reached the river, she desperately sang, and sang, and sang:

"Tezen, Tezen, bon zanmi maven, Tezen lan dlo, bon zanmi maven Tezen, O Zen!"

She was in tears. Tezen did not come up. Instead, the water bubbled and became bright red. She lay on the ground by the river, singing and weeping. She was very worried. Finally she went home, dragging her feet sadly. Everybody was still working in the vegetable garden. She found the dish of fish left for her, confirming her apprehensions. She went behind the hut and sat in a little chair. There, she sang and wept a river of tears that moistened the ground. The little chair progressively sank into the mud as she was singing and weeping.

Ti-Frè was coming from the garden when he saw his sister neck deep into the ground. "Noemi!" he cried.

Noemi did not even glance at him. She was still singing and weeping sadly.

"Tezen, Tezen, bon zanmi maven, Tezen lan dlo, bon zanmi maven Tezen, O Zen!"

By the time Ti-Frè got his parents from the garden, only one braid of her hair was visible. Father pulled on it as hard as he could, but without success. Noemi disappeared completely. Everyone believed that she went into the river to live with Tezen.

Legend says that when the moon is full and the night clear, if you go by the river and listen carefully in the peaceful silence, you can hear the beautiful voice of Noemi singing for Tezen, and you can even see them swimming and frolicking in the clear water of the river.

INTRODUCTION TO HAITIAN COOKING

Chicken in Creole Sauce

Haitian cuisine is Creole and is derived mostly from African and French cuisines, with a dash of Native Indian and Spanish influence. In Creole cooking, food is cooked with a respectable amount of spices and herbs among which tomato, onion, and pepper are customary. Our cuisine includes a few hot dishes but it is not always hot. Very often, the hotness of a dish is left to the cook's discretion and the preference of the table companions. Garlic, onion, shallots, pepper, chives, leeks, cloves, parsley, tomato or tomato paste, thyme, habanero chile, bitter orange, lime, and vinegar are what one would call "must-have" in order to achieve the taste of Haitian cooking. These condiments are found in every open-air market in our country, and fortunately the vast majority of them are available worldwide. Besides that, there are some other imported spices and dried herbs founds in the spice section of supermarkets in Haiti like ground paprika, ground cayenne pepper, cumin, chili powder, chicken bouillon cubes, coriander, oregano, bay leaves, to name a few. Among these chicken bouillon cubes, which are made of dehydrated chicken broth, have literally invaded Haitian groceries and open-air markets. Chicken bouillon cubes are used practically every day in Haitian cooking.

In this book, I use condiments used in the traditional Haitian cooking, except for very few recipes in which I add very little ground paprika and very little ground cayenne pepper. Paprika and cayenne blend nicely with other spices and herbs, and belong in fact to the pepper family which is a constant condiment in Haitian cuisine.

In the traditional Haitian kitchen, you will not find any measuring tool. Food is cooked by taste, sight, and common sense. Even the amount of water to cook rice is evaluated by sight.

Most of the time, when you are getting ready to cook Haitian food, be prepared to boil water. Fortunately, with the help of technology, boiled water is one of the quickest and easiest things "to cook." Many Haitian meat recipes require boiled water, and generally meat intended for braising or stewing is rubbed with bitter orange pulp or lime pulp, then rinsed (not soaked) quickly and carefully with very hot water. In this book, many rice recipes include boiling water as well. My mother always says that, in Haitian cooking, only rice can withstand unboiled water and only when it is being reheated. I absolutely agree with her.

Here is a note about our common way of braising meat and a way to simplify it. Not every cut is suitable for braising but when it is, the meat (beef, pork, goat, lamb, conch) is usually marinated, then sautéed over medium high to high heat. As it browns and as the meat juices evaporates, the marinade diluted with a small amount of boiled water is gradually added, a little at a time, and allowed to evaporate while the meat is being tossed with a large spoon. This is done until the meat gradually reaches a beautiful golden color. This prevents the meat from sticking to the pan, thus avoiding scorching. After the last addition of diluted marinade has evaporated, a small amount of boiled water is added, the pan is covered, and the meat is cooked over medium to medium-low heat until the liquid evaporates. This is what we call in Haitian Creole **"sue vyann."** At this point some meat cuts are already tender. They are then removed from the pan. The sauce is prepared in the same pan. The meat is added later to the strained sauce and allowed to boil for a few more minutes during the reduction of the sauce.

Some other cuts need longer cooking to become tender; so after the "sue," more water is added, the pan is covered, and the meat is allowed to cook longer, until tender. Although still in practice in the traditional Haitian cooking, this method is time-consuming, demanding, and seems complicated. To simplify it, you may skip the whole "sue." Sauté the meat until golden, add the marinade, boiled water if needed, cover, and continue cooking as above over medium to medium-low heat. If necessary, add some more boiled water after the juices evaporate, cover, and cook longer.

Although Haiti is not a large country, its cooking presents some interesting particularities. There are dishes that are specific to the South, dishes specific to the North, . . . etc. For example, *Tonmtonm ak Kalalou Gonbo* is specific to the South, *Chicken with Cashew Nuts* is specific to the North, *Braised Greens with Pork and Crab* is specific to the Vallee de l'Artibonite. Despite that, the taste of Haitian food is very distinctive due to the choice of spices and herbs, the way they are combined in a dish, and the mode of cooking.

Among the basic utensils, the mortar and pestle, the plantain press, strong wooden spoons, good strainers, and a good food mill are tools always found in the traditional Haitian kitchen. Pots and pans in the Haitian kitchen are always heavy (thick), allowing slow cooking and preventing food from scorching; most of them are heavy lidded.

"Le mot de la fin." Keep in mind that the best quality ingredients insures the best quality food. The fresher are your ingredients, the better is your cooking.

UTENSILS USED FOR THE RECIPES INCLUDED IN THIS BOOK

Keep it as simple as possible. A few utensils marked with an asterisk are ones for which you can easily find an alternative. It is best to use heavy pans. It is not essential to have a fancy set of knives, but essential to keep them sharp at all times. Know the capacity of each one of your utensils. This will be helpful when it comes to pouring, boiling down, or a quick estimation.

A set of covered containers
A set of knives
Aluminum foil
An assortment of preserving jars
Baba molds*
Brownie pan
Cake pans (13-x 9-x 2-inch, 9- x 9- x 2-inch)
Can opener
Charcoal grill
Condiment bowl*
Cookie cutters
Double-boiler*
Electric blender
Food mill, or potato ricer, or potato masher
Food processor*
Four-sided grater
Garlic crusher
Hand electric mixer
Hinged grilling baskets
Ice cream maker
Ice pick
Ice trays (3)
Jelly-roll pan and cookie sheets
Kitchen scale
Kitchen scissors
Kitchen thread
Kitchen towels
Large forks
Large spoons (slotted and plain)
Loaf pan (9-inch x 5-inch)
Mandolin slicer (or a vegetable slicer)
Measuring cups and measuring spoons
Meat tenderizer (meat hammer)
Melon baller*
Mortar and pestle (medium and large)
Muffin pans (6 cups and 12 cups)

Pastry bags (or syringes), and nozzles
Plantain press* (see the Glossary)
Plastic bags (or zipper bags), sandwich bags
Plastic wrap
Pressure cooker *
Pudding mold*
Quiche pans and pie pans
Ramekins (6 ounces and 8 ounces)
Roasting pans
Rolling pin
Round cake pans (9 inches in diameter)
Round pans (2, 3, 4, 5, and 8 quarts)
Rubber gloves
Saucepans (2 and 3 quarts)
Scraper
Shaker or any tight-lidded glass jar
Skillets and frying pans (7, 8, 10, 12 inches)
Small, medium, and large mixing bowls
Soufflé mold
Soup pot (12 quarts)*
Spatulas (slotted and plain)
Steamer basket
Stoneware or glass baking dishes (2 to 4 quarts)
Strainers and colander
Tartlet pans
Tea kettle*
Tea strainer (can be a handy sugar sifter)
Tongs
Trays
Tube pan
Vegetable chopper*
Vegetable peeler
Wax bags
Wax paper
Wire racks
Wire whisks

USEFUL EQUIVALENTS

In this section, you will find the more common measurements used in cooking, and a few easy tools to do more conversions. Almost all equivalents listed below are rounded for your convenience.

Oven Temperatures

To convert Fahrenheit (F) to Centigrade, also called Celsius (C), use this equation: [5(F - 32)]: 9

For example, to convert 250 F to Centigrade:

[5 x (250 - 32)]: 9 = 121.11 C.

To convert Centigrade to Fahrenheit: [(C x 9): 5] + 32

For example, to convert 200 C to Fahrenheit: [(200 x 9): 5] + 32 = 392 F~400 F.

When necessary, the result is rounded (121.11 ~ 120, 392 ~ 400). Following is a list of common equivalents.

225 F = 110 C

250 F = 120 C

300 F = 150 C

325 F = 160 C

350 F = 180 C

375 F = 190 C

400 F = 200 C

425 F = 220 C

450 F = 230 C

500 F = 260 C

Volume conversions: 1 fl oz = 30 ml.

To convert fluid ounces to milliliters, use this equation: fluid ounces x 30 = milliliters.

1 teaspoon (tsp.) = 5 milliliters (ml)

2 tsp. = 10 ml

3 tsp. = 1 Tablespoon (Tbsp.) = 15 ml

1/4 cup = 2 fluid ounces (fl oz) = 60 ml

1/3 cup = 75 ml

1/2 cup = 8 Tbsp. = 4 fl oz = 125 ml

2/3 cup = 5 fl oz =150 ml

3/4 cup = 6 fl oz = 175 ml

1 cup = 16 Tbsp. = 8 fl oz = 225 ml

1 quart (qt) = 32 fl oz = 950 ml

Weight Conversions: 1 oz = 30 g.

To convert ounces to grams, use this equation: ounces x 30 = grams.

1/2 ounce (oz) = 15 grams (g)

3/4 oz = 20 g

1 oz = 30 g

2 oz = 55 g

4 oz = 115 g

8 oz = 1/2 pound (lb) = 225 g

12 oz = 3/4 lb = 340 g

16 oz = 1 lb = 450 g

32 oz = 2 lb = 900 g

35 oz = 2.2 lb = 1000 g =1 kilogram (kg)

Specific Weight Conversions

1 cup butter (2 sticks) = 226 g = 8 oz

1 cup powdered sugar = 150 g = 5 oz

1 cup sifted granulated sugar = 225 g = 8 oz

1 cup uncooked rice = 200 g = 7 oz

1 cup uncooked penne rigate = 100 g = 3 oz

1 cup sifted all-purpose flour = 150 g = 5 oz

3 1/2 cups sifted flour = 454 g = 16 oz = 1 lb

1 cup cake flour = 125 g = 4.5 oz

1 cup uncooked dry beans = 200 g = 7 oz

1 cup uncooked cornmeal = 175 g = 6 oz

Linear Conversions: 1 in = 2.5 cm

To convert inches to centimeters, use this equation: inches x 2.5 = centimeters.

1/8 inch (in) = 3 millimeters (mm)

1 /4 in = 6 mm

1/2 in = 1.25 centimeters (cm)

3/4 in = 2 cm

1 in = 2.5 cm

2 in = 5 cm

3 in = 7.5 cm

4 in = 10 cm

THE COOK'S TECHNIQUES
TEKNIK KIZIN
TECHNIQUES DE CUISINE

Malanga, Habanero Chile, and Plantain

HOW TO HANDLE LOBSTER

In Haiti, not only lobster and seafood in general are available in fish markets and supermarkets but interestingly you can also buy very fresh lobster (alive), fresh shelled conch, and fresh fish directly along a few seashores; the "Cote des Arcadins" is one of those places. The fisherman will willingly scale the fish for you and, if you are lucky enough, he will boil the lobster for you in a pot of boiling sea water for a few minutes if you ask. I have done it on my way back from the beach, and I can assure you that sea water is the best when it comes to boiling lobster.

There is more than one way to handle live lobsters. You can boil, steam, or cut them. To boil a lobster, plunge it in a large pot of boiling water, with the head first. Bring to a boil for 1 minute or so. Then drain, and cut as indicated below. In steaming, the lobster does not come directly in contact with the water, and it takes a little longer than boiling.

To cut lobster, hold it down on a cutting board, and insert quickly a sharp knife at the junction of the chest and tail. This will sever the spinal cord and kill the lobster instantly. Then use one of the following methods which can be used for a steamed and a boiled lobster as well. Collect any juice that comes from the lobster. This will be used later with the tomalley (liver) to flavor the sauce.

Twist the claws (if any)* and the legs off. Cut lobster tail and chest lengthwise in two halves with sharp kitchen shears. Remove and discard intestine and stomach, then detach tail halves from the chest, or continue to cut through the head to make 2 lobster halves. Remove and reserve the tomalley (liver). Crack claws and legs open to remove the meat. At this point how you proceed depends on the recipe chosen.

You may also twist the lobster tail from its chest, and work with the two parts separately. To remove flesh from lobster tails without cutting the tails in half, you can boil, steam or use the following method which allows you to have raw lobster meat right out of the shell. Twist off the tail fan situated at the end, then use kitchen shears to cut the ventral part of the shell on both sides where it is attached to the dorsal part of the shell. You must be cautious when handling the spikes at the side of the shell. Carefully slide a blunt knife between the flesh and the dorsal part of the shell. Move the knife from side to side, then push the flesh out. With a sharp paring knife, make a small incision lengthwise in the middle of the back of the tail to remove the intestine.

A quick note about shrimp

To devein shrimp, peel off the shell. Hold shrimp with its back facing you. Slide the tip of a sharp paring knife lengthwise along the black vein on the back to make a shallow slit. Then carefully remove and discard the vein.

*Spiny Lobster, also known as Caribbean lobster and rock lobster, is the only lobster available in Haiti. It is called *oma* in Haitian Creole, and *langouste* in French. Spiny lobster has no claws. Additional information about lobster is provided in the glossary.

CLEANING FISH

Here are some useful definitions:

A drawn fish is a fish that has been eviscerated. That means its entrails and sometimes its gills have been removed.

A dressed fish is a fish that has had its scales removed in addition to being eviscerated. Whole dressed fish generally refers to the whole fish that has been dressed.

Pan-dressed fish generally refers to a dressed fish that has had its head, fins, and tail removed. In Haiti, fish is always sold with its head on, unless it is sliced.

Usually, dressed fish is available in the freezers of fish markets and groceries. Even in this case, I would suggest you review it, particularly the head and the areas under the fins. Sometimes, fish is displayed drawn only. You can ask the fishmonger to remove the scales for you, or you can do it by yourself. Here is an easy way to do it without splashing scales all over your kitchen. Place the whole fish in a plugged sink, then fill it with fresh water to cover fish by 4 to 5 inches. Cut six Persian limes (or 10 to 12 key limes) lengthwise in three portions each. Squeeze their juice into the water. Lift the jaws to remove the gills with a sharp knife, if remaining. Discard the gills. Keeping fish submerged in the water at all times, use a dull knife to quickly remove the scales on the fish skin by scraping from tail to head, lifting and loosening scales as you go. Scales will come off easily and will stay in the water. There are not many scales on the head, but be sure to scrape scales there as well. Cut off the fins and the tail. Finally, rub fish in and out with lime pulp. Rinse under fresh running water. Pat dry. Fish is now ready to be seasoned. A fish scaler is a good tool to scale fish.

DEMYSTIFYING HABANERO CHILE

The majority of Haitian savory recipes include habanero chile mostly for the distinctive taste it gives to the dishes but sometimes also for its fieriness. This chile is among the hottest members of the pepper family which belongs to the *chinense* species which in turn belong to the capsicum genus. The agent responsible for the heat in chile peppers is an alkaloid called *capsaicin*. Its concentration varies depending on the variety of chile. The *capsaicin* is contained in the seeds and the membranes. Generally, the smaller the chile, the hotter it is.

Although habanero chile is easily found in many groceries and supermarkets, many home cooks, unacquainted with such an exotic and hot spice, are reluctant to use it in their cooking. However, once one knows how to handle it, it becomes a true pleasure to cook with this condiment which infuses foods with a unique fruity flavor. Although we do not use them to make desserts in Haitian cooking, there are many sweet dishes made with chiles (Chile Cheese Cake, Chile Sherbet, . . . etc.). To me, this represents the ultimate use of chiles in cooking. There are many books written about chiles. Among them, *The Chile Pepper Encyclopedia*, written by Dave De Witt, offers a very interesting and colorful overview of chiles around the world.

To use habanero chile, wash and put the fruit whole, with its stem attached, in the food being cooked. In this way, the food will have the taste of the chile without its hotness. Since the seeds and the membranes are the hottest parts of the chile, make sure the fruit does not split into the dish, which happens very unfrequently. However if accidentally that happens, remove it immediately. A too hot dish is barely eatable. If cooking for children, you may leave the chile out if you do not feel comfortable. On the other hand, if you wish to release some of its hotness into a dish, poke the chile just moments before removing it, and press it gently with the back of a spoon to bring out some juice, then mix. Milk controls the effect of hot chiles quite well, not water as one would think. It works instantly. Even just one gulp of milk, or a spoonful of ice cream, is effective.

In this book, recipes ask you to cut, seed, and wash habanero chile. Very often we mash habanero chile instead of using it whole. Mashed chile is excellent in marinade. Be aware that the vapor released by the cut chile is strong. To handle such a hot spice, wear rubber gloves, cut the chile lengthwise, remove and discard seeds and membranes, then rub gently under fresh running water for about 15 seconds, or a little longer if you wish. Mash it in a mortar or mince it. Then use soap and water to wash thoroughly the knife, the board, and any other utensils that have been in contact with the chile to avoid transferring the capsaicin to other surfaces, thus avoiding accidental transfer to the eyes. While you are still wearing them, also wash the gloves as if you were washing your hands, or discard them if using disposable rubber gloves. Avoid contact with eyes by all means. If accidentally that happens, flush eyes with fresh running water for a long time. The pain will be intense, but fortunately it will subside very shortly.

In light of what I said above, you may cut, wash, and mince habanero chile for every recipe containing this spice if you wish. Minced chile will release more flavor, as do many other spices when cut. You must be certain that the chile is washed sufficiently to avoid having too hot a dish. Nevertheless, you should refrain from washing it to such a degree that the flavor is washed out.

COOKING WITH TOMATO PASTE

Tomato paste has a very distinctive taste that can overwhelm even the strongest spice. This problem can be efficaciously dealt with by boiling and frying the paste alone or with a spice that may also need to be diluted, such as garlic.

Tomato paste is mixed with water, then boiled with a small amount of oil. When the water evaporates, the paste is then stir-fried for a couple of minutes or so. This makes all the difference. When this is not done, the flavor of tomato paste is strong and can be very unpleasant.

Use the chart below as a guide.

Tomato Paste	Oil	Water
1 tablespoon	1 tablespoon	1 cup
2 tablespoons	1 1/2 to 2 tablespoons	1 cup
3 tablespoons	2 tablespoons	1 cup

Mix tomato paste with the water. Heat oil in a heavy 3-quart pan over medium high setting. Add diluted tomato paste, and boil until water evaporates completely, about 15 to 20 minutes. At this point, tomato paste should be separated from the oil. Reduce heat to medium and stir-fry for 1 to 2 minutes. Then proceed following the recipe chosen.

A Note about storing tomato paste

It can be very annoying to find moldy tomato paste in your refrigerator right when you need to use it. Even stored in the refrigerator, tomato paste gets moldy very rapidly after the can has been opened. Fortunately, there are ways to avoid that.

Once the can is opened, carefully transfer the tomato paste to a tightly covered container (preferably a glass container), making sure that the paste comes in contact with the container only at the bottom and the sides. Cover it with one to two inches of vegetable oil, and store it in the refrigerator. This will prevent the formation of mold. As you use the tomato paste, be sure enough oil remains to cover the paste; add more oil if necessary. Use within two weeks.

Tomato paste may also be preserved by freezing. Transfer the tomato paste to a covered container, and put it in the freezer. This is an excellent way to preserve tomato paste once the can has been opened. The only hitch is that you have to remember to thaw the frozen tomato paste for a short while at room temperature, or in the refrigerator overnight, when you are planning to use it. Once you have used it, remember to put the remaining paste in the freezer. A friend of mine used to freeze it by portions. When frozen, tomato paste will keep indefinitely.

DEALING WITH PLANTAIN, BREADFRUIT, AND ROOTS

To peel green **plantain**, cut and discard about 1 inch at both ends. Once the ends are cut off, it is easy to know how thick the skin is, thus how deep you can cut through the skin. Make a slit through the skin along one of its ridges. Starting at the slit, lift the skin with the tip of a blunt knife, then slide your thumb under the skin and push until completely peeled, helping with the knife whenever necessary. Skin will most likely come off in pieces. Rub peeled plantain with pulp of bitter orange, lemon, or lime, then rinse under fresh running water. To avoid discoloration, place it in a large bowl of water mixed with bitter orange juice, lemon juice, or lime juice until ready to use. Sweet plantain peels more easily and in one piece. Although a fruit, green plantain is eaten as a vegetable.

Brush **breadfruit** under fresh running water. Cut the fruit lengthwise into eight wedges with a strong knife. Start by cutting the fruit in half, then each half in two halves, and so on. Peel and core each piece. The tiny seeds will come off with the core. Rub peeled breadfruit with the pulp of bitter orange, lemon, or lime, then rinse under fresh running water. To avoid discoloration, place it in a large bowl of water mixed with bitter orange juice, lemon juice, or lime juice until ready to use.

To use roots (**cassava, malanga, name root, and taro root**) brush them carefully under fresh running water, then peel, and discard the skin. Rub peeled roots with pulp of bitter orange, lemon, or lime, then rinse under fresh running water. To avoid discoloration, place them in a large bowl of water mixed with bitter orange juice, lemon juice, or lime juice until ready to use. Additional information is provided in the Glossary.

ABOUT COCONUT

A thick, dry, and very fibrous husk has already been removed from the coconut on store shelves where it has a very hard, hairy, dark brown, and oblong shell. When bought, you may store it in the refrigerator for a few days, or you may crack it at once to be sure of its freshness. I recommend the latter since there is no apparent sign indicating that the coconut has gone bad before it is opened. Once the coconut is cracked, remove the flesh from the shell. The brown and thin layer that tightly coats the coconut flesh should not come off with the shell. If that happens, it means invariably that the coconut had gone bad, will taste rancid, and should be discarded. Coconut flesh can be stored in the freezer for a very long time only when intended for coconut milk. I suggest buying the coconut the day before it is to be used, and it is best to use the coconut flesh shortly after it has been taken out of the shell. Coconut flesh can be stored in the refrigerator for one to two days. After that, it starts becoming moldy.

To use coconut, brush vigorously the "coconut eyes" area, located at one of the ends, with soapy water and rinse thoroughly with fresh water. Pat dry. Poke two holes through the "eyes" with an icepick, and strain the sweet coconut water into a glass. To open, crack the shell on a hard surface, or hit with a heavy tool (like a hammer). You will have to break the coconut into pieces in order to take out its flesh. Slide a strong blunt knife between the hard shell and the flesh, and push to detach the flesh from the shell. You may then use the coconut for grated coconut, coconut flakes, coconut slices, or fresh coconut milk. After draining the coconut water, another way to ease the flesh out of the shell is to bake coconut in an oven preheated to 400 degrees Fahrenheit for 15 to 16 minutes, then carefully crack the coconut open to remove the flesh.

Coconuts can be used at different levels of maturation:

There is the very ripe coconut that is common in groceries and supermarkets (described above). It is prefect for grating, flaking, slicing, and making coconut milk.

There are different stages of young coconuts. They are used at different stages of maturation of the young fruit. They are all called **kok ole** or **kokoye ole** in Haitian Creole. The youngest coconut has not yet formed its flesh. It is filled only with coconut water. There is a young coconut whith delicious jelly-like flesh that can be eaten right out of the shell with a spoon. There is also a young coconut which has flexible flesh tightly coated with a thin yellowish beige layer. It is preferably puréed with a liquid in a blender. It has little or no residue. It is used mostly to make desserts and drinks (*Coconut Ice Cream* for example).

All coconuts are filled with a sweet, delicious, and refreshing water that decreases and gets sweeter as the fruits mature on the tree. It is essential that coconut is fresh; otherwise, it will ruin your cooking.

To make 1 cup of **fresh coconut milk**, put 1 cup of finely chopped fresh coconut in a blender with 1 cup of hot water. Process on high speed for 2 minutes. Coconut will look as if it had been grated. Press coconut through a fine strainer to collect the milk. Strain coconut milk again.

You can also grate coconut with a fine grater. Then mix in 1 cup of hot water, and strain coconut as above. For some recipes, you have to cool down the coconut milk completely before using.

You may blend the residue with 1 to 2 cups of hot water to obtain a diluted coconut milk that can be used to replace water in some recipes that ask for coconut milk and water. For example, when cooking *Basic Cornmeal Recipe*, you may replace some of the water with diluted coconut milk.

Additional information is provided in the Glossary.

HOW TO SOAK SALT COD AND SMOKED RED HERRING

Salt cod and smoked red herring must be soaked before they can be used. Soaking will soften the fish flesh and remove most of the salt. Here is a way to do it.

If a large piece of salt cod filet is being prepared, cut it into smaller pieces. For example one pound of salt cod can be cut into 8 pieces, and even smaller pieces depending on use. It is not necessary to cut herring filets before soaking. Whole salt fish, which we treat differently from salt cod, must be soaked whole. Homemade salt cod need less time to soak.

Place salt cod or herring in a large pot of hot boiled water for 10 to 12 hours, changing hot water at least three times (approximately every 2 to 3 hours). Check for saltiness after 8 hours of soaking by tasting a small piece of fish taken from the thicker part. Repeat the process if necessary. Then gently squeeze the fish between sheets of paper towels to remove the excess water. Salt cod or herring is then ready to be prepared according to the chosen recipe.

If you are using the whole smoked herring, you need to remove its skin, head, and as many bones as possible. This is quite easy to do. Pour a lot of boiling water on the herring. Let it soak for 3 minutes, then peel off the skin which should come off easily. Remove and discard the head. Split the fish in half by lifting one side with a spatula. Remove and discard the bones. Soak as above.

SPECIAL CONDIMENTS

Asezonnman Espesyal
Assaisonements Spéciaux

Homemade Salt Cod

Flavored Vinegar and Pickle

Pikliz
Vinaigre Aromatisé et Conserve au Vinaigre

Pikliz is a flavorful condiment made of spices and vegetables marinated in vinegar. Habanero chile represents the key ingredient. There is simply no Pikliz without habanero chile. It can be made with any ordinary vinegar, but I do not recommend using balsamic vinegars as they are already strongly flavored, and constitute a line of special condiments themselves.

A hot condiment, Pikliz must be used with caution. Add it to meat marinade, or use it as a condiment served on the table, or use it in your chicken sandwiches, beef sandwiches, or ham and cheese sandwiches to which it will bring interest. It improves as it ages, and to some degree, vinegar and other spices and vegetables can be added as it is being used. A freshly made Pikliz is always served with *Griyo* in addition to *Sauce Ti Malice*. Learn how to handle habanero chiles in *The Cook's Techniques* chapter.

7 habanero chiles, unseeded, and cut crosswise into about 1/4-inch slices
1/4 cup fresh green beans, trimmed*
3/4 cup thinly sliced white onion
1/4 cup finely sliced red bell pepper
1/2 cup finely sliced shallots
1/2 cup shredded cabbage

1/2 to 1 tablespoon coarsely crushed black peppercorns
1/4 cup thinly sliced carrots
about 2 cups white vinegar, white wine vinegar, or apple cider vinegar
a clean 4-cup glass preserving jar (any glass jar with a tight lid will do)

Layer chiles, green beans, 1/2 cup onion, bell pepper, shallots, cabbage, black peppercorns, carrots, and remaining onion in the jar. Fill the jar with vinegar. Cover, and store in the refrigerator. Allow the flavors to develop and blend for 24 hours at least before using. It keeps forever in the refrigerator.

Yields about 4 cups.

How to use Pikliz

If you use it in marinade, reduce vinegar accordingly. For example, if a recipe asks for 2 tablespoons vinegar, use 1 tablespoon vinegar and 1 tablespoon *Flavored Vinegar* instead. You are free to make your own proportions. Consider substituting *Pikliz* for part of the vinegar as often as possible in any recipe; it will add more interest to your cooking.

As a table condiment, a few drops are enough. You can also make your own proportions.

To use in sandwiches, use a fork to lift out some of the vegetables (not the peppers) to put in meat sandwiches to taste. Use it cautiously as this can be very fiery.

*Use a small paring knife to lightly trim off and discard both sides of the green beans. Snip off and discard both ends. You may substitute frozen French style green beans or regular frozen green beans for the fresh beans.

Pikliz for Griyo and Tasso

Here is the recipe for the *Pikliz* served with *Griyo*, other fried and grilled meats. Do not be duped by the appearance of this pickle. It looks exactly like a fresh coleslaw. In fact, it is the most fiery dish in Haitian cuisine. It is eaten in very small portions and always with a piece of meat. You can also use it in sandwiches, and always with caution. Wash chiles only before slicing.

One 1-pound cabbage, finely shredded
1/2 cup sliced shallots
3 habanero chiles, seeded, and sliced
(read *Demystifying Habanero Chile*)

Juice of 2 Persian limes (about 6 tablespoons)
4 tablespoons white vinegar, or apple cider
vinegar
1/2 cup white onion shavings*

Put all the ingredients in a large covered bowl, and toss to mix thoroughly. Cover tightly, and allow to blend in a cool place for at least 6 hours. Remove and discard the chile pieces and serve with grilled and fried meat. Serve avocado slices on the side. This recipe can be halved.

Serves 12 to 15.

*To make onion shavings, remove and discard the papery skin of an onion, then cut off the top. Use a sharp knife to cut very thin slices of onion crosswise. The thin slices are the shavings.

Cured Pork

Vyann Kochon Sale ak Kwann
Salaison

Used as a condiment, these pieces of cured pork are used mostly to flavor *Rice and Beans*, *Cornmeal and Beans*, *Mayi Tyaka*, and *Bean Purée*. They can be made with almost any part of the pork, but very often they are made with parts with a high fat content. Pork rib tips and pork belly are the best choices. You may remove it from the dish before serving, or choose to serve it. Do not remove it from *Mayi Tyaka*. It is part of the dish.

1/4 cup chopped white onion
3 habanero chiles, seeded, and carefully washed (Read *Demystifying Habanero Chile*)
2 garlic cloves, peeled (see note in *More Tips*)
pinch ground cloves
2 tablespoons chopped fresh flat-leaf parsley

1 tablespoon chopped chives, or 1 chopped scallion
1 sprig thyme (leaves only)
1/4 teaspoon coarsely crushed black peppercorns
1/4 cup fresh bitter orange juice, or fresh lemon juice
1 pound fresh pork rib tips, or fresh pork belly cut into about 3 x 1-inch pieces
1 cup coarse sea salt

With a blender, purée onion, chile, garlic, cloves, parsley, chives, thyme with black pepper, and orange juice. Pour the puréed herbs and spices over the pork pieces in a large bowl. Toss to coat. Cover and marinate in a cool place for 3 hours at least, or in the refrigerator overnight.

Transfer the pork and marinade into a shallow dish. Coat the pork pieces with the salt, then leave them in the shallow dish to dry completely in a well-ventilated area, about 7 to 10 days. Turn pork over every day to allow it to dry on both sides at the same pace. Then store the cured pork with the salt on the lower shelf of the refrigerator in a tightly covered container.

How to Use Cured Pork

Rinse cured pork pieces under fresh running water to remove the excess salt. You may need to reduce the salt a little bit in the dish you are making. Two pieces of cured pork are enough for one recipe of *Rice and Beans*, or one recipe of *Bean Purée*. You will need more for *Mayi Tyaka*.

When using it in *Bean Purée*, boil it with the beans until the beans are cooked. Remove it from the beans. Purée the beans, then add it to the bean purée and proceed as directed.

When using it in *Rice and Beans* and in *Cornmeal and Beans*, boil it with the beans, then also sauté it with the beans. Then proceed as directed in the recipe.

Note: In Haiti, andouille (*andui* in Haitian Creole) and andouillette (*anduiyet* in Haitian Creole) are small pieces of cured pork encased in pork tripe or in pork caul fat. They are mostly used in *Rice and Beans* and in *Mayi Tyaka*.

Homemade Salt Cod

Kijan pou Sale Mori Lakay ou
Methode Simple de Préparation de la Morue Salée

Salt cod adds another dimension to dishes every time it is used in cooking. Its taste is very pleasing and different from that of fresh cod. Once you taste it, you will know the difference, and you will come to appreciate it. In Haiti, we buy salt cod, rather than making it. If we can buy it, why bother making salt cod? Homemade salt cod is a very good alternative to store-bought salt cod, and it is fresher. Surprisingly, throughout the process, the smell is not very invasive.

1 pound fresh skinless cod filets
Scant 1/2 cup sea salt
Shallow dish or a tray
Rack

Sprinkle cod with salt. Make sure cod is well coated. Add more salt if necessary. Arrange cod in the shallow dish and let stand in the salt for 24 to 48 hours, turning occasionally. The cod will give up a lot a liquid. Then place cod on the rack, in the shallow dish, on the kitchen counter for 7 to 10 days or until it is completely dry. Turn cod over every day to allow it to dry on both sides at the same pace. Store in a zippered plastic bag in the refrigerator. It will keep for a very long time.

Learn how to soak salt cod in *The Cook's Techniques* chapter. Additional information is provided in the Glossary.

Spice and Herb Blend

Epis Melanje
Mélange d'Epices

This mixture can reduce considerably the time spent in the kitchen, allowing fresh spices and herbs to be very handy. It is also a good preserving method. Use this preparation mostly to prepare meat, and a guide is given below. You will just add thyme, parsley, and ground cloves when needed, with salt of course, and to rectify the seasoning a little bit. I add a small amount of hot sauce and soy sauce to have some liquid to start in the blender. This is not a hot mixture despite the presence of habanero chile and the addition of hot sauce.

This spice blend keeps forever in the freezer. It will not transfer odor to ice, water, or other food in the refrigerator. This yields about five cups and fills three 12-cube ice trays!

1 1/2 large white onions, chopped (about 2 1/2 cups chopped onion)
2 tablespoons hot sauce
3 tablespoons soy sauce, or Worcestershire sauce
3 tablespoons vinegar
1 large leek, finely sliced
1 1/2 red bell pepper, chopped (about 2 1/4 cups chopped bell pepper)

3 tablespoons chopped chives, or 3 scallions, chopped
14 garlic cloves, peeled (about 2/3 cup)
2 tablespoons prepared yellow mustard
14 chicken bouillon cubes
1 tablespoon ground black pepper
3 habanero chiles, seeded, and carefully washed (read *Demystifying Habanero Chile*)

Carefully wash herbs under fresh running water. Using a blender at high speed, purée part of chopped onion with hot sauce, soy sauce, and vinegar. Remove the filler-cap of the blender, and gradually add remaining herbs and spices through the feeding hole. Blend after each addition, and until smooth. Spoon mixture into three ice trays (with lids if possible). Carefully cover trays with plastic wrap and seal in zipper bags. Freeze until ready to use. Each cube contains 2 tablespoons of spice mixture.

Yields 5 cups (36 cubes).

Note. You may add 1/4 cup fresh flat-leaf parsley to the mixture if you wish.

How to use *Spice and Herb Blend*
As a guide, I recommend using 1 or 2 spice and herb cubes to marinate 2 pounds of beef, pork, or 4 pounds cut-up poultry, or to roast one 4-pound chicken. Use one cube for one pound of chicken liver. For 2 pounds of seafood, one cube should be enough. This can be adjusted to taste.

Do not use this mixture to make *Griyo, Bean Purée, Pea Purée*, or to make recipes in the *Gratins* chapter of this book. This will make delicious fried pork, but not the *Griyo* as we know it.

Tritri and Pisket

Tritri (Haitian Creole word) is a condiment used in Haitian cooking. It is an optional condiment. Tritri is made of really tiny shrimp. The tiny shrimp are thoroughly sun-dried until no trace of moisture remains. Tritri is carried by vendors in open-air markets, or by ambulatory vendors, and it is sold by a special measure. It can be stored in an airtight container at room temperature.

Tritri is not salted. It is often used to add more flavor to dishes that already contain shrimp or other seafood, like *Vegetable Stew*, *Gumbo*, some rice recipes, . . . etc.

Pisket

The Haitian Creole word *pisket*, I believe, comes from the Latin word *pisces* which means fish. Contrary to Tritri, pisket are not a condiment. Each pisket is a very small fresh fish. Available at a few seashores, they are also carried by vendors in open-air markets or by ambulatory vendors.

Before cooking, pisket are rinsed in a solution of fresh water and lime juice, drained, then coated with a highly seasoned marinade. After marinating, they are fried until crispy. They are drained on paper towels to remove the excess oil, then served with *Sauce Ti Malice*, avocado slices, crusty bread, and lime wedges.

SAUCES

Sos
Les Sauces

Sauce Ti Malice

Sauces

Meat and Sauce,

Such a complementary pair

That does not need repair.

The perfect pair!

David Menager

Creole Sauce

Sòs Vyann (Sòs Kreyòl)
Sauce Créole

Haitian meat recipes include the preparation of a sauce. Sauce is part of our everyday meal. We spoon it over meat, rice, plantain, name root, potatoes . . . etc. That tells how important it is in Haitian cuisine, and how much care is taken to make it right.

Creole Sauce is the Haitian Creole tomato sauce. The meat varies accordingly. Use only two tomatoes or 1 tablespoon tomato paste, and lime juice instead of bitter orange juice to make the sauce for poultry and sea food.

Estimated time: 1 hour.

1/4 cup vegetable oil

1/4 cup coarsely chopped meat (any ordinary cut will do)*

4 garlic cloves, peeled, and crushed (see note in *More Tips*)

1/2 cup white onion shavings (see note in *More Tips*)

1 tablespoon chopped chives, or 1 finely chopped scallion

1/4 cup chopped fresh flat-leaf parsley

1/4 teaspoon ground black pepper

pinch of ground cloves

1/2 teaspoon salt

4 Roma tomatoes, chopped, or 2 tablespoons tomato paste

2 1/2 cups boiled water

1 habanero chile

1 teaspoon apple cider vinegar

1 teaspoon fresh bitter orange juice, or fresh lemon juice

1 slice white onion (to finish)

1 slice red bell pepper (to finish)

Heat oil in a heavy 3-quart round pan over medium high setting, and sauté meat until browned. Transfer meat to a plate. Add garlic and sauté for 1 minute. Add onion, chives, parsley, black pepper, cloves, and salt. Continue to sauté for 3 minutes. Add chopped Roma tomatoes (or tomato paste), 1 cup boiled water, and chile. Bring to a boil, then cook over medium high heat until water evaporates, stirring constantly toward the end, about 20 to 30 minutes. Stir-fry for 2 minutes. Add sautéed meat, remaining water, vinegar, and orange juice (or lemon juice). Cover and boil for 15 minutes over medium heat. Remove chile and reserve. Strain through a fine strainer, pressing well on the residue. Discard the residue. Season with additional pepper if desired. Add reserved chile. Reduce sauce uncovered, over medium heat, until thickened, about 8 to 10 minutes. Add onion slice and bell pepper slice at the last minute. Discard chile just before serving. Serve hot.

Yields about 1 cup.

*This sauce is also made without meat; in this case I recommend adding 1 chicken bouillon cube when reducing the sauce.

Hot Creole Sauce

Sos Pikant (Sòs Kreyòl Pike)
Sauce Créole Piquante

This delicious hot sauce stands half-way between *Creole Sauce* and *Sauce Ti Malice*. It is served with grilled or fried meat, poultry, or fish.

1/2 cup finely sliced shallots
1/2 cup finely sliced white onion, or white onion shavings (see note in *More Tips*)
1/4 cup finely chopped flat-leaf parsley
2 tablespoons apple cider vinegar
1 habanero chile, seeded, and washed*
1/4 cup vegetable oil
4 garlic cloves, peeled, and crushed (see note in *More Tips*)

1 tablespoon chopped chives, or 1 chopped scallion
3 Roma tomatoes, chopped**
1 cup boiled water
2 tablespoons bitter orange juice or lemon juice***
1 chicken bouillon cube, crushed
1/2 teaspoon salt

Put shallots, half of the onion, parsley, vinegar, and chile in a sauce boat. Set aside.

Heat oil in a heavy 3-quart pan over medium heat. Add garlic and sauté for 1 to 2 minutes. Add remaining onion, chive, and continue to sauté for 3 minutes. Add chopped tomatoes. Increase heat to medium high and cook uncovered until no liquid remains, about 10 minutes. Add boiled water, bitter orange juice, black pepper, chicken bouillon cube, and salt. Bring to a boil, then lower heat to medium, and reduce until the sauce thickens, about 5 to 7 minutes. Season with additional salt and pepper if necessary. Strain sauce into a bowl. Pour the sauce while still hot into the sauce boat over the herbs and spices. Serve immediately with grilled or fried meat, poultry, or fish.

Yields about 1 cup.

*Wash chile, cut it in half, and remove seeds and membranes. If you wish to have a mild sauce, rub it gently under fresh running water for 15 seconds. Some people slice the chile crosswise and pour the sauce over it without seeding and washing. I do not recommend this because you will not be able to appreciate the sauce if it is too hot.

**Tomato paste can be used instead of the fresh tomatoes.

***Use 2 tablespoons of lime juice instead of the bitter orange juice, and only 2 tomatoes if the sauce is to be served with fish or poultry.

Sauce Ti Malice

Sòs Ti Malis
Sauce Ti Malice

To me, *Sauce Ti Malice* is the hallmark of Haitian sauces. This delicious hot sauce, usually served with grilled or fried meats and seafood, complements well all its partners. It is invariably served with *Griyo*, *Tasso*, and *Grilled Sardines (Pimantad)*. As I previously said, the amount of chile can be adjusted, depending on the table companions.

Generally meat is marinated before grilling or frying. You may choose to use the marinade to make the *Sauce Ti Malice*. To do so, you have to sauté and boil the marinade. In this case, from the ingredient list below you will use only the shallots, parsley, black pepper and mustard to put in the sauce boat, and the oil and the water to boil the marinade. The reduction time may be 1 to 2 minutes longer.

Estimated time: 20 minutes.

1/4 cup finely sliced shallots
1/2 tablespoon chopped fresh flat-leaf parsley
1/2 teaspoon ground black pepper
1 /4 teaspoon prepared yellow mustard
3 tablespoons vegetable oil
3 garlic cloves, peeled, and crushed (see note in *More Tips*)
 1/2 cup finely sliced white onion

1 tablespoon chopped chives, or 1 minced scallion
1 habanero chile, cut and seeded*
2/3 cup boiled water
1 1/2 tablespoon apple cider vinegar
1 1/2 tablespoon fresh lime juice
1/2 teaspoon salt

Put shallots, parsley, black pepper, and mustard in a sauce boat. Set aside.

Heat oil over medium setting in a heavy 2-quart saucepan. Sauté garlic for 1 to 2 minutes, stirring constantly. Add onion, chive, and chile. Continue to sauté for about 4 minutes. Add boiled water, vinegar, lime juice, and salt. Boil over medium setting for about 10 minutes. Strain sauce, pressing well on the residue. Discard the residue. Reduce slightly over medium heat for about one minute. Pour boiling sauce on spice and herbs in sauce boat. Serve immediately.

Yields about 3/4 cup.

*Wash chile, cut it in half, and remove seeds and membranes. If you wish to have a mild sauce, rub it gently under fresh running water for 15 seconds. Some people slice the chile crosswise and pour the sauce over it without washing out some of the hotness under running water. I do not recommend this because you will not be able to appreciate te the sauce if it is too hot.

Variation of Sauce Ti Malice

Sòs Ti Malis
Variation de la Sauce Ti Malice

This delicious *Variation of Sauce Ti Malice* is prepared with the meat cooking liquid. Here the timing for the reduction of the sauce depends on the amount of cooking liquid remaining after the meat has cooked and the thickness of the liquid. You will have to rely on your best judgment. The sauce should be fairly thick. The sauces for *Griyo* and for *Tasso* are made following this recipe.

Estimated time: 10 minutes

1/4 cup finely sliced shallots
1/2 teaspoon ground black pepper
1/2 tablespoon chopped fresh flat-leaf parsley
1 tablespoon vegetable oil

1 cup strained meat cooking liquid (from the meat being prepared)
1 tablespoon fresh lime juice
1 habanero chile, cut and seeded*
Salt to taste (if necessary)

Put shallots, black pepper, and parsley in a sauce boat. Set aside.

Heat oil over medium setting in a heavy 2-quart saucepan. Add meat cooking liquid, lime juice, and chile. Reduce until sauce thickens. Season sauce with salt if necessary. Pour boiling sauce on spice and herbs in sauce boat. Serve hot.

Yields about 3/4 cup.

Note. If the cooking liquid is very thick, which should be the case, dilute it with some boiled water (about 1/2 to 1 cup). Do not make it too thin. If that happens, reduce it until it becomes fairly thick again.

*Wash chile, cut it in half, and remove seeds and membranes. If you wish to have a mild sauce, rub it gently under fresh running water for 15 seconds. Some people slice the chile crosswise and pour the sauce over it without washing out some of the hotness under running water. I do not recommend this because you will not be able to appreciate the sauce if it is too hot.

Vinaigrette

Vinegrèt
Vinaigrette

Vinaigrette is very simple and easy to make. It can be prepared ahead and stored in a tightly covered glass jar in the refrigerator for 1 to 2 days. This will allow the sauce to ripen and thus enhance the flavor of the sauce. Mix it with the salad just before serving to keep the salad from wilting. You can also serve it separately in a sauce boat.

Boiling the garlic for a few minutes reduces its sharpness and makes it easier to mash.

1 small garlic clove (yields 1/4 to 1/2 teaspoon mashed garlic)
1/2 teaspoon salt
1/4 teaspoon granulated sugar
1 teaspoon prepared yellow mustard
1/4 cup sliced shallots, or 3 thin slices (1/8- inch thick) of white onion*

1/2 teaspoon finely ground black pepper
3 tablespoons vinegar (white vinegar, apple cider vinegar, or wine vinegar)
1 tablespoon fresh lime juice
1/2 cup olive oil, or a blend of 1/4 cup each olive oil and vegetable oil

Bring 2 cups of water to a boil. Add unpeeled garlic clove, and boil over high heat for 5 minutes. Peel garlic, then mash it with the back of a spoon until smooth. Put mashed garlic and remaining ingredients in a lidded jar. Screw the lid of the jar tightly, and shake until the sauce thickens, a few seconds. Season with additional salt if necessary. Vinaigrette can be prepared ahead and stored in a tightly covered glass jar in the refrigerator for 1 to 2 days. Bring to room temperature before serving.

Yields 3/4 to 1 cup.

*If you are using onion, you may quarter the slices crosswise to obtain small pieces of onion.

Holy Week Dressing

Sòs Salad pou Semenn Sent
Sauce à Salade de la Semaine Sainte

This sauce is served with the *Holy Week Salad*, which is a cooked vegetable salad. You may add a little more salt if the vegetables are cooked without salt. The vegetables and the sauce will balance each other nicely once they are put together. The recipe for this salad is given in the *Vegetables and Roots* chapter.

1/3 cup olive oil
1 cup sliced white onion (about 1/4 inch thick)
1/3 cup mayonnaise
1 tablespoon fresh lime juice

2 tablespoons apple cider vinegar
1 teaspoon prepared yellow mustard
1/2 teaspoon finely ground black pepper
1 teaspoon Tabasco sauce
1 teaspoon salt

Heat 2 tablespoons oil in a heavy 3-quart pan over medium high setting. Sauté onion for about 1 minute. Remove from heat. Transfer to a medium bowl. Mix in mayonnaise, lime juice, vinegar, mustard, black pepper, tabasco, salt, and remaining olive oil.

Yields about 2 cups.

Roux

Roux is not a sauce, but a blend of fat and flour cooked together on low heat and used as a base for Bechamel and other sauces, and also used as a thickening agent for sauces, stews, and soups. There are White Roux, Blond Roux, and Brown Roux. The cooking time determines the color and type of roux.

For White Roux, the mixture is cooked for about 3 minutes, and the flour should not brown.

For Blond Roux, the mixture is cooked for about 4 minutes or until the flour becomes a light golden color.

For Brown Roux, it is cooked for about 6 minutes or until the flour becomes a brown color.

1 /4 cup butter, margarine, or vegetable oil
1/4 cup all-purpose flour

Heat fat over medium low setting in a 2-quart heavy pan. Mix in the flour, stirring constantly for the desired time (see above).

To make a sauce, remove the roux from heat, add the desired liquid, whisking vigorously. Reduce over medium heat until the desired consistency, whisking constantly.

If you plan to add a roux to a soup, remove it from heat, add some liquid while whisking continuously until a thick and smooth sauce is formed. Then stir the thick sauce into the soup.

Bechamel Sauce

Sòs Bechamèl
Sauce Bechamel

The Bechamel Sauce is a white French base sauce used to make a lot of more elaborate sauces, gratins, and soufflés. It can vary slightly from one cook to another, but the method stays the same. If you are a first time cook (or if you prefer), you may allow the flour to cool down for a few minutes before adding the milk. This way, you will avoid the formation of lumps.

Estimated time: 5 to 7 minutes.

1/4 cup butter, margarine, or vegetable oil
1/4 cup all-purpose flour
1 1/2 cups whole milk
1/4 teaspoon salt

Heat fat over medium setting in a 2-quart heavy pan. Mix in the flour, stirring constantly for 2 to 3 minutes. Flour should not brown. Remove from heat. Using a wire whisk, whisk in milk vigorously until mixture becomes creamy and homogenous. Reduce for 3 to 4 minutes over medium heat to thicken, whisking constantly. The sauce is now ready to be flavored as desired. It can be thickened by stirring it over medium low heat, or thinned by the addition of liquid depending on its use. If you want to double this recipe, use slightly more fat.

Yields about 2 cups.

EGGS AND SOUFFLÉS

Ze ak Soufle
Les Oeufs et les Soufflés

Spinach Soufflé

Eggs

Eggs are for breakfast
And for dinner, I'll take two
Ingredient or meal?

Jean Bernard Ménager, 16

COOKING WITH EGGS

When cooking with eggs, be sure that they are fresh. A cracked egg should be avoided. To know if an egg is fresh, use this easy test. Fill a glass jar or a large glass with fresh tap water. Place the egg on a spoon and carefully dip the egg in the water with the spoon. Remove the spoon.

A fresh egg sinks directly to the bottom of the water and lies on its side.

If the egg stands on its smaller end, its freshness may be questionable. However, that happens also when the egg has a large air chamber. It is best not to use it in recipes asking for very fresh eggs, like a soufflé.

If the egg floats in the middle of the water, it is not very fresh. It should be avoided. If the egg floats at the surface of the water, it is not fresh at all. It must be discarded.

There is no good way to crack an egg. Your way is the best as long as you are satisfied with it, and as long as you reach your goal. However you must pay attention not to break the yolk whenever it is required, as in *Fried Eggs "Sunny Side Up "*. Many recipes ask you to separate the egg white from the egg yolk. These are precisely the cases in which you have to pay particular attention to keep an intact yolk. Personally, I strike the egg with the side of a spoon to make a crack, then I open it with my fingers. I could be considered a bad "egg-cracker," but my way fits perfectly my needs.

Some recipes in this book contain eggs that are not fully cooked. Young children, pregnant women, breast-feeding women, the elderly, and people with a deficient immune system should avoid eating eggs that are not fully cooked which may constitute a risk for their health.

Fried Eggs "Sunny Side Up"

Ze Sou Plat
Oeuf sur Plat

This recipe is just for one egg. You can also cook more than one egg at a time, using a 7- inch non-stick skillet for 1 and 2 eggs, and bigger skillets as you make more eggs. Nonetheless, stay realistic; do not put in the skillet more eggs than you can handle.

1 large egg
1/2 tablespoon vegetable oil
Salt and pepper to taste

Crack egg and drop it in a small individual bowl, or in a condiment bowl. Heat oil over medium low setting in a 7-inch non-stick skillet. Slide egg in the hot oil, being careful not to break the yolk. Cook for 3 minutes. At this point the white should be coagulated and soft, and the yolk should be bright yellow and liquid*. Cover, and cook for 2 minutes. Uncover, and use a slotted spatula to transfer egg to a hot serving plate. The white should still be soft, and the yolk should be soft and covered by a thin white film. Sprinkle with salt and pepper. Serve with toasted bread.

Yields one serving.

Note. Pregnant women, breast-feeding women, elderly, and people with a deficient immune system should avoid eating eggs that are not fully cooked as they may constitute a risk for their health.

*If you want a bright yellow and liquid yolk, serve it after the first 3 minutes of cooking.

Stuffed Omelette

Omlèt Fasi
Omelette Farcie

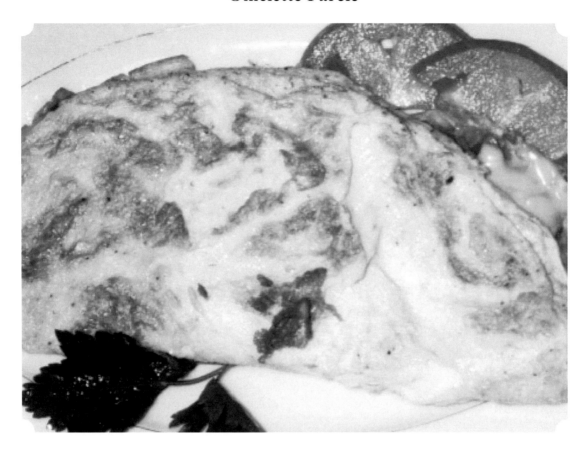

The following recipe serves three to four persons but it may be made individually in a 7-inch non-stick skillet with one to two eggs. Serve it with toasted bread and a fresh cantaloupe salad.

Estimated time: 20 minutes.

1/4 cup vegetable oil
1/4 cup diced white onion
1/2 cup cubed tomatoes
salt and pepper to taste
6 eggs
2 tablespoons milk or water

a few drops of Tabasco sauce
3 individual slices of fully cooked ham, cut into small pieces
3 individual slices of cheese (Cheddar, Gouda, Gruyere), halved

Heat 1 tablespoon oil over medium setting in a small frying pan. Add onion, and sauté for 1 minute. Transfer to a plate and set aside. Heat 1 tablespoon oil in the same pan, add the tomato, and sauté until the juice thickens, about 7 minutes. Sprinkle with salt and pepper to taste. Set aside.

Crack eggs and pour into a medium bowl with milk, and Tabasco. Season with salt, and pepper to taste. With a fork or a wire whisk, beat the eggs vigorously until lightly foamy, about 1 minute.

Heat remaining oil over medium setting in a 12-inch non-stick skillet. Pour in egg mixture, and rotate the skillet gently so the mixture spreads on the bottom of the skillet. Reduce heat to medium low, and cook until omelette is almost set, about 2 to 3 minutes. Using 2 spatulas, flip omelette over, then quickly arrange sautéed onion and sautéed tomato on one half of the omelette. Top with ham pieces and cheese pieces, then immediately fold the other omelette half over the filling. Serve immediately with toasted bread.

Serves 3 to 4.

Note. Do not use an electric mixer to beat the eggs when making omelettes. The electric mixer will allow too many air bubbles to get into the eggs. The omelette will be unpleasantly dry and spongy.

Variation

You may make an omelette with a creamier inside. To do so, do not flip the omelette over. Arrange the filling on one half, then fold the other half over the filling and cook a little longer.

Rolled Stuffed Omelette

Visually divide the omelette in two equal portions. Arrange the stuffing lengthwise near the center of the omelette, so half of the omelette is free of filling on one side, and a smaller flap is free of filling on the other side. Using two spatulas, fold the small flap over the filling, fold again over the other side, and again until a roll is formed. Remove from heat, and serve immediately with toasted bread.

Scrambled Eggs

Ze Bwouye
Oeufs Brouillés

This recipe of Scrambled Eggs is made of yellow and white bits of soft fried eggs. Spices may be added to taste.

Estimated time: 10 minutes.

3 tablespoons vegetable oil
1/4 cup diced white onion (optional)
3 individual ham slices, cut into small
pieces (optional)

6 eggs
salt and pepper to taste
3 tablespoons freshly grated or freshly shredded
Parmesan (optional)

Heat oil over medium setting in a 10-inch non-stick skillet, and sauté onion for 1 minute. Add ham, and continue to sauté for 1 minute. Crack in the eggs. Sprinkle them with salt, then start scrambling after one minute so as to have small lumps of fried eggs. The eggs should start setting before you scramble them. Remove from heat once eggs are set and soft, after about 2 minutes of cooking. Sprinkle with pepper and Parmesan cheese. Serve hot with toasted bread.

Serves 3.

Poached Eggs, Soft-boiled Eggs, Hard-boiled Eggs

Ze Poche, Ze Bouyi Ole, Ze Bouyi Di
Oeufs Pochés, Oeufs Mollets, Oeufs Durs

Poached eggs*

Bring 4 cups of water with 1 tablespoon of white vinegar to a simmer in a small greased pan. Crack one egg at a time, and drop it carefully into a small condiment bowl paying attention to not break the yolk, then slide it in the barely simmering water. Cook for 4 to 5 minutes. Remove from water, and keep warm in a bowl of warm water until all eggs are poached. Using a slotted spoon, transfer poached eggs on a serving dish and pat dry with a sheet of paper towel. Cut off any tail that might have formed around the egg. Egg white should be tender and should coat the yolk which should be soft and creamy. Sprinkle with ground pepper and salt. Serve warm with toasted bread, and butter or a cheese sauce. You can also use an egg poacher to make the task easier.

Soft-boiled eggs*

Bring a medium pot of water to boil over medium setting. Place eggs on a spoon, one at a time, and carefully place them in the boiling water. Cook for 5 to 6 minutes. Remove from heat, and dip them in a large bowl of cold water for 1 to 2 minutes. Peel off the shell immediately. Dip shelled eggs in a bowl of hot water for a few minutes to reheat them if necessary. Egg white should be soft, and the yolk should be soft and creamy. Serve hot with toasted bread, salt, and butter or a cheese sauce.

Oeuf à la Coque is a softer soft-boiled egg served in its shell. An egg-cup is used to hold it. Cook the eggs for 3 to 4 minutes in boiling water. Then dip in cold water for 1 to 2 minutes, and peel off about half of the shell at the smaller end. Place each in an egg-cup. Serve hot with pepper, salt, and toasted bread.

Hard-boiled eggs

Bring a medium pot of water to boil over medium setting. Place eggs on a spoon and carefully put them, one at a time, in the boiling water. Cover, cook for 15 to 18 minutes. Remove from heat, and dip them in a large bowl of cold water for 1 to 2 minutes. Peel off the shell immediately. Dip shelled eggs in a bowl of hot water for a few minutes to reheat them if necessary. Serve hot with toasted bread, and butter or a cheese sauce. Hard-boiled eggs are also used in some salads and sauces, and to garnish a few dishes.

*Pregnant women, breast-feeding women, the elderly, and people with a deficient immune system should avoid eating eggs that are not fully cooked as they may constitute a risk for their health.

Cheese Soufflé and Other Soufflés

Soufle Fromaj ak Lòt Soufle
Soufflé au Fromage et Autres Soufflés

The eggs, particularly the whites, make the soufflé. They must be very fresh. The egg whites must be beaten in a clean bowl, and until stiff to allow the soufflé to puff up properly. As soon as they have been beaten stiff, fold them into the dish and put the dish into the oven. Once the soufflé is in the oven, do not open the oven door at any time during baking. However, you may take a glance after 30 minutes of baking. Soufflé must be served once out of the oven; otherwise it will collapse.

Estimated time: 1 hour

1 tablespoon butter or margarine (to coat the mold)
1 tablespoon flour (to coat the mold)
2 1/2 tablespoons vegetable oil
3 tablespoons all-purpose flour
1 cup whole milk
3/4 teaspoon salt, divided (1/2 teaspoon and 1/4 teaspoon)
1/2 teaspoon finely ground black pepper

1/4 teaspoon ground paprika
4 egg yolks
2 cups freshly shredded Parmesan cheese, or 1 cup Parmesan plus 1 cup extra sharp cheddar
4 egg whites
1 to 2 tablespoons finely grated Parmesan cheese (to sprinkle on the soufflé)

Generously coat a 6-cup soufflé mold with melted butter or margarine. Then coat it with the flour. Set aside. Preheat oven to 375 degrees Fahrenheit.

Heat oil over medium setting. Add flour and cook for 1 to 2 minutes, whisking constantly. Whisk in milk. Continue to cook for 1 to 2 minutes until sauce thickens, whisking continuously. Remove from heat and stir in 1/2 teaspoon salt, black pepper, and paprika. Let it stand to cool a little bit. Then thoroughly mix in the egg yolks and the cheese. Set aside.

Using a hand electric mixer at high speed, in a clean bowl beat the egg whites with remaining salt until stiff. Delicately fold beaten egg whites into the cheese mixture. Transfer to the prepared soufflé mold. Sprinkle with finely grated Parmesan cheese, and bake in the middle of preheated oven until golden and puffed, 30 to 35 minutes. Serve immediately.

Serves 4 to 6.

Other soufflés

To make *Ham Soufflé*, mix 1 1/2 cups finely shredded fully cooked ham to the sauce before adding the egg whites.

For *Fish Soufflé*, see the fish chapter. For *Spinach Soufflé* and *Corn Soufflé*, see the notes at the end of *Creamy Spinach au Gratin* and *Creamy Corn au Gratin* in the *Gratin* chapter.

Potato Soufflé, Breadfruit Soufflé

Soufle Pomdetè, Soufle Veritab
Soufflé de Pomme de Terre, Soufflé de Véritable

Estimated time: 1 hour.

1 tablespoon flour (to coat the mold)
1 tablespoon vegetable oil
1 cup finely diced white onion
1/2 recipe of *Bechamel Sauce*
4 large baking potatoes (about 1 1/2 pounds), peeled, boiled, drained, and mashed
1/4 cup whipping cream
2 chicken bouillon cubes, crushed
1/4 teaspoon finely ground black pepper, or to taste

1/4 teaspoon granulated garlic
1 teaspoon soy sauce
3 egg yolks
1 1/2 cups freshly grated Parmesan cheese
1 cup freshly grated extra sharp cheddar cheese
3 egg whites
1/4 teaspoon salt
1/4 cup freshly grated Parmesan cheese (to sprinkle on the soufflé)

Generously coat a 6-cup soufflé mold with melted butter or margarine. Then coat it with the flour. Set aside. Preheat oven to 375 degrees Fahrenheit.

Heat oil over medium heat. Add onion and sauté until it becomes translucent and very soft. Transfer sautéed onion to a large bowl. Mix in *Bechamel*, mashed potatoes, cream, bouillon cubes, black pepper, garlic, soy sauce, egg yolks, and the cheeses until well blended. Set aside.

Using a hand electric mixer at high speed, beat the egg whites with the salt until stiff. Fold beaten egg whites into the potato-cheese mixture. Transfer to the prepared soufflé mold. Sprinkle with finely grated Parmesan cheese, and bake in the middle of preheated oven until golden and puffed, 40 minutes. Serve immediately.

Serves 4 to 6.

For *Breadfruit Soufflé*, use mashed breadfruit instead of the mashed potatoes. Flake 1/4 pound soaked salt cod filets. Sauté it with the onion, mix it with the mashed breadfruit, then proceed as above. The breadfruit must be firm, ripe and green but not ripened and sweet. Learn how to soak salt cod in *The Cook's Techniques* chapter.

APPETIZERS

Odèv
Les Hors d'Oeuvres

Herring Chiquetaille

Appetizers

Before the first course come the appetizers.
Big ones! Little ones! All sorts of them!
Something to warm up my taste buds.
I think I'll take a few!

Jean Bernard Ménager, 16

Malanga Croquettes

Akra
Croquettes de Malanga

Akra is a delicious fritter made of a mixture of mashed beans and grated malanga, or only with grated malanga. It can go from mild to hot.

Estimated time: 1 hour.

1/2 habanero chile, seeded, and washed*
1/4 cup finely minced fresh flat-leaf parsley
4 garlic cloves, peeled and crushed (see note in *More Tips*)
2 teaspoons salt
1 1/2 cups freshly grated malanga**
1/4 cup milk
1/4 teaspoon finely ground black pepper
1/2 cup all-purpose flour
Vegetable oil for deep-frying

Using a mortar, finely mash chile, parsley, and garlic with the salt. Heat 2 tablespoons oil, in a medium skillet, over medium setting and sauté mashed spices for 1 minute. Transfer to a large bowl and combine with grated malanga, milk, and pepper. Add flour and whisk to form a homogenous mixture. Cover and let stand for one hour. The batter can be refrigerated for up to one day.

In a heavy pan, heat oil over medium setting and drop the mixture by tablespoons in the hot oil. Do not overload. Fry until golden, about 3 to 4 minutes on each side. Drain on paper towels. Garnish with parsley. Serve hot.

Yields about 50.

Note. Remove brown bits in oil, and do not hesitate to change the oil when there is too much deposit at the bottom of the pan. This will prevent the croquettes from tasting burned.

* Read about habanero chile in *The Cook's Techniques* chapter.

**Read note about *malanga* in the glossary of this book.

Breadfruit Croquettes

Kwokèt Veritab
Croquette de Véritable

Breadfruit must be ripe and green, but not ripened and sweet, to be able to make croquettes. These delicious croquettes are crusty on the outside, and soft in the inside. The mash can be prepared in advance and stored in the refrigerator until ready to use.

Estimated time: 1 hour 20 minutes (without soaking time)

1/2 pounds dried salt cod fillet (gives about 2 cups flaked cod)
1 1/2 pounds breadfruit, peeled, sliced, and cored* (gives about 2 1/2 cups of mash)
1 tablespoon chopped chives, or 1 minced scallion
1/2 habanero chile, seeded, and washed (read *Demystifying Habanero Chile*)
1/2 tablespoon crushed garlic
1/2 cup finely minced white onion
1/4 teaspoon finely ground black pepper
salt to taste
1/2 cup all purpose flour
oil for deep-frying

Soak cod for 12 hours, changing water three times, every 4 hours. Taste for saltiness. Repeat if necessary. Drain, and squeeze between 2 sheets of paper towels to remove excess water. Flake and set aside. (Learn how to soak salt cod in *The Cook's Techniques* chapter).

Cook breadfruit in a large pot of boiling water until tender, about 20 to 30 minutes.

Meanwhile, finely mash chives and chile with garlic using a mortar and pestle. Heat 2 tablespoons oil, in a medium skillet, over medium setting and sauté mashed spices for 1 minute. Add onion and black pepper. Continue to sauté for 3 minutes. Add flaked cod and sauté for 3 additional minutes. Season with salt if necessary. Remove from heat and set aside.

Drain breadfruit and mash it while still hot with a 12-inch mortar and pestle. Add sautéed spice and cod mixture. Mix well. This can be prepared ahead and refrigerated for up to one day. Form small balls using about one tablespoon of the breadfruit mixture. Put flour in a large shallow dish. Roll breadfruit balls in the flour. Shake excess flour off breadfruit balls.

Heat oil over medium setting in a heavy pan, and deep-fry breadfruit balls until golden, about 8 minutes. Do not overcrowd. Drain on paper towels. Serve hot.

Yields about 35 croquettes.

Note. Remove brown bits in oil, and do not hesitate to change the oil when there is too much deposit at the bottom of the pan. This will prevent the croquettes tasting burned.

*Read note about breadfruit in the Glossary of this book. Canned breadfruit can be found in African, Caribbean, and Latin-American groceries and markets. Drain, rinse with fresh water, and use as indicated in the recipe. It is an alternative to fresh breadfruit but it will not replace the taste of the fresh fruit. This is particularly true for breadfruit.

Potato Croquettes

Kwokèt Pomdetè
Croquettes de Pommes de Terre

Estimated time: 1 hour 20 minutes.

2 large potatoes (gives about 2 cups of mashed potato)
1/2 cup finely minced white onion
1 tablespoon chopped chives, or 1 minced scallion
1/4 teaspoon black pepper
1/2 tablespoon granulated garlic

1 egg yolk
1 chicken bouillon cube, crushed
1 cup freshly grated Parmesan cheese, or freshly grated extra sharp cheddar cheese
1 teaspoon salt
1/2 cup flour
vegetable oil for deep frying

Cook potatoes in a large pot of boiling water for 20 to 25 minutes.

Meanwhile heat 1 tablespoon oil over medium setting and sauté onion, and chives for 2 minutes. Set aside.

Drain potatoes. Peel and mash them while still hot with a fork, a potato masher, a potato ricer, or a food mill. Add sautéed onion mixture, black pepper, garlic, egg yolk, bouillon cube, cheese, and salt. Form small mashed potato balls using about one tablespoon of mixture. Put flour in a shallow dish. Roll potato balls in flour. Shake excess flour off the potato balls.

Heat oil over medium setting in a heavy pan, and deep-fry potato balls until golden, about 6 to 8 minutes. Do not overcrowd. Serve hot.

Yields about 25 croquettes.

Note. You may prepare the mashed potato in advance, mix it with the spices, but not the egg yolk. It may then be kept refrigerated for up to one day. Moments before rolling the potato balls, mix in the yolk thoroughly.

Remove brown bits in oil, and do not hesitate to change the oil when there is too much deposit at the bottom of the pan. This will prevent the croquettes tasting burned.

Fish Croquettes

Kwokèt Pwason
Croquettes de Poisson

Fish Croquettes can be very delicious. Use a fish that has a tender and fine flesh.

2 Persian limes
1 pound skinless fish filet
2 tablespoons vegetable oil
3 garlic cloves, peeled, and crushed (see note in *More Tips*)
1 habanero chile, seeded, washed, and finely minced (read *Demystifying Habanero Chile*)
1 tablespoon finely minced parsley
1 teaspoon salt

1/4 cup finely minced white onion
1/4 cup finely minced shallot
1/2 teaspoon finely ground black pepper
1/2 cup freshly mashed potatoes
1 large egg, beaten
1 cup of all-purpose flour
vegetable oil for deep-frying
Sauce Ti Malice or *Hot Creole Sauce*, to serve

Cut limes lengthwise in 3 portions. Reserve 1 tablespoon lime juice. Rub fish with lime, then rinse under fresh running water. Pat dry. Place fish in a shallow dish, and drizzle with the lime juice.

Heat 1 tablespoon oil in a non-stick skillet over medium setting, and cook fish in the oil until tender, about 10 minutes. Mash cooked fish with a fork. Set aside.

Using a mortar and pestle, finely mash garlic, chile, and parsley with salt. Heat the remaining tablespoon of oil over medium setting and sauté mashed spices for 1 minute. Add onion, shallot, and black pepper, and continue to sauté for 3 minutes. Remove from heat. Mix in mashed potatoes and mashed fish. Season with additional salt and pepper if necessary. This can be prepared to this point and kept refrigerated for up to one day. Form small balls using about 1 tablespoon of mixture.

Put beaten egg in a small bowl, and flour in a shallow dish. Roll the balls in the beaten egg. Drain excess egg, then roll the balls in the flour. Shake off excess flour.

Heat oil over medium setting in a heavy pan, and deep-fry croquettes until golden, about 6 to 8 minutes. Do not overcrowd. Serve hot with *Sauce Ti Malice* or with *Hot Creole Sauce*.

Serves about 6.

Note. Remove brown bits in oil, and do not hesitate to change the oil when there is too much deposit at the bottom of the pan. This will prevent the croquettes from tasting burned.

Herring "Chiquetaille"

Chiktay Aran Sò
Chiquetaille de Hareng Saur

Chiquetaille de Hareng Saur, made with flaked smoked red herring, is an excellent dish for cocktails. It can be very hot, but you will adjust the amount of habanero chile according to your taste and of course the taste of your guests. Prepare Chiquetaille one day in advance, and store it in the refrigerator to allow the flavors to blend.

Estimated time: 20 minutes (without soaking time).

1/2 cup olive oil
1/4 cup white vinegar, or apple cider vinegar
2 habanero chiles, seeded*
1/2 cup chopped shallots

1/2 cup finely diced white onion
1/2 teaspoon ground black pepper, or to taste
1 pound skinless smoked red herring filets**
salt if necessary

In a large bowl, whisk oil with vinegar until mixture thickens, a few seconds. Add chiles, shallots, onion and black pepper. Cover, and refrigerate until ready to use.

Bring a large pot of water to a boil. Remove from heat. Add herring and soak for 10 to 12 hours, changing water every 3 hours. Check for saltiness. Repeat the process if necessary. Drain carefully. Put herring between sheets of paper towel and squeeze out excess water. Flake herring very finely, and transfer to olive oil mixture. Mix well. Season with salt and additional black pepper if necessary. Then bring to a quick boil on medium heat for 3 minutes. Serve warm or at room temperature with *Homemade Crackers (Biskuit Sèk)*, toasted Kasav***, crackers, or croutons.

Serves 8.

*Wash chile, cut it in half, remove seeds and membranes, then mince finely. If you wish to have a mild Chiktay, rub it gently under fresh running water for 15 seconds.

**Smoked red herring can be found at Caribbean and Latin-American groceries.

***Recipe for *Homemade Crackers* is given in this book. *Kasav*, very popular in Haiti, is a Creole word that designates a dry flat preparation made with yucca (cassava), and is called cassava bread and yucca bread. It is available in Caribbean and Latin-American groceries and markets.

Salt Cod "Chiquetaille"

Chiktay Mori
Chiquetaille de Morue

This delicious cocktail dish made with flaked salt cod can go from mild to hot as for *Chiquetaille de Hareng*. You will adjust the amount of habanero chile according to your taste and of course the taste of your guests. Prepare Chiquetaille one day in advance, and store it in the refrigerator to allow the flavors to blend.

Estimated time: 20 minutes (without soaking time).

1/2 cup olive oil
1 /4 cup white vinegar, or apple cider vinegar
2 habanero chiles, seeded*
1/2 cup chopped shallots
1/2 cup finely diced white onion

1/2 teaspoon ground black pepper, or to taste
1 pound skinless dried salt cod filet**, cut into 6 to 7 pieces
salt if necessary

In a large bowl, whisk oil with vinegar until mixture thickens, a few seconds. Add chiles, shallots, onion and black pepper. Cover, and refrigerate until ready to use.

Soak cod in a large pot of hot boiled water for 12 hours, changing hot water three times, every 4 hours. Check for saltiness. Repeat the process if necessary. Drain carefully. Put cod between sheets of paper towel and squeeze out excess water. Flake cod very finely and transfer to olive oil mixture. Mix well. Season with salt and additional black pepper if necessary. Then bring to a quick boil on medium heat for 3 minutes. Serve warm or at room temperature with *Homemade Crackers (Biskuit Sèk)*, toasted Kasav***, crackers, or croutons.

Serves 8.

*Wash chile, cut it in half, remove seeds and membranes, then mince finely. If you wish to have a mild Chiktay, rub it gently under fresh running water for 15 seconds.

**Salt cod can be found at Caribbean and Latin-American groceries, and also at specialty Italian Import Stores. It is called baccala in Italian, and bacalao in Spanish. A recipe to make salt cod is given in this book.

***Recipe for *Homemade Crackers* is given in this book. *Kasav*, very popular in Haiti, is a Creole word that designates a dry flat preparation made with yucca (cassava), and is called cassava bread and yucca bread. It is available in Caribbean and Latin-American groceries and markets.

Ham "Chiquetaille"And Chicken "Chiquetaille"

Chiktay Janbon ak Chiktay Poul
Chiquetaille de Jambon et Chiquetaille de Poulet

Chiquetaille de Jambon, made with shredded ham, is also an excellent dish for cocktails just like the two preceding chiquetailles. It can be very hot, but you will adjust the amount of habanero chile according to your taste and of course the taste of your guests. Prepare Chiquetaille one day in advance, and store it in the refrigerator to allow the flavors to blend.

1/2 pound fully cooked cured ham, (yields 2 cups packed shredded ham)	1/4 teaspoon finely ground black pepper
2 habanero chiles, seeded*	1/3 cup olive oil
1/4 cup chopped shallots	1/4 cup white vinegar, or apple cider vinegar
1/4 cup finely diced white onion	salt to taste

Shred the ham, then mix it with chile, shallots, onion, and black pepper in a large bowl. Set aside.

Whisk olive oil and vinegar in a medium bowl until the mixture thickens, a few seconds. Drizzle it over ham, and turn to coat. Season with salt to taste. Let stand at least 8 hours in the refrigerator to allow the flavors to blend. Bring to room temperature before serving. Serve with *Homemade Crackers (Biskuit Sèk)*, toasted Kasav**, crackers, or croutons.

Serves 6 to 8.

Chiquetaille de poulet
Replacing the ham with skinless and boneless chicken breast, follow the same recipe to make a delicious *Chicken Chiquetaille*. Poach the chicken breast in chicken broth until cooked through. Remove the chicken from the broth and place on a rack to cool down until easy to handle. Squeeze with paper towel to remove excess liquid. Shred and mince the chicken, then proceed as above. You may also use any leftover from a roast chicken, but you have to make sure to remove all skin, membranes, fat, tendons and cartilage. You may use this recipe to make *Turkey Chiquetaille*.

*Wash chile, cut it in half, remove seeds and membranes, then mince finely. If you wish to have a mild Chiktay, rubit gently under fresh running water for 15 seconds.

**Recipe for *Homemade Crackers* is given in this book. *Kasav*, very popular in Haiti, is a Creole word that designates a dry flat preparation made with yucca (cassava), and is called cassava bread and yucca bread. It is available in Caribbean and Latin-American groceries and markets.

Choux with Seafood Filling

Bouche Fwidmè
Petits Choux aux Fruits de Mer

This filling can be made with shrimp, lobster, scallops, crabs, or a combination of seafood. These choux can also be stuffed with a cheese filling*. It is best to prepare the choux the day they are to be served.

36 to 38 medium choux (Double *Choux Pastry* recipe)
4 tablespoons butter or margarine
1/2 cup sliced shallots
3/4 pound medium shrimp, shelled, deveined, and cut crosswise in 3 pieces each
salt to taste
pepper to taste

2 1/2 cups cream of seafood, cream of mushroom, or cream of chicken
1 1/2 cups (one 12-ounce can) evaporated milk
2 medium turnips, peeled, and diced into about 1/4-inch cubes (yields 2 cups)
minced fresh parsley to garnish (optional)

Keep choux hot until ready to use. They may be put in a warm oven. Heat butter over medium setting in a large skillet. Add shallots and sauté for 2 minutes. Add shrimp and sauté until cooked through, about 2 minutes. Season with pepper and salt to taste. Using a slotted spoon, transfer shrimps and shallot to a plate. Set aside. Add cream of seafood and milk to the same skillet, reduce over medium heat until sauce thickens, stirring constantly 10 minutes. Mix in seafood and shallots. Add turnips, and cook for 3 minutes over medium setting. Remove from heat. Sauce should be very thick.

Cut off the top 1/3 of the choux. Carefully remove and discard the moist dough inside each of them. Fill the choux with the seafood filling. Sprinkle with minced parsley if desired. Cover with the tops. Serve immediately.

Yields 36 to 38 choux.

* For cheese filling:
half the recipe of *Bechamel Sauce*, thickened
1/2 teaspoon finely ground black pepper
3/4 to 1 cup heavy whipping cream
1/2 cup finely diced red bell pepper

2 to 2 1/2 cups of freshly grated Parmesan cheese or extra sharp cheddar cheese
1/4 cup minced white onion
salt to taste

Mix all ingredients in a heavy 2-quart pan, then stir over medium low heat just until smooth, about 3 minutes. Cool until warm, then fill the choux. Serve immediately.

Seafood Barquettes

Tatlèt Fwidmè
Barquettes de Fruits de Mer

1 recipe of *Short Pastry*
1 pound medium shrimp, or a medley of cooked shrimp, crab, lobster, and scallops
1 cup whole milk
2 tablespoons butter, margarine, or vegetable oil
2 tablespoons all-purpose flour
1/2 cup sour cream

1 teaspoon granulated garlic
1/2 teaspoon finely ground black pepper
1 teaspoon salt
1/4 cup thinly diced shallots
1 chicken bouillon cube, crushed
1/4 teaspoon Tabasco sauce
1/2 teaspoon soy sauce
Chopped parsley to garnish, if desired

Have on hand twenty-four 2-inch mini tartlet pans (boat-shaped for barquettes, or any other shape) and a large ungreased jelly roll pan.

Form 24 same-size dough balls with the short pastry, and chill for 30 minutes. Meanwhile, shell and devein the shrimp. Add shells and shrimp to the milk, then boil over medium heat until shrimp are just cooked, about 3 minutes. Transfer shrimp to a plate, leaving the shells in the milk to steep until ready to use. Reserve 24 shrimp. Cut remaining shrimp crosswise in 3 portions. Set aside.

Roll out each dough ball into a 1/8 inch thick circle about 1 inch larger than the pan. Fit each circle into a tartlet pan. Trim excess dough. Pierce bottom and side of crust all over with the tines of a fork. Wrap in wax paper and refrigerate for 30 minutes. This can be done ahead.

Preheat oven to 400 degrees Fahrenheit.

Place tartlet pans on the ungreased jelly roll pan. Bake in the middle of preheated oven until golden, about 20 minutes. Let stand for 3 minutes in the pans, then unmold, and cool completely on a rack. Crust may be prepared in advance and kept in a wax bag at room temperature until ready to use.

Heat butter over medium setting in a 2-quart heavy pan. Mix in the flour, stirring constantly for 2 minutes. Flour should not brown. Remove from heat. Strain the milk over the flour, and whisk vigorously until mixture becomes creamy and homogenous. Reduce for 5 to 7 minutes over medium heat until very thick, whisking constantly. Cool completely. Stir in shrimp, sour cream, garlic, black pepper, salt, shallots, bouillon cube, Tabasco sauce, and soy sauce until creamy. Just before serving, fill each pastry crust with some of the creamy mixture. Top each tartlet with one shrimp, and garnish with parsley if desired. Do not fill the crusts ahead. They will get soggy and unpleasant.

Yields 24 barquettes.

Mini Cheese Sandwiches

Ti Sandwich Fwomaj
Petits Sandwiches au Fromage

An easy way to cut bread slices without messiness is to do that while they are frozen. Your sandwiches will be neat and appealing. Cover the sandwiches with a damp cloth at all times, so they do not dry out. Make sure the cloth is not too wet. The cheese spread can be prepared one day ahead, and yields about one cup. Keep bread refrigerated until ready to use.

4 ounces cream cheese (half of a package), softened
1/2 cup mayonnaise
1 cup freshly grated Parmesan cheese
1 teaspoon Tabasco sauce
1/2 teaspoon finely ground black pepper

1 teaspoon prepared yellow mustard
1/4 teaspoon soy sauce
1/4 cup very finely diced red bell pepper
1/4 cup very finely diced white onion
one bag of sliced white sandwich bread, about 20 slices

Mix all ingredients, except the bread, in a medium bowl until a homogeneous paste is formed. Cover, and refrigerate for at least 3 hours to allow the flavors to blend. This yields about one cup.

Spread cheese paste on one slice of bread, then cover with another slice to form a sandwich. Continue until all the sandwiches are made. Put all the sandwiches in a zippered bag and freeze for 3 hours or more, so they are very firm when you are slicing them.

Place frozen sandwiches, one at a time, on a smooth clean working surface. Trim crust from the sides of the sandwich with a sharp knife, then divide each sandwich in four, cutting crosswise or diagonally, making this way 4 small square-shaped sandwiches or 4 small triangle-shaped sandwiches. Repeat the same procedure until you cut all the sandwiches. Transfer to a large plate, and cover with a damp kitchen cloth as they are being made. Refrigerate until ready to serve. Remove from the refrigerator and bring to room temperature before serving. Remove the damp cloth just before serving.

Yields about 40 mini sandwiches.

Canapés

Kanape
Canapés

These canapés are crispy and delicious. Garnish as you please. Garnishes can be prepared one day ahead, but it is best to prepare the bread the day the canapés are to be served.

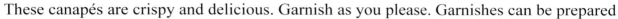

An easy way to cut bread slices without messiness is to do it while they are frozen. Your canapés will be neat and appealing.

Estimated time: 30 minutes.

One bag of sliced white sandwich bread, about 20 slices (keep frozen until ready to use)
8 tablespoons (1 stick) butter or margarine, at room temperature
1/4 cup freshly grated Parmesan cheese (optional)
A 13x 18-inch jelly roll pan, or a 14 x 17-inch cookie sheet

Preheat oven to 250 degrees Fahrenheit. Generously grease the baking sheet with butter or margarine.

Cut off the crust of each slice of bread with a sharp knife. Butter one side of each of them, then cut them into small triangles, small squares, small rounds, or any shape you want, using a sharp knife, or a cookie cutter. Star shapes are particularly appropriate for Christmas. Each slice gives one to four canapés, depending on the size and the shape used. Sprinkle each piece of buttered bread with Parmesan if using. Place the cut bread slices, buttered sides up, in one single layer on the prepared baking sheet. Bake in preheated oven for 15 minutes. Increase oven temperature to 350 degrees Fahrenheit, and bake until slightly golden and crispy, about 7 minutes. Remove from oven, and center each canapé with one or two teaspoons of a garnishing of your choice. Serve immediately.

As garnishing you may use all the Chiquetailles, and the cheese spread used in *Mini Cheese Sandwiches*. Top with a thin slice of red bell pepper. You may make a spread with cooked crab meat, onion, and mayonnaise, and also with cooked fish, onion, and mayonnaise, then top everything with a cooked small shrimp, or a thin piece of smoked salmon. You may also top the canapés with Duck Liver Paté, or Chicken Liver Paté; in this case it is not necessary to sprinkle the bread pieces with the Parmesan.

Bread pieces can be prepared and baked hours in advance. In this case, store in airtight containers. Reheat them at low temperature when ready to serve. Garnish just before serving.

Yields about 20 to 80 canapés.

Cheese Sticks

Ti Baton Fwomaj
Batonnets au Fromage

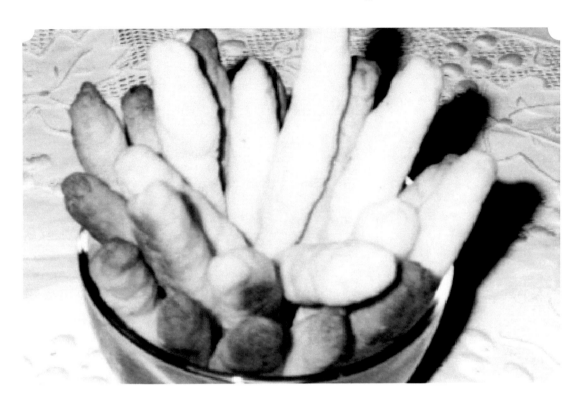

2 cups all-purpose flour
1/4 teaspoon salt
1/4 teaspoon finely ground black pepper
1 teaspoon double acting baking powder

3/4 cup (1 1/2 sticks) cold butter or margarine
2 large eggs, slightly beaten
1 cup freshly grated Parmesan cheese

Preheat oven to 350 degrees Fahrenheit. Have on hand two large ungreased baking sheets.

Mix flour, salt, pepper, and baking powder on a smooth surface. Using your finger tips, mix in butter until mixture resembles coarse meal. Quickly mix in eggs until a firm dough is formed. Refrigerate the dough for one hour. Roll small portions of dough between palms of hands to form 3-inch x 1/4-inch finger-shaped sticks, then transfer them to prepared baking sheets, 1/2 inch apart. Bake in the middle of preheated oven until slightly golden, 15 minutes. Cool on baking sheets for 5 minutes, then transfer to a rack to cool completely. They can be stored in a wax bag and placed in an airtight container.

Yields about 65 cheese sticks.

Meat Fritters

Marinad
Beignets à la Viande

Marinad is very popular in Haiti. It is a spiced fritter containing poultry, salt cod, or smoked red herring. As with *Akra* and the *Chiquetailles*, it can also go from mild to hot.

Estimated time: 45 minutes (batter resting time not included).

2 cups all purpose flour
2 cups plus 1 tablespoon water
4 garlic cloves, peeled and crushed (see note in *More Tips*)
1 tablespoon chopped chives, or 1 minced scallion
1/2 habanero chile, seeded and washed*
2 teaspoons salt
1/2 teaspoon finely ground black pepper, or to taste
2 chicken bouillon cubes, crushed
1 cup chopped cooked chicken, or 1/2 cup soaked and crushed smoked herring fillet, or 1/2 cup soaked and crushed salt cod
3/4 teaspoon baking soda
Vegetable oil for deep-frying

In a large bowl, whisk flour and water to form a fluid batter. Finely mash garlic with chives, chile, and salt until pasty. Add to the batter with black pepper, bouillon cubes, and meat. Mix well. Allow the batter to rest for 20 minutes to one hour at room temperature. Then mix in baking soda.

In a heavy pan, heat oil over medium setting (do not overheat) and drop dough by tablespoons in hot oil. Do not overload. Cook until golden and crisp turning once, about 3 to 4 minutes on each side. Drain on paper towel. Garnish with parsley if desired. Serve immediately. **Yields about 60.**

*Read about habanero chile in the Glossary and in *The Cook's Techniques*.

Papita

More a street snack than an appetizer, *Papita* is a sort of long plantain chip. It is crispy and delicious. Peel bitter orange (or lemon) before using.

Estimated time: 45 minutes

Juice of 1 bitter orange (or 1 lemon, or 1 lime)
3 large green plantains
Vegetable oil for deep-frying

In a large bowl, mix 10 cups water with the juice of the bitter orange. Set aside.

Peel plantains, and thinly slice them lengthwise using a vegetable slicer or a mandolin slicer. Drop plantain slices in water mixture.

Heat oil over medium setting in a heavy pan. Remove plaintain slices from the water and fry them until golden and crispy, 2 to 3 minutes for each side. Drain on paper towel. Sprinkle with salt. Serve warm or at room temperature.

Serves 6.

SOUPS AND STEWS

Soup ak Bouyon
Soupes et Bouillons

Pumpkin Soup

Soups and Stews

Confort in winter.
A treat in spring and summer
Even autumn too!

Jean Bernard Ménager

Pumpkin Soup

Soup Jouwoumou (Soup Joumou)
Soupe de Giraumon

Soup Jouwoumou, the traditional soup of New Year's Day in Haiti, is also a Sunday morning soup. It has a smooth and delicious base filled with pieces of vegetables and meat. It is served at breakfast with toasted bread. The meat can be cooked one day ahead and kept in the refrigerator until ready to use.

Estimated time: 2 hours (including time to cook the meat).

1 recipe of *Beef in Creole Sauce* made with beef brisket with bone, or with beef shank (cross cut)*
one 3 to 3 1/4-pound West Indian pumpkin**
1/4 cup vegetable oil
2 cups chopped white onion
2 medium leeks (white and pale green parts only), sliced crosswise into 1/4-inch pieces
3/4 pound turnips (about 2 medium turnips), peeled, and cut into bite-size pieces
1/2 pound carrots (about 3 medium carrots), peeled, and sliced crosswise into 1/2 inch pieces

1 1/4 pounds potatoes (about 3 medium potatoes), peeled, and cut into bite-sized pieces
1 habanero chile, seeded, washed, and minced (read *Demystifying Habanero Chile*)
3 chicken bouillon cubes, crushed
6 celery ribs, trimmed and sliced crosswise into 1/2 inch pieces***
2 cups coarsely chopped cabbage
7 to 10 radishes, peeled
3 slices red bell pepper
5 to 6 sorrel leaves (sour grass), tied up or 1 tablespoon vinegar
1 cup rigatoni, or penne rigate****

Allow sauce to reduce until very thick when cooking meat. Remove meat from sauce, add 1/2 cup of boiled water to sauce. Remove and discard the sprig of thyme. It is not necessary to strain the sauce. Set the sauce aside.

While the meat is cooking, brush pumpkin very carefully under fresh running water. Cut and core. Cut into eight pieces. Peel with a sharp knife. Discard the skin. Put pumpkin in a large pot of water, cover, and cook over medium heat until tender, about 25 minutes. Drain pumpkin, reserving the cooking liquid. Transfer cooked pumpkin to a blender. Purée pumpkin pulp with 7 to 8 cups of cooking liquid.

Heat 2 tablespoons oil over medium high setting in a heavy 8-quart round pan (or in a soup pot), and sauté onion and leeks for 5 minutes. Add pumpkin purée, turnips, carrots, potatoes, chile, bouillon cubes, celery, cabbage, radish, bell pepper, meat sauce (not meat), sorrel or vinegar, and pasta. Season with salt and pepper if necessary. Boil uncovered until vegetables are tender, about 15 minutes. Do not overcook. Add cooked meat and remaining oil at the last 5 minutes. Discard sorrel if using. Serve hot with toasted bread.

Serves 8 to 10.

*If using shank, choose the middle portion. Precut stew meat can be used as well, along with a few soup bones. You may cook the meat one day ahead and store it in the refrigerator.

**West Indian pumpkin is also called Calabaza squash. Although a poor alternative, acorn squash may be used where West Indian pumpkin is not available. Another alternative would be to use a combination of half acorn and half "pumpkin pie pumpkin". Butternut squash is the closest alternative to West Indies Pumpkin I could find. It makes a creamy, velvety, and delicious soup. It is widely available in the USA.

***The celery found in Haiti looks a lot like flat-leaf parsley. It has the same great taste as celery stalks, but more concentrated. If available and if you want to use it, put two or three large sprigs in the soup. At the end of cooking and before serving, discard it, just as you do the sorrel.

****Traditionally, vermicelli is the pasta used in *Pumpkin Soup*. Frequently people use spaghetti. I use rigatoni or penne rigate because I find them easier to handle in the soup. You can be innovative and use any kind of short plain pasta. If you must use spaghetti, break them into roughly 2-inch pieces.

Vegetable Stew

Bouyon
Bouillon de Légumes

Above all, *Bouyon* is the Haitian stew. It contains meat, seafood, and also vegetables and roots which make it hearty and filling. It is rather a Saturday dish and a regular of midnight suppers.

The meat can be cooked one day ahead. Make sure that the coconut is fresh and does not taste rancid. Whole milk can easily replace coconut milk.

Estimated time: 2 hours (including time for meat and seafood).

1 pound precut stew meat, cooked following *Beef in Creole Sauce* recipe
1/2 pound medium shrimp, shelled, and deveined
1 pound crab legs (to be cooked with the shrimp)
1 large pot of boiled water
salt to taste
2 1/2 cups all-purpose flour (for the dumplings)
1 tablespoon vegetable oil
1 /4 cup chopped red bell pepper
1/2 cup chopped white onion

2 bundles (about 1 1/2 pounds) fresh spinach, chopped
2 bundles fresh watercress, chopped
2 green plantains, peeled and cut crosswise into 3/4-inch pieces
2 large potatoes, peeled and cut into 1 1/2-inch cubes
4 carrots, peeled and cut crosswise into 1/2-inch pieces
1 small white name root*, peeled and cut into 2-inch cubes
1 malanga (yautia)*, peeled and cut into 2- inch cubes
1 cup fresh coconut milk (or whole milk)
3 chicken bouillon cubes, crushed

Cook meat following *Beef in Creole Sauce* recipe. It is not necessary to strain sauce. Remove and discard the sprig of thyme. Set aside.

Cook shrimp and crab together following *Spiny Lobster in Creole Sauce* recipe. It is not necessary to strain the sauce. Set aside.

Mix 1 cup of water with 2 teaspoons salt. Add gradually to the flour to form a smooth dough. Sprinkle palms of both hands with flour, and roll dough into 3-inch long finger-shaped dumpling sticks. Set aside.

Heat oil over medium setting in a heavy 8-quart round pan (or a soup pot), and sauté bell pepper and onion. Add spinach and watercress. Toss to coat with oil. Cover and cook until greens are tender, about 5 minutes. Add 7 cups boiled water, seafood with sauce, meat sauce (not meat), dumpling sticks, plantain, potato, carrots, name root, malanga, coconut milk, and bouillon cubes. Season with salt to taste. Boil until vegetables are tender, about 25 minutes. Add more boiled water if stew is too thick. Add cooked meat, and simmer for 5 additional minutes. Remove from heat. Serve hot.

Serves 8.

*Found in the vegetable section of Caribbean, African, and Latin American markets, and some supermarkets. See note in the Glossary and *The Cook's Techniques* in this book. Where name root is not available, use cassava which is an excellent alternative for name root.

Not having malanga or name root should not keep you from making this stew. Malanga and name root are not optional ingredients, but you can make the stew without them. In fact, nothing in this stew is optional; that is what makes it the stew it is.

Vegetable Consommé

Konsonmen Legim Klè
Consommé de Légumes

This is the kind of light consommé we usually serve during midnight supper on Christmas Eve, or on New Year's Eve. It is sometimes served, along with other soups or stews, as long as the party goes on, or during the cocktail hour, or at the beginning of the main course. A midnight supper menu is given in the menu section of this book.

Estimated time: 1 hour 45 minutes.

2 tablespoons vegetable oil
4 garlic cloves, peeled, and crushed (see note in *More Tips*)
1/2 cup chopped white onion
1 leek, sliced
1 tablespoon chopped chives, or 1 minced scallion
10 cups of boiled water
2 medium potatoes, peeled, and coarsely chopped (yields about 2 1/2 cups)
1 medium carrot, peeled and sliced
1 small turnip, peeled, and cut into small wedges

1/2 cup trimmed green beans (trimmed and chopped snow peas will also do)
1 tablespoon chopped parsley
1/2 teaspoon coarsely crushed black peppercorn
3 chicken bouillon cubes, crushed
1 habanero chile (read *Demystifying Habanero Chile*)
1 tablespoon salt
1/4 cup frozen green peas, thawed
1/4 cup finely diced carrots
1/2 cup finely sliced leeks (white and pale green parts only)
1 tablespoon butter or margarine

Heat oil over medium high setting in a heavy 5-quart pan. Add garlic, onion, leeks, and chives, and sauté for 3 minutes. Add water, and bring to a boil. Add potatoes, carrots, turnip, green beans, parsley, black pepper, bouillon cubes, chile, and salt. Cover, and cook for 1 hour 15 minutes over medium heat, with lid slightly ajar. Remove from heat, discard chile, and strain through a fine strainer without pressing on the vegetables. Reserve cooked vegetables for another use*. Add green peas, diced carrot, and sliced leek. Reduce the consommé in a heavy 3-quart pan over medium heat, 15 minutes. Remove from heat. Mix in butter. Serve hot. This recipe can be doubled.

Yields five 6-ounce servings.

*Make a cream of vegetables by puréeing cooked vegetables with 3 cups of boiled water in a blender at high speed for 2 minutes. Strain. Add 1 tablespoon vegetable oil. Correct seasoning. Reduce over medium heat for a short time.

Cream of Malanga

Konsonmen Malanga Kraze
Potage Purée de Malanga

This creamy and delicious soup can be served as first course during a dinner meal; it can also be served alone with toasted bread for lunch, or to warm a cold night.

Estimated time: 1 hour 30 minutes.

2 tablespoons vegetable oil
6 garlic cloves, peeled, and crushed (see note in *More Tips*)
11 cups of boiled water
6 malanga, peeled and coarsely chopped (yields about 5 cups)
1 leek, sliced (yields about 1 1/2 cups)
2 cups chopped white onion
3 teaspoons salt
1 teaspoon black pepper
4 chicken bouillon cubes
1/2 tablespoon apple cider vinegar
2 tablespoons butter, or margarine

Heat oil over medium high setting in a heavy 8-quart round pan. Sauté garlic for 1 minute. Add 11 cups of boiled water, malanga, leek, onion, salt, black pepper, bouillon cubes, and vinegar. Boil covered with lid ajar over medium high heat until vegetables are very tender, 30 minutes. Remove from heat. Cool at room temperature for 20 minutes.

Purée vegetables with cooking liquid in a blender at high speed, until smooth. Strain through a fine strainer. Bring vegetable purée to a quick boil over medium heat for 3 minutes, stirring constantly. Remove from heat. Mix in butter or margarine. Serve hot. The recipe can be halved.

Serves 8 to 10.

Cream of Potato with Leek and Green Peas

Konsonmen Pomdetè ak Powo ak Pwa Frans
Potage Purée de Pommes de Terre aux Poireaux et aux Petits Pois

This creamy soup is often served as a first course during a dinner meal, and can also be served alone with toasted bread for lunch, or to warm a cold night.

Estimated time: 1 hour 30 minutes.

1/4 cup vegetable oil
4 garlic cloves, peeled, and crushed (see note in *More Tips*)
1/2 cup chopped white onion
10 cups boiled water
3 large baking potatoes (about 2 pounds), peeled, and chopped (yields 4 cups)

1 1/2 cups sliced leeks (white part only)
1/4 cup frozen green peas, thawed
4 chicken bouillon cubes
1/4 teaspoon ground black pepper
3/4 teaspoon salt, or to taste
1/2 cup whole milk (optional)

Heat oil over medium high setting in a heavy 5-quart pan. Sauté garlic for 1 minute. Add onion and sauté for 3 minutes. Add boiled water, potatoes, leeks, green peas, bouillon cubes, black pepper, and salt. Boil covered with lid ajar over medium high heat until vegetables are very tender, 30 minutes. Remove from heat. Cool at room temperature for 15 minutes.

Purée vegetables with cooking liquid in a blender at high speed, until smooth. Strain through a fine strainer. Residue, if any, should be very little. Add milk, if using. Reduce over medium heat for 5 to 10 minutes, stirring very often. Serve hot.

Serves 6.

Cream of Vegetable

Konsonmen Legim Kraze
Potage Purée de Legumes

This creamy soup is often served as a first course during a dinner meal, and can also be served alone with toasted bread for lunch, or to warm a cold night.

Estimated time: 1 hour 30 minutes

1/4 cup vegetable oil
6 garlic cloves, peeled, and crushed (see note in *More Tips*)
14 cups boiled water
2 pounds baking potatoes (5 medium potatoes), peeled and chopped; yields 4 1/2 cups
1 large carrot (about 1/4 pound), peeled, and chopped; yields about 1 cup

1/2 pound turnips (2 medium), peeled, and chopped; yields about 2 cups
1 leek, sliced (yields about 1 1/2 cups)
2 cups chopped white onion
2 celery ribs, sliced (yields about 1 cup)
1 cup frozen green peas, thawed
3 teaspoons salt
1/2 teaspoon black pepper
4 chicken bouillon cubes
1/2 tablespoon apple cider vinegar

Heat oil over medium high setting in a heavy 8-quart round pan. Sauté garlic for 1 minute. Add 11 cups of boiled water, potatoes, carrot, turnips, leek, onion, celery, green peas, salt, black pepper, bouillon cubes, and vinegar. Boil covered with lid ajar over medium high heat until vegetables are very tender, 30 minutes. Remove from heat. Cool at room temperature for 20 minutes.

Purée vegetables with cooking liquid in a blender at high speed, until smooth. Strain through a fine strainer. Bring vegetable purée to a quick boil over medium heat for 3 minutes, stirring constantly. Serve hot. The recipe can be halved.

Serves 8 to 10.

Cream of Vegetable with Beef

Konsonmen Bèf ak Legim
Potage Purée de Légumes à la Viande de Boeuf

This delicious dish can be served as first course during a dinner meal, or alone with toasted bread for lunch, or to warm a cold night.

Estimated time: 1 hour.

1/2 pound precut stew meat, cooked
following *Beef in Creole Sauce* recipe
2 malanga (yautia)*
2 carrots

3 large baking potatoes (about 2 pounds)
2 tablespoons vegetable oil
2 cups chopped white onion
1 leek, sliced
salt to taste if necessary

Cook meat following *Beef in Creole Sauce* recipe. Do not strain sauce. Set aside.

Peel and coarsely cut malanga, carrots, potatoes. Set aside.

Heat oil over medium high setting in a heavy 8-quart round pan (or soup pot), and sauté onion and leek for about 7 minutes. Add 7 cups of water and bring to boil. Add vegetables, meat with sauce and cook until vegetables are tender, about 30 minutes. Purée vegetables, meat and cooking liquid with a blender. Strain in a large pan. Add salt if necessary. Bring to a short boil over medium heat, about 5 minutes. Serve hot.

Serves 6.

*Also called yautia, malanga is found in the vegetable section of Caribbean and Latin-American groceries and markets, and some supermarkets. It is sometimes confused with taro. Read about malanga in the Glossary of this book.

Cream of Vegetable with Seafood

Konsonmen Fwidmè ak Legim
Potage Purée de Légumes aux Fruits de Mer

Just as the preceding recipes, this creamy soup is often served as a first course during a dinner meal, and can also be served alone with toasted bread for lunch, or to warm a cold night.

Estimated time: 1 hour 30 minutes (including cooling time).

1/4 cup vegetable oil
6 garlic cloves, peeled, and crushed (see note in *More Tips*)
1 tablespoon tomato paste diluted with
1 cup boiled water
11 cups of boiled water
2 pounds baking potatoes (5 medium potatoes), peeled and chopped; yields about 41/2 cups
1 large carrot (about 1/4 pound), peeled, and chopped; yields about 1 cup
1/2 pound turnips (2 medium), peeled, and chopped; yields about 2 cups
1 leek, sliced (yields about 1 1/2 cups)

2 cups chopped white onion
2 celery ribs, sliced (yields about 1 cup)
1 cup frozen green peas, thawed
3 teaspoons salt
1 teaspoon black pepper
1 habanero chile (read *Demystifying Habanero Chile*)
3 chicken bouillon cubes
1 tablespoon apple cider vinegar
1/4 pound medium shrimp
1/4 pound scallops
1/4 pound crab legs
one 6.5-ounce can clams in juice

Heat oil ever medium high setting in a heavy 8-quart round pan. Sauté garlic for 1 minute. Add diluted tomato paste, and boil until water evaporates completely, about 15 to 20 minutes. Add 11 cups of boiled water, potatoes, carrot, turnips, leek, onion, celery, green peas, salt, black pepper, chile, bouillon cubes, vinegar, shrimp, scallops, crab legs, and clams. Boil covered with lid ajar over medium high heat until vegetables are very tender, 30 minutes. Remove from heat. Cool at room temperature for 20 minutes. Remove and discard chile.

Using sharp kitchen shears, shell crab legs. Add crab flesh and juice to vegetables in pan, and discard crab shells. Purée vegetables and seafood with cooking liquid in a blender at high speed, until purée is smooth. Strain through a fine strainer. Bring purée to a quick boil over medium heat for 3 minutes, stirring constantly. Serve hot. The recipe can be halved.

Serves 8 to10.

Chicken and Vegetable Stew

Bouyon Poul
Bouillon de Poulet aux Légumes

Estimated time: 1 hour 30 minutes.

8 to 10 cups of boiled water
2 tablespoons apple cider vinegar
4 chicken bouillon cubes, crushed
1 1/2 pounds chicken breast, cleaned and cubed into 1-inch cubes
1/4 cup vegetable oil
2 cups diced white onion
6 garlic cloves, peeled, and crushed (see note in *More Tips*)
2 leeks, sliced (white and pale green part only)
2 tablespoons chopped chives, or 2 minced scallions

1/4 cup all-purpose flour
5 large potatoes, peeled, and cut into bite-sized pieces
2 malanga, cut into bite-sized pieces
1 small turnip, peeled, and quartered lengthwise
4 medium carrots, peeled and sliced
5 celery ribs, trimmed and sliced
7 radishes, peeled
1 habanero chile (read *Demystifying Habanero Chile*)
1/4 heaping teaspoon ground black pepper
3 teaspoons salt

Mix 3 cups of water, vinegar, and bouillon cubes in a 12-inch skillet, add chicken cubes, cover (lid slightly ajar), and cook over medium heat until chicken is tender, 10 to 15 minutes. Remove from heat, and strain, reserving the cooking liquid. Set aside until ready to use.

Heat 1 tablespoon oil over medium heat in a heavy 8-quart pan. Add onion, garlic, leeks, chives, and sauté for 3 minutes. Transfer onion mixture to a plate, and reserve. Heat remaining oil over medium setting in the same pan. Add flour and cook for 3 minutes whisking often. Remove from heat. Using a wire whisk, vigorously whisk in reserved chicken cooking liquid until mixture becomes creamy and homogeneous. Add remaining water, whisking constantly, and bring to a boil. Add potatoes, reserved sautéed spices, malanga, turnip, carrot slices, celery slices, radishes, chile, black pepper, and salt. Cover, leaving lid slightly ajar, and cook over medium heat until vegetables are tender and the stew is fairly thick, about 20 minutes. Add cooked chicken at the last 5 minutes. Remove and discard the turnip wedges and the chile before serving. Serve hot.

Serves 8 to 10.

Gumbo

Kalalou Gonbo
Bouillon au Gombo

Kalalou Gonbo is typical of the south of Haiti. It is served with *Tonmtonm* to such an extent that the combination is called *Tonmtonm ak Kalalou Gonbo*. Meat and seafood can be cooked one day ahead and stored in the refrigerator. Recipe for *Tonmtonm* follows.

Estimated time: 2 hours (cooking time for meat and seafood is included).

1/2 pound medium shrimp, shelled and deveined

1 pound crab legs (to be cooked with shrimp)

1 pound okra (yields slightly more than 4 cups of sliced okra)

1/4 cup vegetable oil

1/2 cup diced white onion

1/4 cup diced red bell pepper

1 large pot of boiled water

1 1/2 pound precut stew meat cooked following *Beef in Creole Sauce* recipe

1/4 teaspoon ground paprika

1 tablespoon apple cider vinegar

1 habanero chile (read *Demystifying Habanero Chile*)

2 chicken bouillon cubes, crushed

1 teaspoon salt

1/4 teaspoon ground black pepper

Cook shrimp and crab together following the recipe of *Lobster in Creole Sauce*. Set aside.

Wash okra under fresh running water. Trim and discard both ends of okra. Slice them crosswise into about 1/3-inch pieces. Cook okra in 5 quarts (20 cups) of unsalted water for 20 minutes. Drain and discard cooking water*. Transfer okra to a large bowl, and mash it with a fork. The small okra seeds should be visible. Set aside.

Heat oil over medium high setting in a heavy 8-quart round pan (or a soup pot), and sauté onion and bell pepper for 3 minutes. Add 10 cups of boiled water, mashed okra, seafood with sauce, meat sauce (but not meat), paprika, vinegar, chile, bouillon cubes, salt, and black pepper. Boil down, uncovered, over medium heat, 25 to 30 minutes. Gumbo should be fairly thick. Add cooked meat during the last 5 minutes. Discard chile. Serve hot with *Tonmtonm*.

Serves 6

*You may choose to use the okra cooking water if you wish to make a heavier Gumbo.

Variation. To make *Black Gumbo*, boil 2 cups of Haitian mushrooms with shrimp shells for 20 minutes in 11 cups of water, over medium heat. Boil the mushrooms before boiling the okra, so they have plenty of time to steep. Strain "black water," and use it instead of the 10 cups of boiled water.

Mashed Breadfruit and Mashed Sweet Potato

Tonmtonm
Purée de Véritable et Purée de Patate

Tonmtonm is the accompaniment for *Kalalou Gonbo*. It is a mash made with breadfruit, and also with sweet potato and name root. The procedure is different from mashed potato because breadfruit has to be mashed a little longer, and very little liquid is added. Besides salt, no seasoning is added to *Tonmtonm* since the *Gumbo* is already very flavorful. You can choose to serve one type of *Tonmtonm* or the three at the same meal.

Traditionally a huge and deep mortar paired with a long pestle are used to make it, and I have always believed that its name comes from the beat produced by the huge pestle stamping in the huge mortar. Use the biggest mortar available to you. Mashed breadfruit is sticky, so the tip of the pestle must be dipped often in water to ease the process. That is about all the liquid added to the mash.

Be sure breadfruit is ripe and green, but not ripened and sweet.

Estimated time: 45 minutes.

- 1 breadfruit, quartered, cored, and peeled, or 8 large dry-flesh sweet potatoes
- salt to taste
- a bowl of cool boiled water to moisten the pestle

For mashed breadfruit

Cut each breadfruit quarter in half lengthwise or crosswise. Cook them in a large pot of boiling salted water until tender, about 20 to 30 minutes. Using a 12-inch (or bigger) mortar with a matched pestle, purée breadfruit by portions while still hot until smooth. Dip the tip of the pestle often in fresh water. Gather mashed breadfruit into a ball. Serve with *Kalalou Gonbo*.

For mashed sweet potatoes

Boil sweet potatoes in a large pot of salted water until tender, 20 to 30 minutes. Peel boiled sweet potatoes, holding them with a kitchen cloth. Follow the above procedure to mash the sweet potatoes while they are still hot. Gather mashed sweet potatoes into a ball. Serve with *Kalalou Gonbo*.

Sweet potatoes can also be puréed through a potato ricer or a food mill, just like potatoes.

Serves 6.

Herring and Dumplings Soup

Soup Aran Sò ak Donmbrey
Soupe à l'Hareng Saur et aux Boulettes de Farine

Here is a very easy and delicious soup. The herring flavor is intense.

Estimated time: 30 minutes (without soaking time).

2 skinless smoked red herring filets, or 1 whole smoked red herring*

2 teaspoons salt (for the dumplings)

1 cup water (for the dumplings)

2 1/2 cups all-purpose flour (for the dumplings)

1/4 cup vegetable oil

4 garlic cloves, peeled, and crushed (see note in *More Tips*)

1/2 tablespoon tomato paste diluted with 1/2 cup of boiled water

1 cup finely diced white onion

1 tablespoon chopped chives, or 1 minced scallion

1 cup thinly sliced leeks (white and pale green parts only)

1 tablespoon all-purpose flour

10 cups boiled water

1/2 teaspoon finely ground black pepper

1 habanero chile (read *Demystifying Habanero Chile*)

2 chicken bouillon cubes, crushed

salt to taste**

Soak herring as indicated in *The Cook's Techniques* chapter. Then cut into bite-size pieces. Remove as many bones as possible.

Meanwhile, prepare the dumplings. Dilute salt in the water. Add gradually to flour to form a smooth dough. Sprinkle palms of both hands with flour and roll dough into 3 to 4-inch long dumpling sticks. Cover and set aside.

Heat oil in a heavy 5-quart pan over medium high setting. Sauté garlic for 1 minute. Add diluted tomato paste and boil uncovered until all liquid evaporates, 6 to 7 minutes. Stir-fry for about 1 minute. Add onion, chives, leeks, and continue to sauté for 3 to 4 minutes, stirring often. Add soaked herring filets, and flour. Sauté for 1 minute. Add 1 cup boiled water, and mix well, then add remaining water, black pepper, chile, bouillon cubes, and salt. Mix well. Bring to a boil, then add dumplings. Reduce over medium heat until soup thickens, about 25 to 30 minutes. Serve hot.

Serves 6.

*To learn how to handle whole smoked herring, read *How to Soak Salt Cod and Smoked Red Herring* in *The Cook's Techniques* chapter.

**The amount of salt will depend on the length of soaking the herring. You can use some of the soaking water if you wish, preferably the last soaking water, and use caution when adding salt to the soup.

BREAD AND PASTRY

Pen ak Patisri
Pain et Patisserie

Choux

Kabich (Cabiche)

     Kabich is a delicious bread stuffed with herring. Prepare the stuffing ahead of time and store it in the refrigerator. Use skinless herring filets, so you do not have to worry about skin, and they are much easier to handle. You may mix the stuffing with the dough while kneading, or use it as a filling as I do it in this recipe, or do both. Mixing the filling with the dough gives a more delicious bread, whereas rolling the dough over the stuffing is more appealing.

     Water and milk must be just warm (between 95 and 100 degrees Fahrenheit). If too hot, the heat will kill the yeast and the bread will not rise. Use an instant-read thermometer to check the water and the milk temperatures. If such a thermometer is not readily available, drop a few drops of water and milk on the back of your wrist; they should feel around normal body temperature. Place dough in a warm place to rise (around 80 to 85 degrees Fahrenheit).

Estimated time: 3 hours 30 minutes (including 2 hours 45 minutes rising time).

1 tablespoon sugar
1/4 cup warm water (between 95 and 100 degrees Fahrenheit)
one 1/4-ounce (2 1/4 teaspoons) package active dry yeast
1 cup warm milk (between 95 and 100 degrees Fahrenheit)
2 1/2 teaspoons salt

4 tablespoons butter or margarine, at room temperature
1 cup warm water (between 95 and 100 degrees Fahrenheit)
6 1/2 cups bread flour
1 recipe of herring stuffing (recipe follows)
2 tablespoons milk (to brush the bread before baking)
2 tablespoons melted butter (to brush the bread after baking)

Grease one large or two small cookie sheets. Grease a large mixing bowl. Set aside.

Dissolve 1 teaspoon sugar in 1/4 cup warm water in a small bowl. Sprinkle with the yeast and let stand for 10 minutes. Then stir.

Put warm milk, remaining sugar, salt, butter in a large bowl. Stir until butter is melted. Add warm water. Mix in yeast mixture. Add 3 cups of flour and mix vigorously with a strong wooden spoon. Mix in gradually 3 to 3 1/2 cups of flour to obtain an elastic dough, using both hands whenever necessary. Knead* dough on a lightly floured surface until smooth, about 8 to 10 minutes. Dough should be smooth and elastic. Form dough into a smooth ball. Transfer dough to the greased bowl. Turn the dough in the bowl to coat it with grease. Cover with plastic wrap and a towel. Let rise in a warm place until doubled, about one hour. Punch down with your fist**. Divide dough into two balls. Roll out each ball into a 12-x 14-inch rectangle, and quickly spread half of herring stuffing on each of them, leaving a 1/2 inch border free of stuffing at each side. Roll dough on the stuffing and away from you, starting with the shorter side facing you. Transfer rolled dough on the prepared baking sheet, seam down. Cover, and let rise until doubled, about one hour. Do not let overrise. Otherwise, the dough will have large air bubbles and the resulting bread could be dry.

Meanwhile, preheat oven to 375 degrees Fahrenheit. After dough has risen, brush it with milk. Bake in the preheated oven for 35 minutes. Brush with melted butter while still hot. *Kabich* can be a good accompaniment for *Holy Week Salad* or *Avocado Salad*.

Yields 2 loaves.

Variation. To make *Sandwich Bread (Pain de Mie)*, do not roll the dough out and do not use the herring stuffing. After dividing the dough in two balls, give each of them roughly a 9-x 5-inch rectangular shape. Fit each into a greased 9-x 5-inch loaf pan, cover, and let rise until doubled. Then bake as above.

*You may also use a fast rising active dry yeast. In this case, reduce the rising times by about half.

**To knead is to work the dough vigorously with the heels of both hands, pushing it away from you, folding it, and turning it. The procedure is repeated until the dough becomes smooth and elastic. Kneading can take 5 to 15 minutes, and can also be done with a mixer equipped with special hooks.

***To punch down is to deflate the dough by pressing it in the middle with your fist. The edges are then folded toward the center until the dough almost returns to its initial volume.

Herring Stuffing for Kabich and Herring Pâté en Croûte

Fas Aran Sò pou Kabich ak Pâté Haran
Farce à L'hareng Saur pour Kabiche et Pate de Hareng en Croûte

Prepare the stuffing one day ahead, and store it in the refrigerator. Use herring filets which are much easier to handle.

1/2 pound smoked red herring filets*
2 tablespoons vegetable oil
3 garlic cloves, peeled, and crushed (see note in *More Tips*)
3 tablespoons tomato paste, diluted with 1 cup of water
1/2 cup finely minced white onion
1 sprig thyme, leaves only

1 habanero chile, seeded, carefully washed, and minced (read *Demystifying Habanero Chile*)
1/2 teaspoon ground black pepper
1 chicken bouillon cube
1/4 cup finely chopped fresh flat-leaf parsley
1 tablespoon vinegar
salt to taste if necessary
1/4 cup mayonnaise (only if the stuffing is to be used as a filling)

Soak herring as indicated in *The Cook's Techniques* chapter. Drain carefully reserving 1/4 cup of the last soaking water. Flake fish with a fork. Set aside.

Heat oil in a heavy 4-quart round pan over medium setting. Sauté garlic for 2 minutes. Add diluted tomato paste and boil over medium high setting until no liquid remains, about 15 to 20 minutes. Reduce heat to medium and stir-fry for about 1 minute. Add onion, thyme, and chile, and sauté for 3 minutes, or until onion is very soft. Add reserved water, herring, black pepper, bouillon cubes, parsley, and vinegar. Reduce over medium high heat until sauce thickens, about 12 minutes. The mixture should be dry. Season with salt if needed. Transfer to a medium bowl and cool at room temperature. If you choose to knead it into the dough, do it preferably at this point (when the stuffing is dry).

To use it as a filling, mix in the mayonnaise thoroughly. The stuffing should be moist and should hold together. This is used in *Herring Pâté en Croûte* and when the kabich dough is rolled over the stuffing. Moist as it is, it is preferably used as a filling, but you can still mix it with the kabich dough; in this case increase the amount of flour to make the bread to 6 3/4 cups.

Yields about 1 1/2 cups.

*You may use whole smoked red herring as well. To learn how to handle whole smoked herring, read *How to Soak Salt Cod and Smoked Red Herring* in *The Cook's Techniques* chapter.

Butter Rolls

Pen Ti Bè
Petits Pains au Beurre

Remember that water and milk must be just warm (between 95 and 100 degrees Fahrenheit). If they are too hot, the heat will kill the yeast and the bread will not rise. Use an instant-read thermometer to check the temperatures. If such a thermometer is not readily available, drop a few drops of water and milk on the back of your wrist; they should feel around normal body temperature. Place the dough in a warm place to rise (around 80 to 85 degrees Fahrenheit).

2 teaspoons granulated sugar
1/2 cup warm water (between 95 and 100 degrees Fahrenheit)
one 1/4-ounce package active dry yeast*
1 cup warm whole milk (between 95 and 100 degrees Fahrenheit)
1 1/4 teaspoon salt

1/4 cup (1/2 stick) butter or margarine, at room temperature
4 1/2 cups bread flour
2 tablespoons whole milk (to brush the rolls before baking)
2 tablespoons melted butter or margarine (to brush the rolls after baking)

Grease one 11x7-inch jelly roll pan. Grease a large mixing bowl. Set aside.

Mix 1 teaspoon sugar with the warm water in a small bowl. Sprinkle with the yeast and let stand for 10 minutes.

Meanwhile, stir warm milk, remaining sugar, salt, and butter in a large bowl until butter is melted. Stir in the yeast mixture. Add 2 cups of flour and mix vigorously with a strong wooden spoon. Mix in gradually the remaining flour to obtain an elastic dough, using both hands whenever necessary. Knead** dough on a lightly floured surface until smooth, about 8 to 10 minutes. Dough should be smooth and elastic. Form dough into a smooth ball. Transfer the dough ball to the greased bowl. Turn dough in the bowl to coat it with grease. Cover with plastic wrap and a towel. Let rise in a warm place until doubled, about 1 hour. Punch down with your fist***. Divide dough into 24 fairly equal balls. Transfer dough balls on the prepared pan, side by side. Brush each roll with milk. Cover with plastic wrap, and let rise in a warm place until doubled, about 45 minutes. Do not let overrise. Otherwise, the roll will have large air bubbles and the resulting bread could be dry.

Meanwhile, preheat oven to 375 degrees Fahrenheit.

Remove the plastic wrap, and bake the rolls in the preheated oven for 15 to 20 minutes, until slightly golden. Brush with melted butter or margarine while still hot.

Yields 24 Butter Rolls.

*You may also use a fast rising active dry yeast. In this case, reduce the rising times by about half.

**To knead is to work the dough vigorously with the heels of both hands, pushing it away from you, folding it, and turning it. The procedure is repeated until the dough becomes smooth and elastic. Kneading can take 5 to 15 minutes, and can also be done with a mixer equipped with special hooks.

***To punch down is to deflate the dough by pressing it in the middle with your fist. The edges are then folded toward the center until the dough almost returns to its initial volume.

Fried Flat Bread

Pate Kòde
Rissole

Flat bread is often made plain, and popularly eaten as a snack. They are particularly delicious when herring or Parmesan is added to the dough. Pastry flour gives a lighter flat bread.

2 teaspoons salt
1 cup water
2 1/2 cups all-purpose flour
2 skinless smoked red herring filets, soaked, and flaked, or 1/2 cup grated Parmesan cheese
vegetable oil for deep-frying

Mix the salt and the water. Put the flour on a smooth surface. Gradually add the water to the flour to form a smooth dough. Knead in the herring or the cheese. Form dough into a ball. Put dough ball in a floured bowl, cover with a damp towel, and let it rest for 1 hour. Divide into 16 to 20 fairly equal portions and form each into a ball. On a floured surface, roll each ball out with a floured rolling pin into a very thin (1/16 to 1/8 inch thick) round, oblong, or irregular shape.

Heat oil over medium setting in a large skillet. Drop the flattened dough in the hot oil, two to three at a time. Fry until golden and crispy, turning once, 4 to 5 minutes. Drain on paper towels. Keep hot. Repeat until all the dough is fried. Serve hot.

Yields 16 to 20 pieces.

Homemade Crackers

Biskuit Sèk
Biscuits Secs

Biskuit Sèk are the Haitian popular crackers. They are made by every "bread making" store in the country. We love to snack on them plain, or with peanut butter and/or jelly. They are also the perfect accompaniments for *Smoked Red Herring Chiquetaille*, *Salt Cod Chiquetaille*, and *Ham Chiquetaille*. This is a home recipe which gives very delicious crackers.

Estimated time: 30 minutes.

1 1/2 cups all purpose flour, or bread flour	2 tablespoons margarine
1/2 teaspoon salt	1/2 tablespoons vegetable shortening
3/4 teaspoon double-acting baking powder	1/2 cup water

Preheat oven to 350 degrees Fahrenheit. Have on hand two to three large ungreased cookie sheets.

Combine flour, salt, baking powder on a smooth surface. Working with hands, mix in margarine and shortening until well blended, then mix in water. Knead for a few minutes just until dough becomes smooth and soft, and does not stick to fingers. Roll out to a thickness of 1/8 inch. Cut with a 2 to 2 1/2-inch round cookie cutter. Roll out each piece of round dough and flatten until very flat. It is all right if they are not perfectly round. Transfer to ungreased cookie sheets, 1/2 inch apart. Poke holes all over each of them with the tines of a fork, and bake in the middle of preheated oven until they are golden and crispy, 10 to 15 minutes. Check them after 10 minutes of baking. Cool at room temperature. They keep for a long time when stored in wax bags.
Yields 40 to 45 Biskuit Sèk.

Note. In Haiti, *Biskuit Sèk* are rather circular. I found that a slight irregularity in their shape adds visual interest, making them more appealing and homey.

Fresh Breadcrumbs

Myèt Pen Griye
Chapelure

Homemade breadcrumbs are easy to make and taste undeniably fresher than commercially made breadcrumbs. Thus, your *Meat Loaf, Bread Pudding, Sweet Potato Pudding II* . . . etc., will taste better. Here the crumbs are made with white bread slices, but any bread or leftover bread will accommodate this recipe, with the exception of heavy fruited sweet loaves which may require more time and a lower temperature. If the bread is not sliced, simply slice it approximately like the sliced bread found at the baker's, or on the grocery shelves (1/2 inch thick).

- 12 slices of white bread
- a 13-x 18-inch jelly roll pan, or a 14-x 17-inch cookie sheet
- one or two racks

Preheat oven to 250 degrees Fahrenheit.

Arrange the bread slices in one layer on the baking sheet. Toast them in the middle of the preheated oven until they are crispy and slightly golden, 35 minutes, flipping them over when they are halfway done. Transfer the bread slices on the rack, and cool at room temperature. Grate toasted bread slices with a fine grater, or use a food processor to crumble them. Sift to eliminate large crumbs. Store breadcrumbs in a tightly closed wax bag. They will keep in the freezer for a very long time.

Yields 2 cups.

Molasses Bread

Bonbon Siwo I
Pain à La Mélasse

Bonbon Siwo is the common Haitian snack. There are two recipes for it in this book. This one is more doughy. The other one, which is in the dessert section, is more like a cake.

4 1/2 cups all-purpose flour	1/2 cup vegetable shortening
2 teaspoons baking soda	1/2 cup brown sugar
1/2 teaspoon salt	1 cup unsulphured molasses
1 teaspoon ground cinnamon	1 1/2 cups water

Preheat oven to 350 degrees Fahrenheit.
Grease and flour a 13- x 9-inch brownie pan. Set aside.

Mix flour, baking soda, salt, and cinnamon in a medium bowl. Set aside.

Cream shortening, sugar, and molasses in a large bowl. Mix in water. Mix in the flour mixture until creamy. Pour into the prepared pan and bake in the preheat oven for 30 to 35 minutes. Cool for 10 minutes in the pan, then unmold. Cool on a rack. Cut into lozenges or square shapes. Serve warm or at room temperature.

Yields about 20 to 30 pieces.

Muffins

Maspen (Ponmkèt)
Muffins

These baked goods lie between bread and cake. They are called *Maspen* or *Ponmkèt* in Haitian Creole, and they are eaten as snacks, but they are not as popular as *Ginger Bread* and *Molasses Bread*.

2 cups all-purpose flour	1 teaspoon pure vanilla extract
2 teaspoons double-acting baking powder	1 cup milk
1 cup sugar	1/2 cup butter or margarine, softened, or vegetable oil
1/4 teaspoon salt	
2 eggs, slightly beaten to mix	1 cup raisins

Preheat oven to 400 degrees Fahrenheit. Grease eighteen 1/3-cup muffin cups, or eight 3/4-cup muffin cups with butter or margarine, and set aside.

Mix flour, baking powder, sugar, and salt in a large bowl. Set aside. In another large bowl, beat eggs slightly. Mix in vanilla extract, milk, butter (or margarine or vegetable oil), and raisins. Quickly stir this egg mixture into the flour mixture to just combine them. Do not over mix. The mixture should be somewhat lumpy. Fill prepared pans with batter 2/3 of the way to the top. Fill empty muffin cups halfway with water to prevent burning. Bake in the middle of preheated oven for 15 to 20 minutes for 1/3-cup muffin cups and 25 minutes for 3/4-cup muffin cups. Unmold and cool on a rack.

Yields 18 small muffins, or 8 large muffins.

Konparèt

Konparèt is a speciality of Grande-Anse, Haiti. It is a dense (but not heavy) and delicious cake-like bread in which coconut, ginger, and cinnamon represent the distinctive ingredients. It can be served with either coffee or tea, and even with a glass of milk. Make sure that the coconut is fresh and does not taste rancid. Otherwise, it will ruin the *Konparèt*.

Estimated time: 1 hour.

3 cups all purpose flour
1 tablespoon ground cinnamon
1/2 teaspoon salt
2 teaspoons double-acting baking powder
1/2 cup (1 stick) butter or margarine, at room temperature
1/2 cup light brown sugar
1/2 cup honey
2 eggs
1 cup crystallized ginger, finely chopped (about 6 ounces)
1 3/4 cups packed freshly grated coconut*
1 teaspoon pure vanilla extract
1/2 teaspoon pure almond extract
2 to 3 tablespoons fresh ginger juice**
2 teaspoons freshly grated lime zest

Preheat oven to 375 degrees Fahrenheit.
Lightly grease a large cookie sheet with butter or margarine. Set aside.

In a large bowl, mix flower, cinnamon, salt, and baking powder. Set aside.

Cream butter in a large bowl. Mix in sugar and honey until creamy and homogenous. Add eggs one by one, mixing well after each addition. Mix in crystallized ginger, coconut, vanilla extract, almond extract, ginger juice, and lime zest. Stir in flour mixture with a strong wooden spoon until a sticky dough is formed. Transfer dough onto a lightly floured surface. Working with floured hands, divide dough into five balls. Transfer dough balls to the prepared baking sheet, 3 inches apart. Bake in preheated oven for 30 minutes.

Yields 10 to 15 servings (5 Konparèt).

*Before grating the coconut, use a vegetable peeler to remove and discard the thin brown coat that covers the coconut flesh.

**Fresh ginger juice: Peel, then grate ginger with a fine grater. Strain the juice through a fine strainer, pressing on the residue. Discard the residue.

Frying Batter I for Savory Fritters

Premye Pat pou Marinad
Pâté à Frire I pour Beignets Salés

This batter is used for savory fritters like *Meat Fritters*. Commonly in Haiti, water is used to hold the ingredients together for savory fritters, whereas for sweet fritters, milk is used.

2 cups all purpose flour
2 cups plus 1 tablespoon water
2 teaspoons salt
3/4 teaspoon baking soda
Vegetable oil for deep-frying

In a large bowl, whisk flour, water, and salt to form a fluid batter. Mix in seasoning and meat*. Let rest for 20 minutes. Then mix in baking soda thoroughly.

In a heavy pan, heat oil over medium setting and drop dough by tablespoons in hot oil. Do not overload. Cook turning once until golden and crisp, about 8 minutes. Serve hot.

Yields about 60 fritters.

*For seasoning, use 4 cloves garlic (crushed), 1 tablespoon finely minced chives, 1 habanero chile (seeded, washed, and minced), 1/2 teaspoon ground black pepper, 2 chicken bouillon cubes. For meat, use 1 cup chopped or finely shredded cooked chicken, or 1/2 cup soaked and crushed smoked red herring filet, or 1/2 cup soaked and crushed salt cod filet.

Frying Batter II for Savory Fritters

Dezyèm Pat pou Marinad ak Vyann Pane
Pâte à Frire II pour Beignets Salés et Viande Panée

These fritters are made by dipping meat in the batter instead of mixing them together. The batter can serve to prepare small pieces of meat, seafood, or cheese (appetizers), or it can be used for large pieces of meat (breaded chicken for example).

1 1/2 cup all-purpose flour
1 teaspoon salt
2 chicken bouillon cubes, crushed
1/4 teaspoon finely ground black pepper
2 teaspoons double-acting baking powder

3/4 cup water
2 eggs, beaten
vegetable oil for deep frying
about 60 meat pieces, seafood pieces, or cheese pieces*

Mix flour, salt, bouillon cubes, pepper, baking powder in a large bowl. Mix in water and beaten eggs until smooth.

Heat oil over medium setting in a heavy deep frying pan. Holding meat or cheese with a fork (hold shrimp by the end of the tail), dip it in the batter to coat. Drop it in the hot oil, and cook until golden turning once, 1 to 2 minutes per side. Do not overload. Drain on paper towels. Serve hot.

Yields about 60 fritters.

*For meat, seafood, and cheese, use bite-sized cooked chicken breast, or blanched, shelled, deveined medium and jumbo shrimp (leave the tail on), or bite-sized hard cheese like Swiss cheese.

Frying Batter I for Sweet Fritters

Premye Pat Dous pou Beniyè
Pâte à Frire I pour Beignets Sucrés

1 cup all-purpose flour
1/4 teaspoon baking soda
1/4 teaspoon salt
1 cup pure fruit purée (well-ripened banana,
mango, apricot, peach)
1/4 cup whole milk
1/2 cup granulated sugar
vegetable oil for deep-frying
granulated or powdered sugar for dusting

Mix flour with baking soda and salt. Set aside.

In a large bowl, mix mashed fruit with milk, and sugar until smooth. Combine with flour mixture and stir until smooth. If you are making mango beignets, strain the purée if necessary.

Heat oil over medium high setting and drop batter by 1/2 tablespoons in hot oil. Do not over load. Fry until golden, about 1 minute for each side. Use a slotted spoon to remove from the pan. Squeeze the oil out by gently pressing them on the slotted spoon with the back of a tablespoon. Drain on paper towels. Sprinkle with granulated or powdered sugar. Serve hot.

Yields 25 to 30 beignets.

Frying Batter II for Sweet Fritters

Deziem Pat Dous pou Beniyè
Pâte à Frire II pour Beignets Sucrés

1 1/2 cups all-purpose flour
1/2 cup granulated sugar
2 teaspoons double-acting baking powder
3/4 teaspoon salt
1/2 cup milk
1/4 cup dark Haitian rum (Rhum Barbancourt)*
2 eggs, beaten
vegetable oil for deep frying
ripe but firm fruit slices (bite-sized banana, pineapple, apricot, apple, or peach)
granulated or powdered sugar for dusting

Mix flour, sugar, baking powder, and salt in a large bowl. Mix in milk and eggs until a smooth batter is formed.

Heat oil over medium setting in a heavy deep frying pan. Dip fruit slices in the batter to coat them. Using a spoon, drop them in the hot oil, and cook until golden, turning once, 1 to 2 minutes per side. Do not overload. Drain on paper towels. Dust with sugar. Serve hot.

Yields about 60 beignets.

*You may use strained fresh pineapple juice, strained fresh orange juice, or apple juice instead.

Sugar Doughnuts and Lady Thighs

Beniyè Kanaval ak Kuis Danm
Beignets de Carnaval (Beignets au Sucre) et Cuisses de Dame.

These delicious doughnuts, along with *Sweet and Soft Banana Fritters*, are enjoyed by everyone during the Mardi-gras (*Carnaval*) in Haiti thus the name *Beignets de Carnaval*.

2 cups plus 1 tablespoon all-purpose flour
1/2 cup granulated sugar
1/4 teaspoon salt
1/2 tablespoon double-acting baking powder
1/4 cup (1/2 stick) butter or margarine, softened
2 eggs, yolks and whites separated
1 teaspoon freshly grated lime zest
2 tablespoons dark Haitian rum (Rhum Barbancourt)*
1 tablespoon milk
vegetable oil for deep frying
1/4 cup granulated sugar mixed with 1 teaspoon ground cinnamon, or
1/4 cup powdered sugar (to coat the doughnuts)

Mix flour with sugar, salt, and baking powder on a smooth surface. Set aside.

In a medium bowl, mix melted butter, egg yolks, lime zest, rum, and milk. Set aside.

In another medium bowl, beat egg whites until stiff. Mix with the butter-yolk mixture. Make a well in the center of the flour mixture and pour in the egg mixture. Mix until a smooth pliable dough is formed. Knead for a few minutes on a lightly floured surface just until dough is homogeneous. Gather dough into a ball. Roll it out to 1/4 inch thickness with a rolling pin. Then, cut flattened dough into 2-inch round shapes with a cutter, remove the center of the round with a small 1-inch round cutter, or make any other shapes you want.

Heat oil over medium setting in a heavy deep frying pan, drop dough shapes into hot oil and fry until golden and puffed, turning once, about 1 minute per side. Do not overload. Use a slotted spoon to remove doughnuts from oil. Drain on paper towels. Roll doughnuts in sugar-cinnamon mixture. Serve warm or at room temperature. *Doughnuts* and *Lady Thighs* can be stored in an airtight container at room temperature for up to one week.

Yields about 35 doughnuts.

Note. To make *Cuisses de Dame*, roll small portions of dough between the palms of your hands to form 2-inch x 3/8-inch sticks, then fry as above.

*If you do not want to use the rum, use strained fresh pineapple juice, strained fresh orange juice, or apple juice.

Pancakes

Krèp
Crêpes

2 large eggs
2 tablespoons granulated sugar
1/4 cup (1/2 stick) butter or margarine, at room temperature
1 teaspoon pure vanilla extract

1/2 teaspoon salt
2 cups flour
2 1/4 cups milk
1/2 cup vegetable oil, or 1/2 cup (1 stick) butter or margarine

Using a hand electric mixer, beat eggs, sugar, butter, vanilla extract, and salt together, in a medium bowl, until homogeneous. Beat in the flour and the milk alternately in three to four additions. The batter should be creamy and fluid. Cover and let it stand for one hour.

To make one crepe, heat 1 teaspoon vegetable oil or butter in a heavy non-stick 7-inch skillet or frying pan over heat set halfway between medium and medium low. Scoop 3 tablespoons batter into the skillet using a 3-tablespoon ladle, and gently rotate the skillet so the batter spreads on the bottom of the pan and forms a thin layer. Cook for 1 to 2 minutes on each side, using a spatula to flip the pancake over. Pancakes will be about 6 inches in diameter. Add oil to pan by teaspoons as needed. Use a lightly greased griddle to make more than one pancake at a time. Keep pancakes warm as they are being made. Serve warm with a warm fruit sauce or syrup, or with warm thinned jelly.

Yields about 24 thin pancakes.

Note. Replace 1/4 cup milk by 1/4 cup dark Haitian rum (Rhum Barbancourt) to make more delicious pancakes.

Choux Pastry and Choux

Pat pou Bouche ak Bouche
Pâte à Choux et Choux

This pastry, with its very particular preparation, is used to make delicious savory appetizers, sweet and delicious cream puffs, profiteroles, and other delicacies. Mix one tablespoon of sugar with the boiling water if you are making choux for dessert (cream puffs for example).

Choux can be prepared in advance, and frozen. To use, reheat at 400 degrees Fahrenheit, for 3 to 5 minutes. But they are best when they are made the day they are to be served.

1 cup boiling water
1/2 cup butter or margarine (1 stick)
1 cup all-purpose flour
4 eggs
pinch of salt

Preheat oven to 400 degrees Fahrenheit. Grease a large cookie sheet, and set aside.

Put boiling water in a heavy 3-quart saucepan, add butter, and stir until the butter melts completely. Bring to a boil over medium heat. Add flour and stir vigorously with a wooden spoon until the resulting dough does not stick to the pan. Remove from heat, stir in salt, then eggs one at a time, mixing vigorously with a strong wire whisk after each addition. The dough should hold together and be very sticky.

For small choux, drop dough by rounded teaspoon on the prepared baking sheet. Wet your index finger to smooth the dough balls if necessary. Bake in the middle of preheated oven for 30 minutes.

Cut the top of each choux, discard its moist contents and stuff with a filling of your choice. See *Choux With Seafood Filling* in the Appetizers section, and *Cream Puffs* in the Desserts section.

Yields 32 to 36 small choux.

Pastry Cream

Krèm Patisiyè
Crème Patissière

Pastry Cream is a rich and delicious cream used as filling for fruit tarts and tartlets, layer cakes, cream puffs, eclairs, ... etc. It can be flavored with chocolate, fruit syrup, rum or some other liquors. Its texture can also be lightened by the addition of whipped cream.

Estimated time: 15 minutes.

1 tablespoon butter or margarine	1/4 cup all-purpose flour
1/2 cup granulated sugar	1 cup milk
pinch of salt	1 cup evaporated milk
4 egg yolks	2 teaspoons pure vanilla extract

Cream butter in a large heat resistant bowl. Using a wire whisk, mix in the sugar, salt, and the yolks. Whisk in the flour by tablespoons until well blended. Set aside.

Mix milk, evaporated milk, and vanilla extract in a heavy 2-quart pan and heat over medium setting until just beginning to bubble. Gradually pour hot milk onto egg mixture, whisking continuously. Transfer into a heavy 3-quart pan, and bring to a boil, whisking continuously. When boiling starts, reduce heat to medium low. Boil down until very thick, whisking continuously, 5 to 7 minutes. Transfer to a bowl, and cool completely before using.

Yields about 2 cups.

Variation.

To add chocolate, mix four tablespoons of unsweetened cocoa powder with the sugar. To add fruit syrup (1/4 cup) or liquor (2 tablespoons), reduce the pastry cream slightly longer; cool the pastry cream completely, then mix the fruit syrup or the liquor of your choice into the pastry cream.

To add whipping cream, add 2 additional tablespoons of sugar to the recipe. Chill the beaters of an electric hand mixer, and a small mixing bowl. Cool pastry cream completely in the refrigerator. Put one cup whipping cream in the chilled bowl, and whip with the mixer at medium speed until stiff peaks are formed, 1 to 2 minutes, then fold it in the pastry cream. For this small amount of whipping cream, you will get better results by using a chilled 2-cup glass measuring cup.

Pastry Dough (Short Pastry)

Pat Brize
Pâte Brisée

Freshly made pastry dough is readily available by the pound in a few pastry shops in our country, and frozen dough is also carried by some supermarkets.

Do not overwork the dough because it will toughen. If you are making the dough for a dessert, add 2 tablespoons of powdered sugar to the flour.

2 cups all-purpose flour
1/2 teaspoon salt
6 tablespoons (3/4 stick) cold butter or margarine, cut into small pieces
6 tablespoons cold vegetable shortening, cut into small pieces
1/3 cup very cold water

Mix flour with salt on a smooth surface. With tips of fingers, quickly combine flour with shortening and butter until it resembles a coarse meal (grainy appearance). Add 3 tablespoons of cold water, and knead quickly to form a dough. Dough should hold together. Add the remaining water, a little at a time, if necessary. Form a ball with the dough, then flatten it into a thick disk with the palm of your hand. Refrigerate for 30 minutes. Then lay flattened dough between 2 large sheets of wax paper and roll it out into a 1/8 inch thick circle with a rolling pin. Remove one sheet of wax paper. Using the other sheet of wax paper as a guide, fit dough in the pastry pan of your choice. Cover with wax paper, and refrigerate until ready to use. This can be prepared one day ahead and kept in the refrigerator. It can also be frozen for a longer time.

Yields about 1 pound, enough for one single-crust 10-inch pie, one double-crust 9-inch pie, or 12 tartlet shells.

Variation. Mix one large egg yolk with the flour-fat mixture, just before adding the water. Use this for pie, tarts, quiches, . . . etc.

Note. Wrap in wax paper and plastic and freeze any leftover *Short Pastry*. It keeps nicely in the freezer. Remember to thaw before using.

Herring Pâté en Croute

Pate Aran
Pâté de Hareng en Croute

one recipe of *Short Pastry* (with egg yolk)
one recipe of *Herring Stuffing for Kabich and Herring Pâté en Croûte*
1 egg yolk diluted with 1 tablespoon of water, or 1 tablespoon of milk (glaze)

Preheat oven to 350 degrees Fahrenheit. Have on hand a large ungreased baking sheet.

Form a ball with the dough, then flatten it into a thick rectangular shape with the palm of your hand. Lay flattened dough on a piece of aluminum foil, then roll it out into a 1/4-inch thick rectangle, with the shorter side facing you. Do not worry if your rectangle is not perfect. Following the long sides and without cutting through the dough, draw two lines on the dough with the tip of a knife to mark it into three rectangular strips. It is best to make the center strip slightly narrower (fig. 1).

Fig. 1   Fig. 2.

Cut each side strip (left and right) into 1-inch wide bands, cutting through the dough but not separating the bands from the center strip (fig. 2).

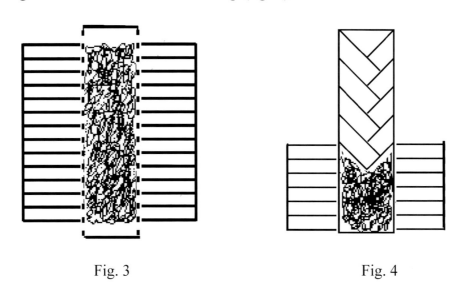

Fig. 3   Fig. 4

Remove the two first and the two last dough bands. Reserve these to make pastry decorations to garnish the pâté en route (bows, flowers, . . . etc.). Place the stuffing on the center strip, leaving a wide margin at both ends (fig. 3). Fold the ends of the center strip over the stuffing, then start braiding; fold left and right bands alternately over the stuffing at a downward angle until all the stuffing is encased in a dough braid (fig. 4). Brush the braid with the glaze. Pick up the dough in the foil and place it on the baking sheet. Bake in the middle of the preheated oven until golden, 1 hour to 1 hour and 15 minutes. Serve warm.

Serves 6 to 8.

Variation. Fillings may vary. Use the *Cooked Stuffing for Poultry, Rabbit, Beef, and Pork* for a delicious variation. Puff Pastry makes also a delicious Herring Pate en Croute

Onion Quiche

Tat Zonyon
Tarte à l'oignon

This delicious quiche is a regular on our New Year's Day dinner table.

Estimated time: 45 minutes.

For crust:

2 cups all-purpose flour
1/2 teaspoon salt
6 tablespoons (3/4 stick) cold butter or margarine, cut into small pieces

6 tablespoons cold vegetable shortening, cut into small pieces
1/3 cup very cold water
One 10-inch quiche pan

For filling:

4 large white onions, cut into about 1/4-inch thick slices
2 tablespoons vegetable oil
one 8-ounce package cream cheese, softened

2 large eggs
3/4 cup heavy whipping cream
1/2 teaspoon salt
1/4 teaspoon black pepper

Crust. Mix flour with salt. With tips of fingers, quickly combine flour with shortening and butter until it resembles a coarse meal (grainy appearance). Add 3 tablespoons of cold water, 1 tablespoon at a time until dough holds together. Add remaining water, a little at a time, if necessary.

Form a ball with dough, then flatten it into a thick disk. Put dough between 2 sheets of wax paper and roll it out into a 1/8 inch thick circle with a rolling pin. Remove one sheet of wax paper. Using the other sheet of wax paper as a guide, fit dough into the quiche pan. Cover with wax paper, and refrigerate for one hour. Crust can be prepared one day ahead, and stored in the refrigerator until ready to use.

Preheat oven to 400 degrees Fahrenheit. Pierce bottom and side of the crust all over with the tines of a fork. Bake crust in the middle of oven until slightly golden, 10 to 15 minutes. Keep oven hot.

Filling.

Quarter onion slices crosswise. Heat oil over medium setting in a large pan, add onion pieces, and sauté until they become translucent and tender, about 5 to 7 minutes. Remove from heat.

In a large bowl, whisk cream cheese and eggs until well blended. Add heavy cream, salt, and pepper. Whisk until a homogeneous mixture is formed. Mix in sautéed onion. Season with additional salt if necessary. Pour into prepared crust. Bake in the middle of preheated oven until golden, about 30 minutes. Serve warm.

Serves 6 to 8.

Variation. Make *Onion Tartlets* by using 12 tartlet pans.

Make a delicious *Leek Quiche* by substituting 4 cups sliced leeks for the onion. Use the white parts only.

Spinach Quiche

Tat Zepina
Tarte aux Epinards

For crust:

Make one recipe of *Short Pastry*. Fit it in a 10-inch quiche pan and cook as for *Onion Quiche*. Set aside.

For filling:

2 tablespoons vegetable oil
2 cups diced white onion
1 pound fresh spinach, trimmed, washed, drained, and torn (or ready-to-use 9-ounce bagged spinach)
1 1/2 cups grated Parmesan cheese

one 8-ounce package cream cheese, softened
2 large eggs
3/4 cup heavy whipping cream
1/2 teaspoon salt
1/4 teaspoon black pepper

Prepare the filling while the crust is baking. Heat oil over medium setting in a large pan, add onion, and sauté for 3 minutes. Mix in spinach. Cover and cook until spinach is tender, about 5 minutes. Uncover, increase heat to medium high, and stir-fry until almost no liquid remains, about 15 to 20 minutes. Remove from heat. Transfer to a bowl, and add the cheese. Then proceed as for *Onion Quiche*.

Serves 6 to 8.

Chicken Quiche

Tat Poulè
Tarte au Poulet

Estimated time: 1 hour.

For crust:

2 cups all-purpose flour
1/2 teaspoon salt
6 tablespoons (3/4 stick) cold butter or margarine, cut into small pieces

6 tablespoons cold vegetable shortening, cut into small pieces
1/4 cup very cold water
one 10-inch quiche pan

For filling:

2 cups water
2 chicken bouillon cubes, crushed
1 /4 teaspoon ground cayenne pepper
1/2 teaspoon ground black pepper
4 skinless chicken breasts, cubed
2 tablespoons vegetable oil

3 cups quartered white onion slices
6 ounces cream cheese, softened
2 large eggs
3/4 cup heavy cream
1/2 teaspoon salt

Crust

Mix flour with salt. With tips of fingers, quickly combine flour with shortening and butter until it resembles a coarse meal (grainy appearance). Add 3 tablespoons of cold water, 1 tablespoon at a time until dough holds together. Add remaining water, a little at a time, if necessary. Form a ball with dough, then flatten it into a thick disk. Put dough between 2 sheets of wax paper and roll it out into a 1/8 inch thick circle. Remove one sheet of wax paper. Using the other sheet of wax paper as a guide, fit dough into the quiche pan. Cover with wax paper, and refrigerate for one hour. Crust can be prepared one day ahead, and stored in the refrigerator until ready to use. Preheat oven to 400 degrees Fahrenheit. Pierce bottom and sides of the crust all over with the tines of a fork. Bake crust in the middle of oven until slightly golden, 10 to15 minutes. Keep oven temperature at 400 degrees Fahrenheit.

Filling

Bring water to a boil in a in a 12-inch skillet. Add bouillon cubes, cayenne pepper, black pepper, and chicken cubes, cover (lid slightly ajar), and cook over medium heat until chicken is tender, 10 minutes. Remove from heat, and strain, reserving the cooking liquid for another use. Set aside until ready to use.

In a heavy 3-quart pan, heat oil over medium setting, and sauté onion until translucent and tender, about 5 minutes. Remove from heat and add to chicken. Mix and set aside.In a large bowl, beat cream cheese and eggs until well blended. Add heavy cream, and salt. Stir until a homogeneous mixture is formed. Mix in chicken. Season with additional salt if necessary. Pour into prepared crust. Bake in the middle of preheated oven until golden, about 30 minutes. Serve warm.

Note. Make *Chicken Tartlets* by using 12 tartlet pans.

Tropical Seafood Quiche

Tat Fwidmè
Tarte aux Fruits de Mer

This delicious quiche may also be made with only one variety of seafood instead of an assortment of seafood.

Estimated time: 1 hour 15 minutes.

For crust:

2 cups all-purpose flour
1/2 teaspoon salt
6 tablespoons (3/4 stick) cold butter or margarine, cut into small pieces

6 tablespoons cold vegetable shortening, cut into small pieces
1/3 cup very cold water
one 10-inch quiche pan

For filling:

1/2 pound medium shrimp
1 pound crab legs
2 tablespoons vegetable oil
1/2 pound lobster meat, cut into about 1/2-inch pieces
1/2 pound conch, cleaned, cut into 1/2 inch pieces, and boiled in plain water*
1/4 teaspoon ground cayenne pepper

1/2 teaspoon ground black pepper
1/2 teaspoon salt
2 cups quartered white onion slices
1 cup sliced shallots
1/2 cup diced red bell pepper
6 ounces cream cheese, softened
2 eggs
3/4 cup heavy cream

Crust

Mix flour with salt. With tips of fingers, quickly combine flour with shortening and butter until it resembles a coarse meal (grainy appearance). Add 3 tablespoons of cold water, 1 tablespoon at a time until dough holds together. Add remaining water, a little at a time, if necessary. Form a ball with dough, then flatten it into a thick disk. Put dough between 2 sheets of wax paper and roll it out into a 1/8 inch thick circle with a rolling pin. Remove one sheet of wax paper. Using the other sheet of wax paper as a guide, fit dough into the quiche pan. Cover with wax paper, and refrigerate for one hour. Crust can be prepared one day ahead, and stored in the refrigerator until ready to use.

Preheat oven to 400 degrees Fahrenheit. Pierce bottom and sides of the crust all over with the tines of a fork. Bake crust in the middle of oven until slightly golden, 10 to 15 minutes. Keep oven at 400 degrees Fahrenheit.

Filling

Bring 1/2 cup of water to a boil. Add shrimp and crab legs. Boil for 1 minute. Drain. Reserve boiling liquid for another use. Shell shrimp and crab legs. Devein shrimp. Cut into 1/2 inch pieces.

Heat 1 tablespoon oil over medium setting in a heavy 2-quart pan, and sauté shrimp, crab, and lobster together for 2 minutes. Add conch, cayenne pepper, black pepper, and salt. Sauté for 1 additional minute. Transfer to bowl and set aside.

In the same pan, heat remaining oil over medium setting, and sauté onion, shallots, and bell pepper for 5 minutes. Remove from heat and add to seafood.

In a large bowl, beat cream cheese and eggs until well blended. Add heavy cream. Stir until a homogeneous mixture is formed. Mix in seafood. Season with additional salt if necessary. Pour in prepared crust. Bake in the middle of preheated oven until golden, about 30 minutes. Serve warm.

Serves 6 to 8.

Note. Make *Seafood Tartlets* by using 12 tartlets pans.

*Conch must be boiled until tender, about 2 hours, or use two 6 1/2-ounce cans of chopped clams in juice.

Fruit Barquettes

Tatlèt Fwi
Barquettes de Fruit

1 recipe of *Short Pastry* (with powdered sugar added)
1 recipe of *Pastry Cream* flavored with a *Fruit Syrup* (may be prepared in advance)
1/2 cup heavy whipped cream, whipped (see note at the end of Pastry Cream recipe)
2 to 3 cups bite-sized fresh fruit slices (pineapple, mango, kiwi, strawberries, . . . etc.)
Fresh Fruit Syrup (or other fruit syrup or thinned marmalade) to glaze the barquettes

Have on hand twelve 3 3/4 x 2 1/4-inch boat-shaped tartlet pans and a large ungreased jelly roll pan.

Form 12 same-sized dough balls with the short pastry, and chill for 30 minutes.

Between two pieces of wax paper, roll out each dough ball into a 1/8 inch thick circle about 1 inch larger than a tartlet pan. Peel back one sheet of wax paper. Using the other piece of paper as a guide, fit each circle into a tartlet pan. Wrap in wax paper and refrigerate until ready to use. This can be done ahead.

Preheat oven to 400 degrees Fahrenheit.

Pierce bottom and sides of crust several times with the tines of a fork. Place tartlet pans on the ungreased jelly roll pan. Bake in the middle of preheated oven until golden, about 20 minutes. Let stand for 5 minutes in the pans, then unmold, and cool completely on a rack. Crust may be prepared in advance and kept in a wax bag at room temperature until ready to use.

Mix *Pastry Cream* with whipped cream (see note at the end of *Pastry Cream* recipe). Just before serving, fill each pastry crust with cream mixture.

Top with as many fruit slices as desired. Brush fruit slices with the fruit syrup.

Yields 12 barquettes.

Note. You can use one kind of fruit or use an assortment of fruits.

You may bake the crusts ahead, and store them in wax bags placed in an airtight container. You may prepare the cream ahead, and store it covered in the refrigerator. Just before serving, fill the crusts with cream, top with fruit slices, and brush with the fruit syrup to glaze.

Do not fill the crusts ahead. They will become soggy and unappetizing.

Coconut Tartlets

Kokonèt
Tartelettes à la Noix de Coco

The Haitian Creole word "kokonet" seems to come from the English word "coconut," and in this particular case it is probably a short word for "Coconut Pie." This recipe is delicious, light, and very pleasing.

Estimated active time: 40 minutes.
Chilling time: 1 hour.
Cooking time: 1 hour 15 min.

Crust:

2 cups all-purpose flour
2 tablespoons powdered sugar
1/2 teaspoon salt
6 tablespoons cold vegetable shortening, cut into small pieces

6 tablespoons cold margarine, cut into small pieces
1/3 cup very cold water
twelve 3 1/2-inch round tartlet pans (fluted or plain)
a large ungreased jelly roll pan

Filling:

5 cups freshly grated coconut*
2 cups evaporated milk
1 teaspoon pure vanilla extract

1 cup granulated sugar
pinch ground cinnamon
pinch of salt

Crust

Mix flour with sugar and salt. With finger tips, quickly combine flour mixture with shortening and margarine until it resembles a coarse meal. Add 3 tablespoons cold water, 1 tablespoon at a time until dough hold together. Add remaining water, a little at a time, if necessary. Form 12 same-size dough balls, and chill for one hour.

Preheat oven to 400 degrees Fahrenheit

Between two pieces of wax paper, roll out each dough ball into a 1/8 inch thick circle about 2 inches larger than a tartlet pan. Peel back one sheet of wax paper. Using the other piece of paper as a guide, fit each circle into a tartlet pan. Pierce bottom and sides of the crust all over with the tines of a fork. Place tartlet pans on the ungreased jelly roll pan. Bake in the middle of preheated oven until golden, about 20 minutes. Remove from the oven. Keep the crusts in the tartlet pans, and set aside.

Reduce oven temperature to 275 degrees Fahrenheit.

Filling

Mix coconut, milk, vanilla extract, sugar, cinnamon, and salt in a heavy 2-quart saucepan. Stirring often, boil over medium heat until thickened, about 30 minutes.

Spoon coconut mixture, while still hot, in baked crusts. Bake in the middle of oven until filling is slightly golden, about 45 minutes. Cool at room temperature. Yields 12 *kokonets*.

*Make sure that the coconut is fresh and does not taste rancid. Before grating the coconut, use a vegetable peeler to remove the brown thin layer that coats it. Four cups of bagged sweetened coconut flakes can also be used. In this case reduce sugar to 1/2 cup.

Puff Pastry

Pat Feyte
Pâte Feuilletée

Time and patience are about all you need to make this *Puff Pastry*. It is well worth it. Once you master this recipe, you may never buy puff pastry from the store freezers anymore. Use it to make pâtés en croûte, tarts, cornets, napoleons, turnovers, and bouchées. They will be light, airy and delicious. Puff pastry can be frozen, but it is at its best when used shortly after the last turn. If you wish to make a "Galette des Rois," use *Puff Pastry* after the fifth turn. "Galette des Rois" is a layered pastry cake filled with *Pastry Cream* and in which a small heat resistant non-toxic trinket is placed.

Estimated time: 7 hours.

2 teaspoons salt
1/2 teaspoon granulated sugar
1 cup water

1 1/2 teaspoons fresh lime juice
3 cups pastry flour
2 3/4 cups vegetable shortening*

In a bowl, mix salt and sugar with the water until dissolved. Mix in lime juice. Set aside.

Sift flour on a large smooth surface. Working with both hands, mix 1/4 cup shortening with flour. Make a well in the center of the flour-shortening mixture, add the liquid and mix to form a smooth and pliable dough. Roll into a ball, wrap it in wax paper, then wrap again in a damp kitchen towel. Refrigerate the dough ball for 20 minutes.

Divide the remaining shortening into 10 portions and keep refrigerated. Pat the dough into a square. Then roll it out into a 1/4-inch-thick rectangle. Visually divide dough crosswise into three sections. Spread one portion of shortening on 2/3 of the rectangle. Fold the dough rectangle into three, as you would fold a business letter: Beginning with the part without shortening, fold it on the middle third, then fold the last third over. Wrap in wax paper, and in a damp kitchen towel. Refrigerate 30 minutes. This constitutes one turn.

Roll folded dough out into a 1/8-inch-thick rectangle. Repeat the above procedure until all the shortening is used, and for a total of 10 turns. Then make two other turns without shortening. If not to be used at once, Puff Pastry can be refrigerated after the 10th turn for up to 3 days, or frozen for several days. Then make the two last turns before using.

Bake recipes made with Puff Pastry on an ungreased baking sheet, or in an ungreased mold, on an upper rack of an oven preheated to 450 degrees Fahrenheit. Bake until puffed and golden, 15 to 20 minutes.

Yields about 2 pounds of Puff Pastry.

Note. Wipe working surface between each turn to remove shortening that might have oozed out. Keep working surface and rolling pin floured at all times.

*Use the butter-flavored shortening for a better taste. Do not use liquid shortening.

Chicken Turnovers and Other Turnovers

Pate Poulè ak Lòt Pate
Chaussons au Poulet et Autres Chaussons

Estimated time: 45 minutes (cooking time for Chicken in Creole Sauce is not included).

1/2 recipe of *Chicken in Creole Sauce*
2 tablespoons finely chopped fresh flat-leaf parsley
1 habanero chile, seeded, carefully washed, and thinly minced*

1/4 cup finely diced white onion
one recipe of *Puff Pastry*
1 egg slightly beaten with 2 tablespoons water (glaze)

When cooking chicken, scale down ingredients accordingly. After cooking the chicken, remove the meat from the bones. Discard the bones, then finely chop the cooked chicken. Combine chopped chicken with its sauce, parsley, chile, and onion. Stir-fry chicken mixture on medium heat to allow sauce to thicken completely, about 5 to 7 minutes. Set aside to cool completely.

Preheat oven to 450 degrees Fahrenheit. Have on hand a large baking sheet.

Roll out *Puff Pastry* into a 1/4-inch thick round on a lightly floured surface. Using a 3 1/2-inch cookie cutter, cut out as many round pastry pieces as possible. Roll out each round into a 4-inch round. Visually divide each round in two. Place one tablespoon of prepared chicken on one half of each round. Brush pastry edges with water, fold the other side over the filling, then seal pressing well on the edges with the tines of a fork.

Place pastry on the large baking sheet. Poke small holes on top of each pastry with the tines of a fork. Brush with egg-water glaze and bake pastry in the upper third rack of preheated oven until puffed and golden, 15 to 20 minutes. Serve warm.

Yields about 10 turnovers.

*Read *Demystifying Habanero Chile* in *The Cook's Techniques* chapter.

Variation: Use 1/2 of *Cooked Stuffing for Poultry, Rabbit, Beef, and Pork* recipe to make *Beef Turnovers*. Use *Salt Cod Chiquetaille* to make *Cod Turnovers*. Use *Smoked Red Herring Chiquetaille* to make *Herring Turnovers*. Mix grated Parmesan cheese with a small amount of butter or mayonnaise to make *Cheese Turnovers*.

You may also make 3- x 3-inch squares, roll out, fill, fold the two opposite corners, then seal as above. Cut smaller pastry rounds or squares, and use less filling to make appetizers; roll out, fill, cover with other pastry rounds or squares, then seal as above. Fill the pastry with jam (confiture) or with fruit compote to make sweet turnovers. You may use the *Guava Preserves* or the *Pineapple Preserves* recipe in this book, or any other preserves that suit your taste. Use leftover puff pastry to make savory or sweet *Pastry Twists*.

VEGETABLES AND ROOTS

Legim ak Viv
Légumes et Vivres Alimentaires

Potato, Beet, and Carrot Salad

Roots! Roots! Roots!

So many roots!
I stick 'em in my boots,
I stick 'em on my chair,
Even in my hair!
I love a fresh beet.
Will it taste better than meat?

Rachel Ménager, 11

Coleslaw

Salad Chou
Salad de Chou

This salad is not hot. *Pikliz* adds interest and excitement to the dish. In Haiti, it is also improperly called choucroûte, which is the French word for sauerkraut.

Estimated time: 40 minutes.

1/4 cup olive oil
2 tablespoons fresh lime juice
1 1/2 tablespoons vinegar or *Pikliz*
1/2 teaspoon granulated garlic
1/2 teaspoon finely ground black pepper
1 1/2 teaspoons salt
1/2 cup sliced shallots
1/2 cup diced white onion
1 /4 cup diced green bell pepper
3 tablespoons mayonnaise (optional)
1/2 tablespoon prepared yellow mustard
(optional)
one 1 1/2 pound cabbage, freshly shredded
(yields about 5 cups shredded cabbage)
1 1/2 to 2 cups freshly shredded carrots
(about 2 large carrots)

Make a vinaigrette by whisking olive oil, lime juice, vinegar or *Pikliz*, garlic, black pepper, salt, shallots, onion, and bell pepper until well blended. Whisk in mayonnaise and mustard if using. Let stand at room temperature for 15 minutes to allow the flavors to blend.

Mix cabbage and carrots in a large bowl. Add the vinaigrette and toss to coat. Season with additional salt and pepper if necessary. Cover with plastic wrap and store in refrigerator for 3 hours, or so. Serve slightly chilled, or bring to room temperature before serving.

Serves 6.

Potato, Beet, and Carrot Salad

Salad Pomdetè, Bètrav, ak Kawòt
Salade de Pommes de Terre, Carottes et Betteraves

This salad is a pleasure not only for the palate but also for the eyes. It takes its amazing color from the beets. Even though it contains *Pikliz* and Tabasco sauce, this is not a hot salad. These two condiments add interest and excitement to the dish.

Estimated time: 45 minutes.

3 large potatoes (about 2 pounds)	1/2 tablespoon *Pikliz*
4 medium carrots (about 1 pound)	1/2 teaspoon prepared yellow mustard
2 medium red beets (about 1 pound)	1/4 teaspoon finely ground black pepper
2 tablespoons vegetable oil	1 teaspoon Tabasco sauce
1/2 cup diced white onion	1 1/4 teaspoon salt
1/2 cup diced red bell pepper	2 tablespoons olive oil
1/4 cup mayonnaise	1 head of romaine lettuce
1 tablespoon fresh lime juice	Parsley to garnish
1/2 tablespoon apple cider vinegar	

Cook potatoes (for about 20 to 30 minutes) and carrots (for about 12 minutes) together in a large pot of boiling water. Do not overcook. Cook beets in another pot of boiling water for 25 to 30 minutes.

Meanwhile, heat vegetable oil over medium high setting and sauté onion and bell pepper for about 3 minutes. Remove from heat. Transfer to a large bowl. Mix in mayonnaise, lime juice, vinegar, *Pikliz*, mustard, black pepper, Tabasco, salt, and olive oil. Set aside.

Remove and wash the lettuce leaves under fresh running water. Put them in a large bowl, cover, and refrigerate until ready to use.

Drain and peel vegetables. Cut potatoes and beets into about 3/4-inch cubes. Slice carrot crosswise into 1/3-inch pieces. Gently mix vegetables with mayonnaise mixture. Season with additional salt and pepper if desired. Mound in a serving dish on a bed of the lettuce. Garnish with parsley. Serve warm with additional olive oil if desired.

Serves 6.

Note. You can mix cubed potatoes, cubed beets and slice carrots together with the sauce or you can mix them separately with sauce as it is shown on the photograph.

Holy Week Salad

Salad Semenn Sent
Salad de la Semaine Sainte

More than ninety percents of Haitians are Catholics. As we observe the fast preceding Easter, we eat fish along with lots of vegetable and roots. The following salad is served as an accompaniment for *Salt Fish* or for *Holy Week Cod*. *Pikliz* and Tabasco add interest and excitement to the dish

Estimated time: 45 minutes.

one small cabbage (1 to 1 1/4 pounds), washed, cut into eight wedges, and cored
3 cups fresh green beans, trimmed*, or 3 cups frozen French style green beans
3 large potatoes (about 2 pounds), peeled, and cut crosswise into 1/3-inch thick slices
4 medium carrots (about 1 pound), peeled, and cut crosswise into 2 pieces each
3 medium red beets (about 1 1/2 pound)
1/3 cup olive oil
1 cup sliced white onion (about 1/4-inch slices)

1/3 cup mayonnaise
1 tablespoon fresh lime juice
2 tablespoons apple cider vinegar, or 1 tablespoon each *Pikliz* and apple cider vinegar
1 teaspoon prepared yellow mustard
1/2 teaspoon finely ground black pepper
1 teaspoon Tabasco sauce
1 1/2 teaspoons salt
4 hard-boiled eggs, sliced crosswise or quartered lengthwise

Steam cabbage over medium heat, about 3 minutes. Uncover the pan, add the beans and continue to steam for 8 additional minutes, until vegetables are tender. To keep hot, uncover the pan and keep over barely simmering water.

Steam potato slices and carrot pieces together over medium heat for about 20 minutes. Do not overcook. Keep hot.

Cook beets in a pot of boiling water until cooked through, 25 to 30 minutes. Do not over cook.

Meanwhile, heat 2 tablespoons oil in a heavy 3-quart pan over medium high setting. Sauté onion for about 1 minute. Remove from heat. Mix in mayonnaise, lime juice, vinegar, mustard, black pepper, Tabasco, salt, and remaining olive oil. Set aside. The sauce may taste a bit too salty, but since the vegetables are unsalted, they will balance each other nicely once they are put together.

Slice carrot pieces into about 1/3-inch slices. Drain beets. Peel and slice them into about 1/3-inch pieces. Arrange the vegetables concentrically onto one or two large round serving dishes, carrots in the center, then potatoes, then beets, then green beans. Garnish with cabbage wedges and egg slices. Take onion slices from the sauce and arrange them on top of the vegetables. Then drizzle the dish with the sauce. Serve warm.

Serves 8.

*Use a small paring knife to lightly trim off both sides of the beans. Snip off both ends.

Potato Salad

Salad Pomdetè
Salade de Pommes de Terre

Estimated time: 45 minutes.

6 large potatoes (about 4 pounds)
2 tablespoons vegetable oil
1/2 cup finely diced white onion
1/2 cup finely diced red bell pepper
1 tablespoon fresh lime juice
1/2 tablespoon apple cider vinegar
1/2 tablespoon *Pikliz*
1/4 teaspoon finely ground black pepper

1 teaspoon Tabasco sauce
1 1/4 teaspoon salt
1 teaspoon prepared yellow mustard
3 tablespoons olive oil
3 hard-boiled eggs, finely diced
1 head of romaine lettuce
3 tablespoons mayonnaise
Chopped parsley to garnish

Cook potatoes in a large pot of boiling water until cooked through, about 20 to 30 minutes. Do not overcook.

Meanwhile, heat vegetable oil over medium high setting and sauté onion and bell pepper for about 3 minutes. Remove from heat. Transfer to a large bowl. Mix in lime juice, vinegar, *Pikliz*, black pepper, Tabasco, salt, mustard, and olive oil. Gently mix in the egg pieces. Set aside.

Remove and wash the lettuce leaves under fresh running water. Put them in a large bowl, cover, and keep in the lower portion of the refrigerator until ready to use.

Drain and peel potatoes. Cube potatoes into bite-size pieces. Add the mayonnaise to the sauce, and mix to blend. Then add the potato cubes. Gently mix to coat the potato cubes with the sauce. Season with additional salt and pepper if desired.

Arrange the lettuce leaves on a shallow serving dish. Mound the Potato Salad on the lettuce. Garnish with parsley. Serve warm.

Serves 6.

Potato, Ham, and Pasta Salad
Salad Boulanjè
SaladeBoulangère

Salade Boulangère is a cooked salad frequently found in large Haitian gatherings, often alongside Potato, Beet and Carrot Salad. I could compare it to the rich American Potato Salad that, I notice, honors tables at many if not all large American celebrations. It is delicious.

Estimated time: 1 hour.

3 large potatoes, about 2 pounds	1 tablespoon fresh lime juice
1 ½ cups macaroni elbow*	½ tablespoon vinegar
1 ½ cups frozen green peas	¼ teaspoon black pepper
¼ cup olive oil	1 teaspoon Tabasco sauce
1 cup finely diced white onion	1 teaspoon prepared yellow mustard
1 habanero chile, seeded and washed**	¾ teaspoon salt
½ cup finely diced red bell pepper	¾ pound cooked cubed ham***
½ cup finely diced green pepper	1 to 1 ¼ cups mayonnaise

Cook potatoes in a large pot of boiling water until cooked through, about 20 to 30 minutes. Boil pasta according to package directions. Cook peas according to package directions. Do not overcook.

Meanwhile, in a medium pan, heat oil over medium high setting and sauté onion, habanero chile, and bell peppers for 3 to 4 minutes. Remove from heat. Transfer to a large bowl. Mix in lime juice, vinegar, black pepper, Tabasco sauce, mustard, and salt. Set aside.

Drain and peel potatoes. Cube potatoes into bite-size pieces. Drain macaroni and peas. Add potato cubes, cooked pasta, cooked peas, cubed ham, and mayonnaise to the onion-bell pepper mixture, and mix gently. Season with additional salt and pepper if desired. Salad should be very moist and clumpy. Discard habanero chile. Serve warm, at room temperature, or cold.

Serves 10 to 12.

Note. Sometimes people add a can of corn (drained), a cup of shredded Parmesan cheese, and a can of thinly sliced stuffed olives to the salad.

* You can also use small shell pasta, pasta wheels, pasta twists, or any small pasta that suit your taste.

** Cut chile in half lengthwise, remove the seed and membranes, and then wash under running water for 10 to 15 seconds. Read about habanero chile in The Cook's Techniques chapter and in the Glossary.

***Ham is found already cubed and packed in supermarkets' freezers.

Avocado Salad

Salad Zaboka
Salade d'Avocat

Estimated time: 20 minutes.

2 tablespoons fresh lime juice
1 tablespoon *Pikliz**
1 tablespoon apple cider vinegar
1/2 tablespoon prepared yellow mustard
1/2 teaspoon salt

1/4 cup sliced shallots
1/2 teaspoon granulated garlic
1/4 teaspoon finely ground black pepper
3 tablespoons vegetable oil
6 cups 1-inch avocado cubes**

Put lime juice, *Pikliz*, vinegar, mustard, salt, shallots, garlic, black pepper, and oil in a jar. Cover the jar with lid and screw tightly. Shake the jar until dressing thickens, about 15 to 30 seconds.

Put avocado cubes in a salad bowl, or on a bed of lettuce. Drizzle with the prepared dressing. Garnish with lime wedges if desired. Serve immediately.

Serves 6.

*If *Pikliz* is not available, use half of a seeded, washed, and minced habanero chile, and vinegar instead. Learn how to handle habanero chile in *The Cook's Techniques.*

**Use Florida avocado (also called choquette) whenever possible. It has a smooth skin, tastes better, and yields at least three times as much as a California avocado. Be sure not to use overripe avocados. Cut avocados in half lengthwise, then remove the pit and peel. Cut avocado into about 1-inch cubes. You can slice the avocados instead of making cubes, then arrange the slices on the lettuce leaves. Learn how to remove the avocado pit in the Glossary of this book.

Avocado Salad with Shrimp and Crab

Salad Zaboka ak Kribich ak Crab
Salade d'Avocat aux Crevettes et au Crabe

Estimated time: 30 minutes.

1/2 pound medium shrimp*
1 /4 cup vegetable oil
1/2 pound fresh crab meat*
1/2 cup sliced shallots
1 teaspoon granulated garlic
1/2 teaspoon finely ground black pepper
3 tablespoons apple cider vinegar
3/4 teaspoon salt

1 habanero chile, seeded and washed**
1/2 teaspoon prepared yellow mustard
1 cup cubed boiled white name root (yam),
or boiled cassava (1/2-inch cubes)
3 Florida avocados, halved lengthwise, pitted, and sprinkled with lime juice***

Quickly blanch shrimp in 4 cups of boiling water for 1 minute in a 3-quart heavy pan. Drain. Discard water, or reserve it for another use. Peel and devein shrimp. Discard shells. Cut each shrimp crosswise into 3 to 4 pieces. Heat 2 tablespoons oil over medium heat in the same pan. Add shrimp and crab, and sauté for 3 minute. Add half of the shallots, half of the granulated garlic, half the black pepper, 1 tablespoon vinegar, and 1/2 teaspoon of salt and sauté for 3 additional minutes. Remove from heat. Keep hot.

Put remaining oil, remaining shallots, remaining garlic, remaining black pepper, remaining vinegar, remaining salt, chile, and mustard in a jar. Cover jar with lid and screw tightly. Shake jar until dressing thickens, about 15 to 30 seconds. Pour into shrimp-crab mixture and mix well. Thoroughly mix in the cubed yam. Season with additional salt and black pepper if necessary. Put avocado halves on a serving plate, poke a few holes in the flesh with a fork. Remove and discard chile, then fill avocado halves with the shrimp-crab mixture. Serve immediately (with small spoons).

Serves 6.

*Use fresh crab meat instead of the shrimp-crab combination to make *Avocado Salad with Crab*. You may also use a more complex seafood combination to stuff the avocado halves.

**Wash chile, cut it in half, and remove seeds and membranes. Then rub it gently under fresh running water for 15 seconds. Read about habanero chile in *The Cook's Techniques* chapter.

***Use Florida avocado (also called choquette) whenever possible. It has a smooth skin, and is a lot bigger and tastier than California avocados. If you are using California avocados, you will need six avocados instead of three. Be sure not to use overripe avocados. Cut avocados in half lengthwise, then remove the pit. Learn how to remove the avocado pit in the Glossary of this book.

Braised Spinach

Toufe Zepina
Epinard Braisé

Easy and simple, *Braised Spinach* makes a great accompaniment for *Fish au Gratin*.

Estimated time: 35 minutes.

3 tablespoons vegetable oil
3 garlic cloves, peeled, and crushed (see note in *More Tips*)
2 cups finely diced white onion (about 1/2 large onion)

1/2 habanero chile, seeded, and washed (read *Demystifying Habanero Chile*)
4 pounds (about 6 bundles) fresh spinach, washed, and torn (or use ready-to-use bagged spinach)
1/2 teaspoon freshly ground black pepper
1/2 teaspoon salt, or to taste

In a heavy 4-quart round pan, heat 2 tablespoons oil over medium setting. Add garlic, and sauté for one minute. Add onion and chile, and sauté for 3 additional minutes. Add spinach and toss to coat with oil. Cover and cook until spinach is tender, about 5 minutes. Uncover, increase heat to medium high, add black pepper, and stir-fry until almost no liquid remains, about 15 to 20 minutes. Add salt to taste and remaining oil at the last 3 minutes. Discard chile. Serve hot.

Serves 6.

Green Bean Salad

Legim Pwa Tann
Salade Chaude de Pois Tendres

2 pounds trimmed green beans*
1/2 habanero chile, seeded, and washed
(read *Demystifying Habanero Chile*)
2 garlic cloves, peeled (see note in *More
Tips*)

3 tablespoons vegetable oil
1 teaspoon ground black pepper
2 chicken bouillon cubes, crushed
1 teaspoon Tabasco sauce
1 teaspoon salt

Bring 7 cups of water to boil. Add beans, chile, and garlic. When boiling restarts, reduce heat to medium, cover, and boil until the beans are just tender, about 5 to 7 minutes. Drain carefully. Remove garlic cloves and mash them with the back of a spoon to form a smooth paste. Set aside.

Heat oil over high setting in a 4-quart pan. Add cooked mashed garlic, beans, salt, pepper, bouillon cubes, habanero chile, and Tabasco sauce. Sauté for about one minute. Discard chile. Serve hot.

Serves 8 to10.

*Use a paring knife to lightly trim off the sides and snip off both ends of the beans. You may use the frozen trimmed green beans (French style green beans) found in the freezer of most supermarkets.

Plantain, Roots, Breadfruit

Bannann, Patat, Yanm, Malanga, Mazoumbèl, Manyòk, Veritab
Banane Plantain, Patate, Igname, Malanga, Mazoumbelle, Manioc, Véritable

These vegetables and roots can be boiled, fried, baked, and grilled. Plantains and sweet potatoes are boiled unpeeled, in salted water just like potatoes. Name root, malanga, taro root, cassava, and breadfruit are peeled before boiling in salted water.

They should be completely immersed in water when they are boiling to ensure uniform cooking. To be sure they are cooked, insert a fine knife in the middle of their flesh. The consistency should be the same as boiled potatoes. They are served with meat and lots of sauce just like potatoes.

Brush **plantains** under fresh running water. Do not peel*. Cut both ends and make a slit in the skin along one of the ridges. Bring a large pot of salted water to a boil. Add plantains and boil for 20 minutes, more or less, depending on their size. Drain, and discard water. Peel while still hot, holding with a clean cloth. Clean lightly by running a knife over their surface. Serve hot. Sweet plantains take less time to prepare. Usually one boiled plantain **yields two servings**.

Brush **sweet potatoes** under fresh running water. Do not peel. Bring a large pot of salted water to boil. Add potatoes and boil for 20 minutes, more or less, depending on their size. Drain, and discard water. Peel them while still hot, holding them with a clean cloth. Serve hot. Usually one boiled sweet potato **yields one to two servings**.

Always peel and wash **name root**, **malanga**, **taro root** and **cassava** with the pulp of bitter orange, lime, or lemon before boiling to avoid discoloration. Rinse well. If they are large, cut them into about 3 to 4 inch long pieces. Bring a large pot of salted water to a boil. Add them and boil for 20 to 30 minutes, more or less, depending on their size. Drain, and discard the cooking water. Clean lightly by running a knife over their surface, if necessary. Cassava has a slightly fibrous core that is removed after cooking; to do so, halve the boiled cassava lengthwise and take the core out with a small knife. Serve hot. Name root and taro root vary greatly in size. Usually one boiled malanga **yields one to two servings**, as does one boiled cassava.

Brush **breadfruit** under fresh running water. Cut the fruit in eight wedges lengthwise with a strong knife. Start by cutting the fruit in half lengthwise, then each half in two halves, and so on. Peel and core each wedge. Bring a large pot of salted water to a boil. Add breadfruit wedges, and cook until tender, about 20 to 30 minutes, more or less, depending on the size of the wedges. Drain, and discard water. If necessary, clean them lightly by running a knife over their surface. Serve hot. One boiled breadfruit **yields about 8 to 12 servings.**

---

*Although a fruit, plantain is eaten as a vegetable. Plantain is more tender and neater when it is boiled with its skin on. Whether plantain is peeled before or after boiling is a matter of taste. If peeled, plantain must be carefully rubbed with the pulp of bitter orange, lime, or lemon before boiling to avoid discoloration. Boiled green banana is a fair alternative to boiled green plantain.

Twice Fried Pressed Plantains

Bannann Peze
Bananes Frites et Pressées

Bannann Peze is a Creole name for a dish made from green plantains. "Bannann" means plantain. Literally translated, "Bannann peze" is "Pressed Plantain." It is always served with *Griyo*, and *Tasso* and also with some fried seafood.

The plantain press I talk about in the Glossary of this book is the key tool for this preparation. It is made out of two pieces of wood attached together by two hinges. Pieces of fried plantain are put on one of the pieces of wood, one at a time, then they are flattened by the other piece of wood. If such a utensil is not available, the smooth backs of two solid saucers or of two small plates can be used. Use saucers or plates without ridges on the back. A tortilla press is a good alternative.

Estimated time: 30 minutes

1 tablespoon salt
1/2 teaspoon granulated garlic
4 cups water
3 large green plantains

1 bitter orange, or 1 lemon, peeled and cut
in half
Vegetable oil for deep-frying

Mix salt and garlic with water. Set aside.

Cut plantains at both ends and make a slit along one of the ridges to peel them. Discard peels and tips. Rub peeled plantains with bitter orange or lemon then rinse well under fresh running water. Pat dry. Cut each plantain diagonally into five 3-inch pieces.

Put oil in a heavy pan, and add plantain sections. Set the pan over medium setting, allowing plantains and oil to heat together. Cook until plantains become tender, slightly crusty, and golden, about 7 minutes. They should not become too crusty. Check if the plantain is cooked by introducing a skewer (or the tines of a fork) in the middle of each plantain section. The skewer should penetrate and come out easily. Using a slotted spoon, remove plantains from oil, and press immediately into a 1/4-inch thick oblong shape with a plantain press. Dip each pressed piece of plantain rapidly in the prepared water (about 10 seconds), then drop it in hot oil over medium heat until golden and crispy, about 5 to 7 minutes. Do not overload. Serve immediately.

Yields about 15 Bannan Peze.

Note: When frying the plantain pieces the first time, make sure that they do not brown too fast. Otherwise you will be forced to remove them from the pan to prevent them from burning; they will not cook in the center, and they will crumble somewhat when you flatten them.

Fried Sweet Plantains

Bannann Jonn Fri
Bananes Mures Frites

These do not need any special preparation, and yet they are delicious. They make a great accompaniment for beef or pork roasts. If sliced lengthwise and sprinkled with sugar, they are eaten after dinner as an easy dessert. Use a mandolin slicer to slice the plantains lengthwise.

Estimated time: 30 minutes.
4 sweet plantains (well ripened but still firm)
Vegetable oil for deep-frying
Sugar (optional)

Brush plantains under fresh running water. Peel and slice them lengthwise, from beginning to end, into 1/4-inch thick stripes, or cut them diagonally into 1 to 2-inch pieces.

Heat oil in a heavy pan over medium heat, add plantain pieces, and deep-fry them until golden, about 5 to 10 minutes. Transfer to plate and serve warm.

Sliced lengthwise, they can be sprinkled with sugar if desired, and served warm at the end of dinner as dessert.

Yields about 16.

Fried Breadfruit

Veritab Fri (Akòdeyon)
Véritable Frit

Breadfruit must be ripe and green, but not ripened and sweet. *Fried Breadfruit* is delicious.

8 cups water
2 tablespoons salt
1 bitter orange (or 2 lemons), peeled and halved crosswise
1 breadfruit
Vegetable oil for deep-frying

Season the water with the salt and 2 tablespoons bitter orange (or lemon) juice. Set aside.

Quarter breadfruit lengthwise. Core and peel the wedges. Rub with orange, rinse under fresh running water, then slice lengthwise into thin slices (between 1/8 and 1/4 inch thick). As they are cut, put breadfruit slices into the seasoned water.

Heat oil over medium heat in a heavy pan. Drop breadfruit slices into hot oil, and cook until golden and crispy, about 5 to 7 minutes. Do not overload. Drain on paper towels, and serve immediately. The recipe can be scaled down.

Yields about 50 slices.

Variation. Slice the breadfruit into small sticks and fry them just like French fries.

Fried Sweet Potatoes

Patat Fri
Patates Frites

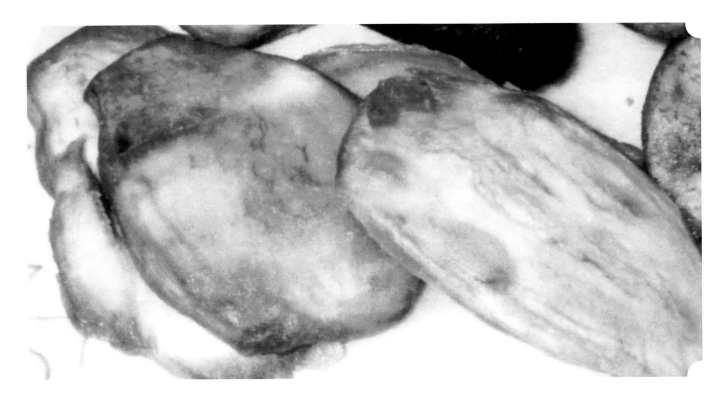

Make sure to use the dry-flesh sweet potatoes. The dark orange sweet potato will provide a soggy result, because they are too moist. Read about sweet potatoes in the Glossary.

Estimated time: 45 minutes
1 1/2 tablespoons salt
6 cups water
2 limes
3 large white sweet potatoes (dry-flesh sweet potatoes)
oil for deep-frying

Dilute salt in water, add juice of one lime, and set aside.

Peel potatoes, and rub them with lime. Rinse potatoes under fresh running water. Pat dry. Slice them into 1/4 to 1/5-inch thick pieces. Soak slices in salted water solution for about 5 minutes.

Heat oil in a heavy pan over medium setting. Drop potatoes in hot oil. Do not overload. Cook until they form a crisp and golden crust, about 7 to 8 minutes. Drain on paper towels. Serve immediately.

Serves 6 to 8.

BEEF

Bèf
Le Boeuf

Beef in Creole Sauce

Beef or Pork

Beef or Pork,
On my fork.
Do you want a leaf?
I'll also have beef.

Rachel Ménager, 11

Beef in Creole Sauce

Vyann Bèf lan Sòs
Boeuf à la Créole

Meat cooked "a la Creole" brings to mind a meat that is cooked in its sauce with a respectable amount of spices and herbs. This is the way we cook meat for soups, stews, . . . etc. Use lemon if bitter orange is not available, and do not forget to peel either of them.

Estimated time: 2 hours (including marinating time).

2 pounds beef (Rump Pot Roast, Sirloin Tip, or any beef cut suitable for braising)
1 bitter orange, or 2 lemons (reserve 1 1/2 tablespoons juice)
1 1/2 tablespoons apple cider vinegar
1 habanero chile (read *Demystifying Habanero Chile*)
1/4 teaspoon ground black pepper
  pinch of ground cloves
1 tablespoon chopped chives, or 1 minced scallion
1/2 teaspoon salt

1 cup white onion shavings (see note in *More Tips*)
1/4 cup chopped fresh flat-leaf parsley
1 sprig thyme
1/4 cup vegetable oil
5 garlic cloves, peeled, and crushed (see note in *More Tips*)
1 tablespoon tomato paste diluted in 1 cup boiled water
4 cups boiled water, or more**
1 slice white onion (for sauce)
1 slice red bell pepper (for sauce)

Trim excess fat from beef. Cut meat crosswise into six fairly equal pieces. Rub meat with bitter orange. Rinse quickly with very hot water. Drain carefully. Put meat in a bowl and coat with orange juice, vinegar, chile, black pepper, cloves, chives, salt, onion, parsley, and thyme. Cover with plastic wrap, and marinate in a cool place for 30 minutes to 1 hour or in the refrigerator overnight.

Heat 2 tablespoons oil in a heavy lidded 5-quart pan over high setting. Reserving marinade, add meat, and sauté until beginning to brown, about 10 minutes. Add marinade, reduce heat to medium, cover, and cook until juice thickens, about 10 to 12 minutes.

Meanwhile, heat remaining oil in a heavy 3-quart pan over medium high setting. Add garlic and sauté for 1 minute. Add diluted tomato paste and boil uncovered until all liquid evaporates, 15 to 20 minutes. Stir-fry for about 1 minute. Add 3 cups of boiled water to tomato paste, mix well, and pour it over the meat. Cover and cook until all liquid evaporates, about 45 minutes**. The sauce should be thick. Remove meat and chile from the sauce. Season sauce with additional salt and pepper if desired. Add 1 cup boiled water to the sauce, and strain. Add meat and reserved chile to the sauce. Reduce, uncovered, over medium heat until sauce thickens, about 5 to 7 minutes. Add onion and bell pepper slices during the last minute. Discard chile. Serve hot.

Serves 6.

Note. The same recipe can be used to cook *Goat in Creole Sauce*. You will then use goat meat instead of the beef. Goat is particularly popular in Plateau Central, Haiti.

When using this recipe for soups or stews, remove the chile before adding meat to the vegetables, and use diced onion instead of the onion shavings. If you use diced onion, you will not need to strain the sauce.

To make "Beef with Okra", sauté 2 cups of sliced okra in a separate skillet until slightly golden; add the sautéed okra slices to the dish before reducing the sauce at the end of the recipe.

*Read note about bitter orange in the Glossary of this book.

**The meat may need more water and more time to become tender. It depends on the cut chosen and the size of the pieces. For small pieces like cuts for stew or soup, the water and the time are less. In this case, add water 1 cup at a time. Sometimes no water is necessary; the meat cooks in its juice.

Sautéed Beef / Pork Tenderloin

Filè Bèf ak Filè Kochon Sote
Filet de Boeuf et Filet de Porc Sautés

In Haiti, the beef tenderloins displayed whole in the meat section of the groceries are the perfect size for sautéing. They weigh about 2 pounds, very rarely heavier than that. If you cannot find a 2-pound beef tenderloin, use 2-inch thick tenderloin slices. Then the time for sautéing will be less.

Estimated time: 1 hour (including marinating time).

One 2-pound whole beef tenderloin (or two 1 1/2-pound pork tenderloins)
1 tablespoon apple cider vinegar
1 tablespoon bitter orange juice (or lemon juice)*
1/2 teaspoon prepared yellow mustard
1 tablespoon ketchup
1/2 teaspoon ground black pepper
1 sprig thyme (leaves only)
Pinch ground cloves
2 chicken bouillon cubes, crushed

4 garlic cloves, peeled, and crushed (see note in *More Tips*)
1/2 cup white onion shavings (see note in *More Tips*)
1/4 cup chopped red bell pepper
1 habanero chile, seeded, and washed**
1 tablespoon chopped fresh flat-leaf parsley
1/4 cup vegetable oil
1 slice white onion (to finish)
1 slice red bell pepper (to finish)
salt to taste

Trim and discard excess surface fat and membranes from the tenderloin. Transfer it to a large bowl. Coat it with vinegar, orange juice (or lemon juice), mustard, ketchup, black pepper, thyme, ground cloves, bouillon cubes, and garlic. Add onion shavings, chopped red bell pepper, chile, and parsley.

Poke the tenderloin with the tines of a fork or a thin knife to allow flavors to penetrate the meat. Cover with plastic wrap, and marinate in a cool place for 30 minutes to 1 hour.

Prepare the sauce before sautéing the tenderloin. Use the marinade to make the sauce following *Creole Sauce* or *Sauce Ti Malice* recipes, and keep it hot.

Heat oil on medium high setting in a 12-inch nonstick skillet, add meat and sauté for 3 minutes so the juice stays trapped inside the meat. Reduce heat to medium and continue to sauté as desired, about 10 minutes for rare, 12 minutes for medium-cooked, and 15 to 20 minutes for well done. At the last minute, stir in remaining onion slice, red bell pepper slice, and sprinkle with salt and pepper. Serve immediately with baked potatoes, or potatoes sautéed in butter.

Serves 6.

*Read note about bitter orange in the Glossary of this book.

**Read *Demystifying Habanero Chile* in *The Cook's Techniques* chapter.

Stuffed Beef / Pork Tenderloin

Filè Bèf ak Filè Kochon Fasi
Filet de Boeuf et Filet de Porc Farci

Here is an elegant and impressive dish. It is also very delicious. The stuffed tenderloin can be sautéed or roasted. The sautéed version is quicker. You will find both methods below.

Estimated time: 1 hour 30 minutes.

1/4 cup chopped white onion
1 habanero chile, seeded, and carefully washed (read *Demystifying Habanero Chile*)
1/4 cup chopped red bell pepper
2 garlic cloves, peeled
pinch ground cloves
2 tablespoons chopped fresh flat-leaf parsley
1 tablespoon chopped chives, or 1 minced scallion
1 sprig thyme (leaves only)
1 chicken bouillon cube, crushed
1 teaspoon salt

1/4 teaspoon ground black pepper
1 tablespoon fresh bitter orange juice, or fresh lemon juice*
1 tablespoon apple cider vinegar
1/3 cup vegetable oil
one 2-pound beef tenderloin**, or one 1 1/2-pound pork tenderloin
1/2 cup *Cooked Stuffing for Poultry, Rabbit, Beef, and Pork*
1 1/2 cups boiled water
ingredients for *Variation of Sauce Ti Malice* (see the Sauces chapter)

With a blender, purée onion, chile, bell pepper, garlic, cloves, parsley, chives, and thyme with bouillon cube, salt, black pepper, bitter orange juice, and vinegar. Heat 3 tablespoons of oil over medium setting in a small pan. Add puréed spices-herbs mixture, and sauté until golden, stirring constantly, lowering the heat toward the end to avoid scorching, about 5 minutes. Set aside.

Trim and discard excess surface fat and membranes from tenderloin. Using a sharp knife, slit the tenderloin lengthwise starting at one end, going 3/4 of the way through the thickness of the meat. Be careful not to cut all the way through. This is called butterflying. Open the tenderloin flat, and make a few slits in the thicker parts of the meat, being careful not to make holes. Spread sautéed spice mixture on both sides of the butterflied tenderloin. Then spoon the stuffing in the center of the butterflied tenderloin lengthwise. Roll up tenderloin as if you were restoring its shape. Using kitchen thread, tie up the stuffed tenderloin at about 2 inch intervals.

Heat remaining oil in a 12-inch nonstick skillet on medium high setting, add meat and sauté for 3 minutes so the juice stays trapped inside the meat. Reduce heat to medium and continue to sauté on all side until juice runs clear and tenderloin is slightly golden, about 20 minutes. Let stand for about 10 minutes before slicing. Serve with baked potatoes, potatoes sautéed in butter with a dash of garlic, *Mashed Potato au Gratin*, or *Scalloped Potatoes* and a crisp tomato-lettuce salad.

Deglaze the pan used for the spices and herbs, and the pan used for the meat to prepare *Variation of Sauce Ti Malice*. Serve hot with the meat.

How to Roast the Stuffed Tenderloin

The tenderloin may be roasted in a preheated oven (350 degrees Fahrenheit). Deglaze the pan used for the spices and herbs with 1 cup of boiled water and pour in a roasting pan. Place stuffed tenderloin on a rack on the roasting pan, so that it does not touch the water. Roast for 1 to 1 hour 30 minutes in the middle of preheated oven, turning the tenderloin after the first hour of roasting. Add more boiled water to roasting pan if necessary. Let stand for about 10 minutes before slicing. Serve as above.

During the standing time, use the pan used for the spices to prepare the sauce with the drippings. Follow the recipe for *Sauce for Roast Chicken*.

Serves 6.

*Read note about bitter orange in the Glossary of this book.

**If you cannot find a 2-pound tenderloin, use a portion of the tenderloin; ask the butcher to cut the amount needed.

Beef Kabob

Bwochèt Bèf
Brochettes de Boeuf

Here the meat is first cooked in its juice, then quickly grilled. The grilling adds that extra flavor and makes the brochettes more appealing. This can be also done under the oven broiler; unfortunately you will miss the particular taste imparted by the charcoal.

2 pounds beef tenderloin
1/4 cup vegetable oil
5 garlic cloves, peeled, and crushed (see note in *More Tips*)
1 tablespoon tomato paste diluted with 1 cup boiled water
1 1/2 tablespoons bitter orange juice, or lemon juice
1 1/2 tablespoons apple cider vinegar
1 habanero chile, seeded, carefully washed, and minced (read *Demystifying Habanero Chile*)
1/4 teaspoon ground black pepper

pinch of ground cloves
1 tablespoon chopped chives, or 1 minced scallion
1/2 teaspoon salt
1 cup white onion shavings (see note in *More Tips*)
1 sprig thyme
2 red bell peppers, cut into 1-inch pieces
2 green bell peppers, cut into 1-inch pieces
1 white onion, cut into 1-inch pieces
ingredients for *Variation of Sauce Ti Malice* (see the Sauces chapter)
6 to 8 skewers (metal or wood)

Trim and discard excess surface fat and membranes from the tenderloin. Using a sharp knife, cube the meat into about 1 1/2-inch pieces.

Heat oil over medium high in a 5-quart heavy pan. Add garlic, and sauté for 2 minutes. Add diluted tomato paste. Boil uncovered until all liquid evaporates, 15 to 20 minutes. Stir-fry for 2 minutes. Add meat, orange juice, vinegar, chile, black pepper, ground cloves, chives, salt, onion shavings, and thyme. Toss with a large spoon. Reduce heat to medium. Cook until the sauce thickens and coats the meat, turning occasionally, about 20 minutes. The meat should be tender. Remove from heat. Remove the meat from the sauce. Remove and reserve 2 tablespoons of oil from the sauce. Add 1/2 cup or so of boiled water to the sauce and strain to prepare *Creole Sauce* or *Hot Creole Sauce*.

Get a charcoal grill ready. On each skewer, thread 2 pieces of onion, one piece of red pepper, one piece of meat, 2 pieces of onion, one piece of green pepper. Continue with meat, onion, red pepper, then meat, onion, green pepper, and so on. Brush the brochettes with the reserved oil, and grill them for a few minutes close to the fire, just until the meat and vegetables are golden. Serve immediately with the sauce.

Serves 6 to 8.

Pepper Steak

Estek Opwav
Steak au Poivre

Estimated time: 1 hour.

one 3-pound beef tenderloin cut into 1 to 1 1/2-inch thick slices, or 3 pounds of beef tenderloin cut into 1 to 1 1/2-inch thick slices
2 tablespoons coarsely ground black pepper
3 tablespoons vegetable oil
salt to taste
1/4 cup finely diced white onion
1/2 cup boiled water

1/2 teaspoon finely ground black pepper
2 chicken bouillon cubes, crushed
1/2 cup dry white or red wine
1/2 tablespoons white balsamic vinegar, or apple cider vinegar
1 teaspoon prepared yellow mustard
3 tablespoons heavy whipping cream

Coat tenderloin slices on both sides with coarsely ground black pepper. Heat oil in a heavy 12-inch skillet over medium high setting. Add meat and sauté 1 minute on each side. Then reduce heat to medium and continue to sauté to the desired doneness (7 minutes on each side for medium). Do not crowd the skillet; otherwise the juice rendered by the meat will not be able to evaporate, and the meat will boil in its juice instead of sautéeing. Sprinkle with salt to taste. Transfer meat to a plate, and keep it warm.

Sauté onion until translucent in the same skillet, about 1 minute. Add water, ground black pepper, bouillon cubes, wine, vinegar, mustard, and cream. Reduce the sauce until it thickens, stirring occasionally, 7 to 8 minutes. Season with additional salt if necessary. Spoon some of the sauce over the steaks, and serve immediately. Serve remaining sauce in a sauce boat.

Serves 6.

Ground Beef

Vyann Moulen
Bifteck Haché

The following preparation can be used as a base to make turnover fillings, meat sauce for pasta, chili, and lots of other recipes asking for ground beef. It makes a delicious filling for homemade ravioli. Work raw ground beef with a large spoon or a fork to undo the small string-like pieces of meat, so it cooks evenly. As before, lemon can be used instead of bitter orange. Peel and seed orange (or lemon) before using. Marinating is not necessary.

Estimated time: 50 minutes.

1/4 cup vegetable oil
6 garlic cloves, peeled, and crushed (see note in *More Tips*)
1/3 cup tomato paste, diluted with
1 1/2 cups boiled water
1 1/2 cups finely diced white onion
1 tablespoon chopped chives, or 1 minced scallion
1 habanero chile, seeded, and washed (read *Demystifying Habanero Chile*)
1/4 cup chopped fresh flat-leaf parsley

1 sprig thyme (leaves only)
1/4 teaspoon ground black pepper
pinch ground cloves
1 pound ground beef (preferably extra lean)
1 1/2 tablespoons apple cider vinegar
1 tablespoon fresh bitter orange juice (or lemon juice)*
1 1/2 teaspoons salt
1/4 cup diced red bell pepper

Heat oil in a 3-quart heavy pan over medium high heat, add garlic, and sauté for 1 to 2 minutes. Add diluted tomato paste, cover partially, and cook until all liquid evaporates, about 25 to 30 minutes, stirring occasionally. Stir-fry for 4 to 5 minutes. Add onion, chives, chile, parsley, thyme, black pepper, and cloves, and sauté for 5 additional minutes. Tomato paste-spice mixture should be very thick. Then add ground meat, working vigorously with a strong spoon to avoid formation of lumps until meat is no longer pink. Then add vinegar, bitter orange juice (or lemon juice), and salt. Cover and cook for 10 to 15 minutes, stirring occasionally. Season with additional salt and pepper if necessary. Add bell pepper, and cook uncovered for 3 to 5 minutes, stirring occasionally. Discard chile. Serve hot.

Serves 3 to 4.

*Read note about bitter orange in the Glossary of this book.

Meat Balls

Boulèt Vyann Bèf
Boulettes De Boeuf

Meat balls should not be larger than 1 1/2 to 2 inches or the center may not cook properly. Make sure oil is hot enough before dropping in meat balls. Peel and seed orange (or lemon) before using.

Estimated time: 45 minutes.

1 pound baking potatoes (about 2 large), boiled and peeled (hot)
5 garlic cloves, peeled, and crushed (see note in *More Tips*)
1/2 cup minced white onion
1/4 cup chopped red bell pepper
1 sprig thyme, leaves only
1/4 cup chopped fresh flat-leaf parsley
1 tablespoon chopped chives, or 1 minced scallion

1 habanero chile, seeded, and washed (read *Demystifying Habanero Chile*)
2 chicken bouillon cubes, crushed
1 teaspoon salt
1/4 teaspoon ground black pepper, or to taste
pinch ground cloves
1 pound ground beef (preferably extra lean)
1 1/2 tablespoon apple cider vinegar
1 1/2 tablespoons fresh bitter orange juice (or lemon juice)*
1/2 cup all purpose flour
vegetable oil for deep-frying

With a fork, finely mash potatoes while still hot, making sure to mash every bit. Set aside.

Heat 1 tablespoon oil on medium setting, add garlic, onion, bell pepper, thyme, parsley, chives, and chile and sauté for about 3 minutes. Add bouillon cubes and sauté for one more minute. Add salt, black pepper, and ground cloves. Discard chile. Remove spice mixture from heat, and allow it to cool down for about 15 minutes. Add meat, vinegar, bitter orange juice, and mashed potato. Mix thoroughly. Form 1 1/2-inch balls, then roll them in flour. Remove excess flour from meat balls.

Heat oil in a heavy pan over medium setting and carefully drop meat balls in hot oil. Fry them for about 15 to 20 minutes. Watch closely, lowering heat whenever necessary to avoid burning. Drain on paper towels. Serve hot, with *Creole Sauce* or with *Hot Creole Sauce* if you wish. After being fried, meat balls can also be simmered in the *Creole Sauce* for 3 to 5 minutes.

Yields about 30 to 35 meat balls.

Note. Remove brown bits from oil, and do not hesitate to change the oil when there is too much deposit at the bottom of the pan. This will prevent the meat balls from tasting burned.

*Read note about bitter orange in the Glossary of this book.

Meat Loaf

Pendvo
Pain de Veau

Estimated time: 1 hour 30 minutes.

1/4 cup vegetable oil
6 garlic cloves, peeled, and crushed (see note in *More Tips*)
1/3 cup tomato paste, diluted with
1 1/2 cups boiled water
2 cups finely diced white onion
1/4 cup diced red bell pepper
2 tablespoons chopped chives, or 2 minced scallions
1 habanero chile, seeded, washed, and minced (read *Demystifying Habanero Chile*)
2 tablespoons finely chopped fresh flat-leaf parsley

1 sprig thyme (leaves only)
1/4 teaspoon ground black pepper
Pinch ground cloves
1 1/2 pounds ground beef
1 1/2 tablespoons apple cider vinegar
1 tablespoon fresh bitter orange juice (or lemon juice)
1 1/2 teaspoons salt
2 large eggs, slightly beaten
1 cup *Fresh Bread Crumbs* (recipe given in this book)
1 slice of white onion (for the sauce)

Heat oil in a 4-quart heavy pan over medium high heat, add garlic, and sauté for 1 to 2 minutes. Add diluted tomato paste, cover partially, and cook until all liquid evaporates, about 25 to 30 minutes. Stir-fry for 4 to 5 minutes. Add onion, bell pepper, chives, chile, parsley, thyme, black pepper, and cloves, and sauté for 5 additional minutes. Remove from heat. Tomato paste-spice mixture should be very thick. Allow it to cool down.

Meanwhile, preheat oven to 350 degrees Fahrenheit. Grease lightly a 9x5-inch loaf pan, and set aside. Then, in a large bowl work raw ground beef with a large spoon or a fork to undo the small string-like pieces of meat. Mix in the tomato paste-spices mixture, then vinegar, orange juice, salt, eggs, and bread crumbs. Work vigorously with a spoon or a fork to obtain a homogeneous mixture. Transfer it to the prepared pan. Cover with aluminum foil, and bake in the middle of preheated oven for 50 minutes. Uncover. If the meat loaf is surrounded with juice, drain the juice into a 2-quart pan to prepare a sauce. Continue baking the meat loaf, uncovered, for 10 to 15 additional minutes.

Meanwhile, skim and discard excess fat from the meat juice if any, and reduce it over medium heat until it thickens. Add onion slice at the last minute.

Allow the meat loaf to set in the pan for 10 minutes before unmolding. Serve hot with the sauce or with *Creole Sauce*.

Serves 6.

Salt Beef

Vyann Bèf Sale
Boeuf Salé

There was a time when salting and drying were the only ways to preserve meat. In Haiti nowadays, people still enjoy a good dish of salted meats, and sometimes it is still the only way to preserve meat. Salt beef is available at some butcher's shops, and if you are craving *Salt Beef*, you can prepare it following the method to make *Cured Pork*, substituting beef for the pork in the recipe.

Boil the meat in plenty of water to remove the excess salt. *Salt Beef* is usually served with avocado slices, watercress, boiled name roots and/or boiled plantains.

Estimated time: 1 hour 45 minutes (soaking time not included).

2 pounds salt beef (1/2-inch thick), cut into six servings (or salt beef tongue)
1/3 cup vegetable oil
3 garlic cloves, peeled, and crushed (see note in *More Tips*)
1 tablespoon chopped chives, or 1 minced scallion
pinch of ground cloves
1/4 heaping teaspoon ground black pepper

2 habanero chiles, seeded, carefully washed, and cut into thin strips*
1/2 teaspoon prepared yellow mustard
1/2 tablespoon mayonnaise
1 1/2 tablespoons apple cider vinegar
salt to taste
3 to 4 white onion slices (about 1/4 inch thick each)

Rinse the meat under fresh running water to remove the excess salt. Soak it in a large pot of water for 12 to 14 hours, changing the water every 3 hours. Soak longer if necessary. This will remove most of the salt and soften the meat. Drain and discard the soaking water.

Bring 16 cups of water (more if possible) to a boil in a pot, add meat, and boil covered (lid slightly a jar) on medium high heat until the meat is tender, about 1 hour 30 minutes. Be sure not to overcook it. Remove from heat. Drain, reserving 1 cup cooking liquid.

Heat 3 tablespoons of oil in a 12-inch skillet over medium setting. Add garlic, and sauté for 2 minutes stirring constantly. Add 3/4 cup cooking liquid, meat, chives, cloves, black pepper, half of the chile, mustard, mayonnaise, and vinegar. Boil 5 minutes. Remove meat from sauce. Strain sauce. Put meat and sauce in the skillet. Reduce over medium heat until sauce thickens, 5 minutes. Season with salt. Transfer to a serving plate. Keep it hot. Sprinkle with additional pepper if desired.

Heat remaining oil in a small skillet over medium high setting. Add onion slices and remaining chile, and sauté for 1 minute. Pour, hot, over the meat. Serve immediately.

Serves 6.

*Read *Demystifying Habanero Chile* in *The Cook's Techniques* chapter.

Tasso

Tasso is very popular in Haiti. It is not a condiment as it is in the south of Louisiana (USA), but a dish in itself usually made with beef or goat, or sometimes turkey. *Tasso* is traditionally made with meat that has been cut into strips, spiced, then sun-dried for two to three days. This way of preserving meat in Haiti comes from the Indian and buccaneer legacy. In this recipe, I use fresh beef which gives a *Tasso* as delicious as the traditional one*. *Tasso* is always served with *Sauce Ti Malice*, *Twice Fried Pressed Plantains*, avocado slices, and a fresh watercress salad.

Estimated time: 1 hour (marinating and standing time not included).

2 pounds beef rump, pot roast, or chuck steak (or any part suitable for braising)
1 bitter orange (or lemon)**, peeled
1 habanero chile (read *Demystifying Habanero Chile*)
1/2 cup chopped shallots
1/2 cup vegetable oil

4 garlic cloves, peeled, and crushed (see note in *More Tips*)
1 tablespoon tomato paste, diluted with 1 cup boiled water
chopped shallots to garnish
chopped parsley to garnish

Cut bitter orange and express 1/4 cup juice. Strain and set aside.

Trim excess fat from meat. Cut into 1/2 -inch x 4-inch strips. Marinate meat with orange juice, chile, and shallots in the refrigerator for 5 to 7 hours, or overnight.

Heat oil over medium setting in a heavy lidded 5-quart pan. Add garlic, and sauté for 2 minutes. Add diluted tomato paste and cook until no liquid remains, about 15 to 20 minutes. Stir-fry for 1 to 2 minutes. Add meat and marinade. Cook covered, for about 30 minutes. Transfer meat to plate and let it cool for about 30 minutes. Discard chile or use it to prepare the sauce.

Reserving the cooking liquid, spoon the oil into a large skillet. Heat oil over medium high setting. Add meat, and sauté until golden brown. Drain on paper towels. Garnish with chopped shallot and chopped parsley. Serve hot with sauce. The recipe for the sauce follows.

Serves 6.

*To make the *Traditional Tasso*, use dried salted meat. Rinse the meat under fresh running water to remove the excess salt. Soak it in a large pot of water for 12 to 14 hours, changing the water every 3 hours. Soak it longer if necessary. Drain and discard the soaking water. Cut the meat into strips, as above. Bring 16 cups of water to a boil in a pot, add meat, and boil covered (lid slightly ajar) on medium high heat until the meat is tender. Marinate meat and proceed as indicated above. Because it is made with salted meat, *Traditional Tasso* will take much longer to prepare.

**Read note about bitter orange in the Glossary of this book.

Sauce Ti Malice for Tasso

Sòs Ti Malice pou Tasso
Sauce Ti Malice pour Tasso

This delicious sauce served with *Tasso* is usually very hot, but its fieriness can be adjusted, depending on the table companions.

Estimated time: 10 minutes.

1/2 teaspoon ground black pepper
1/2 cup finely sliced shallots
1/2 tablespoon chopped fresh flat-leaf parsley
1 tablespoon oil from *Tasso* cooking liquid

1 cup cooking liquid from *Tasso*
1 1/2 tablespoon apple cider vinegar
1 tablespoon fresh lime juice
1 habanero chile, cut, and seeded*
salt to taste

Put black pepper, shallots, and parsley in a sauce boat. Set aside.

Heat oil in a heavy 2-quart saucepan over medium setting. Add cooking liquid, vinegar, lime juice, and chile. Boil until sauce thickens. Pour boiling sauce over spices and herbs in the sauce boat. Spoon out excess oil if necessary. Serve hot, with *Tasso*.

Yields about 3/4 cup.

*Wash chile, cut it in half, and remove seeds and membranes. If you wish to have a mild sauce, rub it gently under fresh running water for 15 seconds.

BEEF GIBLETS

Tonbe Bèf
Les Abats de Boeuf

Beef Tongue in Creole Sauce

Beef Liver in Creole Sauce

Fwa Bèf nan Sos
Foie de Boeuf à la Créole

Liver is a very delicate meat when it is raw, so it must be handled gently, particularly when cleaning. Make sure that the membrane that coats the meat is removed. In Haiti, liver is often served with boiled green plantains, avocado slices, and watercress and sometimes constitutes a breakfast dish. Most of us like to eat "à la fourchette" in the morning, particularly those of us who need to get a good start for the day.

Estimated time: 1 hour 20 minutes.

juice of 2 bitter oranges, or 3 lemons
2 pounds sliced beef liver (1/4-inch thick slices)
2 tablespoons apple cider vinegar
1 habanero chile (read *Demystifying Habanero Chile*)
1/4 heaping teaspoon ground black pepper
pinch of ground cloves
1 tablespoon chopped chives, or 1 minced scallion

1 cup white onion shavings (see note in *More Tips*)
1/4 cup chopped fresh flat-leaf parsley
1 sprig thyme
3 tablespoons vegetable oil
5 garlic cloves, peeled and crushed
1 tablespoon tomato paste diluted in 1 cup boiled water
1 cup boiled water
1 teaspoon salt or to taste
1 slice white onion (for sauce)
1 slice red bell pepper (for sauce)

Reserve 1 1/2 tablespoons bitter orange (or lemon) juice for marinade. Put liver in a large bowl, and pour bitter orange (or lemon) juice on it. Toss to coat. Rinse quickly with very hot (almost boiling) water. Drain carefully. Peel off and discard any remaining membrane from the liver. Transfer liver to a large bowl and add reserved orange juice, vinegar, chile, black pepper, cloves, chives, onion, parsley, and thyme. Cover and marinate in a cool place for 30 minutes.

Heat oil in a heavy 12-inch-covered skillet over medium high setting . Add garlic, and sauté for 1 minute. Add diluted tomato paste and boil until liquid evaporates completely, about 15 to 20 minutes. Reduce heat to medium and stir-fry for 1 to 2 minutes. Add liver and marinade, cover, and cook for 20 minutes. Remove from heat and transfer liver and chile to plate. Add 1 cup of boiled water and salt to sauce, and boil covered over medium high for 5 minutes. Strain sauce. Add liver and reserved chile, and reduce over medium high until sauce thickens, about 3 to 4 minutes. Add onion slice and red pepper slice at the last minute. Discard chile. Serve hot.

Serves 6.

Sautéed Beef Liver with Onion

Fwa Bèf Sote ak Zonyon
Foie de Boeuf Sauté à l'Oignon

Liver contains a lot of juice. In order to trap the juice inside and keep it moist, liver must be sautéed at high temperature. Reduce the temperature toward the end of cooking to avoid scorching.

juice of 3 Persian limes
1/4 cup finely chopped white onion
1 habanero chile, seeded, washed, and minced (read *Demystifying Habanero Chile*)
1/4 cup finely chopped red bell pepper
3 garlic cloves, peeled, and chopped (see note in *More Tips*)
pinch of ground cloves
2 tablespoons finely chopped fresh flat-leaf parsley

1 tablespoon chopped chives, or 1 minced scallion
1 sprig thyme (leaves only)
1 chicken bouillon cube, crushed
1/4 teaspoon ground black pepper
1 pound beef liver slices (four 1/4-inch slices)
1/4 cup vegetable oil
3 tablespoons apple cider vinegar
1/2 teaspoon salt or to taste
4 thin white onion slices

Estimated time: 30 minutes.

Bring a large pot of water to boil.

Meanwhile, purée onion, chile, bell pepper, garlic, cloves, parsley, chives and thyme with the bouillon cube, black pepper, and 2 tablespoons lime juice using a blender. Set the purée aside.

Put liver slices in a large heat-resistant bowl and pour the remaining lime juice on them. Toss to coat the liver with juice. Pour very hot water on the liver, then drain immediately through a strainer. Set aside in the strainer over a bowl.

Heat oil in a large skillet over medium setting. Add the puréed spice-herb mixture, and sauté until golden, lowering the heat toward the end to avoid scorching, about 5 minutes. Increase heat to medium high. Add beef liver to pan, two slices at a time. Sprinkle with vinegar. Sauté until liver just begins to brown and no juice remains, about 7 minutes on each side, lowering the heat to medium toward the end to avoid scorching. Do not overcook. Overcooking will toughen the liver. Add onion slices during the last 3 minutes. Sprinkle with salt and additional pepper. Serve hot with a crisp salad and crusty bread.

Serves 4 to 6.

Beef Kidneys in Creole Sauce

Ronyon lan Sòs
Rognon à la Creole

Just like liver, kidney is a delicate meat when it is raw, and must be handled gently when cleaning. Make sure that the membrane that covers the meat is removed. In Haiti, the kidney lobes are usually separated, and all the fat and vessels are removed and discarded. Kidneys are often served at breakfast just like liver.

Estimated time: 1 hour 20 minutes.

3 beef kidneys (about 3 1 /2 pounds)
juice of 3 bitter oranges, or 6 lemons (reserve 1/4 cup juice)
1/4 cup apple cider vinegar
1 1/4 teaspoons salt or to taste
1 habanero chile (read *Demystifying Habanero Chile*)
1/2 teaspoon ground black pepper
pinch of ground cloves
1 tablespoon chopped chives, or 1 minced scallion

1 1/2 cups white onion shavings (see note in *More Tips*)
1/4 cup chopped fresh flat-leaf parsley
2 sprigs thyme
3 tablespoons vegetable oil
6 garlic cloves peeled and crushed
2 tablespoons tomato paste diluted in 1 cup boiled water
1 cup boiled water
2 slices white onion (for sauce)
1 slice red bell pepper (for sauce

Bring a large pot of water to boil. Separate kidneys into lobes with a sharp knife. Discard fat and vessels. Put kidney lobes in a large bowl. Add bitter orange (or lemon) juice, and toss to coat. Rinse quickly with very hot water. Drain carefully. Peel and discard any remaining membrane from kidneys. Transfer to a large bowl and add reserved bitter orange juice, vinegar, salt, chile, black pepper, cloves, chives, onion, parsley, and thyme. Cover and marinate in a cool place for 30 minutes to 1 hour.

Heat oil in a heavy 5-quart covered pan over medium high setting. Add garlic, and sauté for 1 minute. Add diluted tomato paste and boil until liquid evaporates completely, about 15 to 20 minutes. Reduce heat to medium and stir-fry for 1 to 2 minutes. Add kidneys and marinade, cover, and cook over medium high setting until meat is tender, about 40 minutes. Remove from heat. Transfer kidneys and chile to plate. Add 1 cup of boiled water to sauce, strain, add kidneys, and reserved chile. Reduce over medium high until sauce thickens, about 10 minutes. Add onion and red pepper slices at the last minute. Discard chile. Serve hot.

Serves 6.

Beef Tongue in Creole Sauce

Lang Bèf lan Sòs
Langue de Boeuf à la Créole

Tongue is a very delicious meat. When correctly cooked, it is a real pleasure for the palate. If overcooked, it will be unpleasantly mushy. Tongue is entirely covered by a membrane that must be peeled off. This is easy to do after boiling. There is no marinating. Take advantage of the boiling time to prepare your condiments.

Estimated time: 2 hours.

one whole 2 1/4-pound beef tongue
1 bitter orange, or 2 lemons (reserve 1 tablespoon juice)
3 tablespoons vegetable oil
7 garlic cloves, peeled and crushed
1 tablespoon tomato paste diluted in 1 cup boiled water
2 tablespoons white balsamic vinegar
1 habanero chile (read *Demystifying Habanero Chile*)
1/4 heaping teaspoon ground black pepper

1/8 teaspoon ground cloves
1 tablespoon chopped chives, or 1 minced scallion
1 teaspoon salt
1 1/2 cups white onion shavings (see note in *More Tips*)
1/4 cup chopped fresh flat-leaf parsley
1 sprig thyme
2 cups boiled water
1 slice white onion (for sauce)
1 slice red bell pepper (for sauce)

Bring a large pot of water to boil. Discard fat and vessels at the cut end of the tongue, if any, then rub tongue carefully with bitter orange (or lemon). Rinse thoroughly with fresh running water. Add tongue to boiling water, and boil until tongue is cooked through, 1 hour 30 minutes. Drain and discard water. Cool tongue at room temperature. Peel tongue starting at the cut end. The membrane should come off very easily. Slice tongue diagonally into about 1 1/2-inch pieces. Set aside.

Heat oil in a heavy 5-quart covered pan over medium high setting. Add garlic, and sauté for 1 minute. Add diluted tomato paste and boil until liquid evaporates completely, about 15 to 20 minutes. Reduce heat to medium and stir-fry for 1 to 2 minutes. Add sliced tongue, vinegar, chile, black pepper, cloves, chives, salt, onion, parsley, thyme, and 1 cup boiled water. Cover, and boil over medium heat for 20 minutes. Remove sliced tongue and chile from sauce, and transfer to plate. Add 3/4 cup of boiled water to sauce, strain. Add sliced tongue, reserved chile, and reduce over medium heat until sauce thickens, about 10 minutes. Season with additional pepper if desired. Add onion and red pepper slices at the last minute. Discard chile. Serve hot.

Serves 4 to 5.

PORK

Kochon
Le Porc

Braised Greens with Pork and Crab (served with White Rice)

Pork in Creole Sauce

Vyann Kochon lan Sòs
Porc à la Créole

Estimated time: 2 hours (including marinating time).

2 pounds boneless fresh ham, or fresh pork shoulder
1 bitter orange, or 2 lemons (reserve 1 1/2 tablespoon juice)
1 1/2 tablespoons apple cider vinegar
1 habanero chile (read *Demystifying Habanero Chile*)
1/4 teaspoon ground black pepper
pinch of ground cloves
1 tablespoon chopped chives, or 1 minced scallion
1 chicken bouillon cube, crushed

1/2 teaspoon salt
1 cup white onion shavings (see note in *More Tips*)
1/4 cup chopped fresh flat-leaf parsley
1 sprig thyme
3 tablespoons vegetable oil
5 garlic cloves, peeled and crushed
1 tablespoon tomato paste diluted in 1 cup boiled water
3 cups boiled water
1 slice white onion (for sauce)
1 slice red bell pepper (for sauce)

Trim excess fat from pork. Cut meat crosswise into six fairly equal pieces. Rub meat with bitter orange. Rinse quickly with very hot water. Drain carefully. Put meat in a bowl and coat with orange juice, vinegar, chile, black pepper, cloves, chives, bouillon cube, salt, onion, parsley, and thyme. Cover with plastic wrap, and marinate in a cool place for 30 minutes to 1 hour or overnight in the refrigerator.

Heat 2 tablespoons oil in a heavy lidded 5-quart pan over high setting. Reserving marinade, add meat to oil, and sauté until beginning to brown, about 10 minutes. Add marinade, reduce heat to medium, cover, and cook until juice thickens, about 10 to 12 minutes.

Meanwhile, heat remaining oil in a heavy 3-quart pan over medium high setting. Sauté garlic for 1 minute. Add diluted tomato paste and boil uncovered until all liquid evaporates, 15 to 20 minutes. Stir-fry for about 1 minute. Add 3 cups of boiled water to tomato paste, mix well, and pour it over the pork. Cover and cook until all liquid evaporates and meat is tender, about 30 to 40 minutes. Sauce should be thick. Remove meat and chile from the sauce. Season sauce with additional salt and pepper if desired. Add 1 cup boiled water to sauce, and strain. Add meat and reserved chile. Reduce until sauce thickens, about 5 to 7 minutes. Add onion and bell pepper slices during the last minute. Discard chile. Serve hot.

Serves 6.

Braised Chayote Squash with Pork

Legim Militon ak Vyann Kochon
Mirliton Braisé avec Viande de Porc

This is a delicious vegetable and meat dish. It is worth the time spent to make it. You will need a heavy lidded 8-quart round pan (12 x 4 inches). Peel bitter orange (or lemon) before using.

In this recipe (and in all the other recipes calling for chayote squash in this book), I used the squash commonly available on the United States market; they are not fully mature. Very mature chayote squash yield more mash, making it possible to make the dish with fewer squash.

Estimated time: 2 hours 20 minutes (including marinating time)

2 pounds fresh pork shoulder, fresh ham, or fresh pork ribs

1 bitter orange*, or 2 lemons (reserve 3 tablespoons juice for marinade)

1 1/2 cups white onion shavings (see note in *More Tips*)

1/2 cup minced red bell pepper

1 tablespoon chopped chives, or 1 minced scallion

1/4 cup finely chopped fresh flat-leaf parsley

1 habanero chile (read *Demystifying Habanero Chile*)

2 chicken bouillon cubes, crushed

1/2 tablespoons salt

1/8 teaspoon ground cloves

1/4 heaping teaspoon ground black pepper

2 tablespoons apple cider vinegar

8 to 9 pounds chayote squash (about 15 to 18 squash)

1/3 cup vegetable oil

7 garlic cloves, peeled, and crushed (see note in *More Tips*)

2 tablespoons tomato paste, diluted in 1 1/2 cups boiled water

3 cups or so of boiled water (squash cooking water will do)

3 carrots, peeled, and sliced into 1/2-inch pieces

Trim excess fat from pork and cut into 2-inch cubes. Rub meat with orange and rinse well with very hot water. Drain well. Marinate meat in a large bowl with orange juice, onion, bell pepper, chives, parsley, habanero chile, bouillon cubes, salt, ground cloves, black pepper, and vinegar for 30 minutes in a cool place or overnight in the refrigerator.

Peel, halve, and seed squash. Cut each half into 2 pieces. Bring a large pot of water to boil over high heat. Add the squash pieces and boil until cooked through, 25 to 30 minutes.

Drain, reserving boiling liquid. Mash well with a fork, discarding all fibers, if any. Set aside.

Heat 2 tablespoons of oil over medium heat in a heavy lidded 8-quart round pan (12 x 4 inches). Add pork, and sauté until golden brown, about 15 to 20 minutes. Transfer pork to a plate.

Add 1 tablespoon of oil in the same pan over medium heat. Add garlic, and sauté for 2 minutes. Add diluted tomato paste and boil on medium high heat until all liquid evaporates, about 25 to 30 minutes. Stir-fry for 1 minute. Add sautéed pork, marinade, and 1 cup of boiled water. Cover, and boil until liquid evaporates and pork is tender, stirring occasionally, about 30 minutes. Add mashed squash, and cook uncovered for about 15 minutes, stirring often. Add carrots and remaining oil. Continue to cook until sauce thickens, no liquid runs from the mash, and carrots are cooked through, 15 additional minutes. Discard habanero chile. Garnish with parsley if desired. Serve hot with white rice.

Serves 6.

Variation. For a delicious variation, add 1 pound crab legs to make *Braised Chayote Squash with Pork and Crab*.

*Read about bitter orange in the Glossary of this book.

Braised Eggplant, Chayote Squash, and Cabbage with Pork

Legim Berejenn, Militon, Chou ak Vyann Kochon
Aubergine, Mirliton et Chou Braisés avec Viande de Porc

This recipe is just as delicious as the preceding one.

Estimated time: 2 hours (including marinating time)

2 pounds fresh pork shoulder, fresh ham, or fresh pork ribs
1 bitter orange*, or 2 lemons, peeled (reserve 3 tablespoons juice for marinade)
1 1/2 cups white onion shavings (see note in *More Tips*)
1/2 cup chopped red bell pepper
1 tablespoon chopped chives, or 1 minced scallion
1/4 cup finely chopped fresh flat-leaf parsley
1 habanero chile (read *Demystifying Habanero Chile*)
2 chicken bouillon cubes, crushed
1 tablespoon salt
1/8 teaspoon ground cloves
1/4 heaping teaspoon ground black pepper
2 tablespoons apple cider vinegar

3 chayote squash, peeled, halved, and seeded
2 eggplant, peeled, and cut into 1/2-inch slices
1 pound (about 4 1/2 cups) cabbage, cut into small wedges
1/3 cup vegetable oil
7 garlic cloves, peeled, and crushed (see note in *More Tips*)
6 Roma tomatoes, peeled, seeded, and chopped**
2 tablespoons tomato paste, diluted in 1 cup of boiled water
3 cups or so of boiled water (cooking liquid of vegetables will do)
3 carrots, peeled, and cut into 1/2-inch slices

Trim excess fat from pork, and cut into 2-inch cubes. Rub meat with orange and rinse well with very hot water. Marinate meat in a large bowl with orange juice, onion, bell pepper, chives, parsley, habanero chile, bouillon cubes, salt, ground cloves, black pepper, and vinegar for 30 minutes in a cool place or overnight in the refrigerator.

Bring a large pot of water to boil over medium high heat. Add squash, cover, and cook 20 minutes. Then add eggplant, and continue to boil for 5 additional minutes. Drain. Mash vegetables together with a fork in a large shallow dish. Set aside.

Steam cabbage wedges until tender, about 10 minutes. Transfer cabbage to a plate, and cut the wedges into bite-size pieces. Set aside.

Heat 1 tablespoon of oil over medium heat in a heavy lidded 8-quart round pan (12 x 4 inches). Add pork and sauté until golden brown, 15 minutes. Transfer pork to a plate. Set aside.

Heat 2 tablespoons of oil in the same pan over medium setting. Add garlic and sauté for 1 minute. Add tomatoes and diluted tomato paste. Boil over medium high heat until no liquid remains. Stir-fry for 2 minutes. Add sautéed pork, marinade, and 1 cup of boiled water. Cover and boil until pork is tender, stirring occasionally, about 30 minutes. The sauce should be thick. Transfer pork to a plate, leaving the sauce in the pan. Add mashed vegetables and steamed cabbage to the sauce, and cook uncovered for about 15 minutes, stirring often. Add carrot, pork, and remaining oil. Continue to cook until sauce thickens and no liquid runs from the mash, about 15 minutes. Discard chile. Garnish with parsley if desired. Serve hot with white rice.

Serves 6 to 8.

Variation. For a delicious variation, add 1 pound crab legs to make *Braised Eggplant, Chayote Squash, and Cabbage with Pork and Crab*.

*Read about bitter orange in the Glossary of this book.

**Bring a large pot of water to a boil, add tomatoes and blanch for 1 minute. Drain, and put hot tomatoes in a large pot of cold water for 1 minute. Drain. Peel the skin, which should come off very easily. Halve tomatoes crosswise, then seed, and chop them.

Braised Greens with Pork and Crab

Fèy
Legumes Verts Braisés avec Porc et Crab

Fèy is a speciality of "Vallee de l'Artibonite" of Haiti. Different kinds of greens are used to make one dish. Among those greens, spinach, "lalo," purslane (**koupye** in Haitian Creole), and watercress are always used. But any kind of greens can do, and *Fèy* can even be made with spinach only. Meat can be cooked one day ahead. You will need two heavy 4-quart pans for the meat and the crab, and a heavy lidded heavy 8-quart round pan (12 x 4 inches) for the entire dish.

Estimated time: 2 hours (including cooking time for meat and crab).

7 pounds torn fresh mixed greens*
1 1/2 pounds fresh pork (pork shoulder, fresh ham, or pork ribs), cooked following *Pork in Creole Sauce* recipe
1 pound crab legs, cooked following *Lobster in Creole Sauce* recipe
2 tablespoons vegetable oil
Salt and pepper

Trim excess fat from pork, cut into 2-inch cubes, and cook it following *Pork in Creole Sauce* recipe. It is not necessary to strain the sauce. Set aside.

Cook crab following *Lobster in Creole Sauce* recipe. It is not necessary to strain sauce. Set aside.

In a heavy lidded 8-quart round pan (12 x 4 inches), heat oil over medium setting. Add greens to the pan. You will have a large pack of greens, so you will have to add greens to the pan gradually in 2 to 3 portions. Cover for 2 to 3 minutes until the first addition of greens is wilted, then add another portion into the pan, and so on until all greens are added. Sauté for 5 minutes. Cover, and cook until greens are tender, about 10 minutes. Add pork and crab with their sauces. Season with salt and pepper if desired. Cook uncovered for 10 to 15 minutes until sauce thickens, stirring occasionally. Serve hot with white rice.

Serves 6.

Note. Since they are cooked separately, pork, crab, and greens can be cooked almost simultaneously, reducing the cooking time for the whole dish. The meat and seafood can also be cooked one day ahead.

*If you are using only spinach to make the dish, you will need about 10 bundles to have 7 pounds. You may as well use ready-to-use fresh bagged spinach. This is available in the vegetable section of groceries and supermarkets.

Braised Greens with Oxtail, Pork, and Crab

Fèy
Légumes Verts Braisés avec Beuf, Porc et Crab

This recipe differs from the preceding one because the dish is cooked practically in one step, the meat is different, and it takes longer to cook because of the pig's feet it contains. There are a lot of bones which contribute to the flavor of the dish. There is no addition of water. This takes about three hours to cook, but it does not need to be watched closely, and it is worth all the effort. You will need a heavy lidded 8-quart round pan (12 x 4 inches).

Estimated time: 3 hours 30 minutes.

1 teaspoon ground black pepper
1/4 teaspoon ground cloves
1 teaspoon ground cayenne pepper
2 teaspoons ground paprika
3 teaspoons salt
2 pounds fresh oxtails
1 pound fresh pork neck bones
2 pounds fresh pig's feet
3 bitter oranges or 6 lemons
2 tablespoons vegetable oil
12 garlic cloves, peeled, and crushed (see note in *More Tips*)
2 tablespoons tomato paste diluted in 1 cup of boiled water
1/2 to 1 pound crab legs

8 tablespoons (1/2 cup) apple cider vinegar
juice of 1 bitter orange or 2 lemons (about 1/2 cup)
7 pounds torn spinach, or torn mixed greens*
4 tablespoons chopped chives, or 4 minced scallions
1 cup chopped fresh flat leaf parsley
2 leeks, sliced (white and pale green parts only)
4 sprigs thyme (leaves only)
4 chicken bouillon cubes, crushed
4 cups diced white onion
1/2 cup diced red bell pepper
1 cup chopped shallots

Bring a large pot of water to boil.

Mix black pepper, cloves, cayenne pepper, paprika, and salt in a small bowl. Set this spice mixture aside.

With a sharp knife, remove excess fat from oxtail and pork neck. Plug the kitchen sink and place oxtails, pork neck, and pig's feet in it. Rub them with bitter orange. Rinse quickly with the boiling water. Drain carefully.

Heat oil in a heavy lidded 8-quart round pan (12 x 4 inches) over medium high heat. Add garlic and sauté for 1 minute. Add diluted tomato paste, and boil until liquid evaporates completely, about 8 minutes. Reduce heat to medium and stir-fry for 1 to 2 minutes. Add oxtails, pork neck and feet, and crab. Drizzle with vinegar and bitter orange juice (or lemon juice). Cover meat and crab with a portion of the greens. Cover with the lid to allow the greens just to wilt, 2 to 3 minutes. Uncover, sprinkle with the spice mixture, chives, parsley, leeks, thyme, bouillon cubes, onion, bell pepper, and shallots. Cover with another portion of the remaining greens. Cover with lid until greens are wilted, 2 to 3 minutes. Add remaining greens in the same manner, until all greens are added to the pan. Cover with lid, and when boiling restarts, reduce heat to medium low, and cook stirring and scraping the bottom of the pan occasionally, until the pig's feet are tender, about 3 hours. Increase heat to medium, and reduce uncovered until sauce thickens, scraping the bottom of the pan often, about 10 to 15 minutes. Spoon out and discard any excess oil. Serve hot with white rice.

Serves 8.

Note: The dish may contain small bones.

*If you are using spinach only to make the dish, you will need about 10 bundles of fresh spinach to have 7 pounds. You may also use ready-to-use fresh bagged spinach, or frozen spinach. Both are available in the vegetable sections of groceries and supermarket. With frozen spinach there is no need to wilt the spinach.

Pork Ragout

Ragou Pye Kochon
Ragoût de Porc

Pork Ragout takes a long time to cook, but it is worth it, and fortunately it does not need to be watched closely. You will need a heavy lidded 8-quart round pan (12 x 4 inches). You can also use a pressure cooker to shorten the time.

Estimated time: 3 hours 30 minutes (without a pressure cooker).

3 pounds fresh pig's feet, sliced crosswise in to 3-inch pieces
2 bitter oranges or 3 lemons, peeled (reserve 2 tablespoons juice)
2 tablespoons apple cider vinegar

1/4 teaspoon ground black pepper, or to taste
1/2 teaspoon salt, or to taste
pinch ground cloves
2 chicken bouillon cubes, crushed
1 medium white onion, chopped (about 2 1/2 cups chopped onion)
1 medium leek, chopped
1 habanero chile, seeded, and washed (read *Demystifying Habanero Chile*)
1 slice red bell pepper
2 small sprigs thyme
2 tablespoons chopped chives, or 2 minced scallions
2 tablespoons chopped parsley
1/4 cup vegetable oil
10 garlic cloves, peeled, and crushed
2 tablespoons tomato paste, diluted with 1 cup boiled water
a large pot of boiled water

Rub pig's feet with bitter oranges (or lemon). Rinse well with very hot water. Drain. Transfer the feet to a large bowl and coat them with orange juice, and vinegar. Add black pepper, salt, ground cloves, bouillon cubes, onion, leek, habanero chile, bell pepper, thyme, chives, parsley. Toss to coat. Set aside.

Heat oil over medium setting in a large heavy 8-quart pan. Add garlic and sauté for 2 minutes. Add diluted tomato paste and cook until no liquid remains, 15 to 20 minutes. Stir-fry for 2 minutes. Add pig's feet with marinade, and 10 to 12 cups of boiled water. Cook covered over medium high heat for 2 1/2 to 3 hours until pork is tender, stirring occasionally. Transfer pork to a plate, leaving sauce in the pan. Add 2 cups of boiled water to the sauce. Strain. Discard the residue. Add the pig's feet. Reduce until sauce thickens, about 20 to 30 minutes. Discard chile. Serve hot.

Serves 6.

Note. Sometimes sliced carrots, cubed potatoes, name root (1 cup each), and 1/2 cup sliced leeks (white part only) are added at the last 20 to 30 minutes for a more hearty dish.

*Read note about bitter orange in the Glossary of this book.

Griot (Griyo)

Griyo is a delectable dish made of pieces of pork cooked in the juices produced by the meat, then deep-fried in oil produced mostly by the meat. It is always served with *Sauce Ti Malice*, *Pikliz*, and *Twice Fried Pressed Plantain* (Bannan Peze). Boneless fresh ham and boneless fresh pork shoulder are the best choices to make *Griyo*.

The amount of oil used in *Griyo* may seem a lot, but all the oil is used to fry the meat, then discarded (or reserved for another purpose), and the meat is drained on paper towels. Whole chiles are used and they should be monitored very carefully to avoid scattering the seeds in the pan, thus to control the level of hotness. Prepare the sauce while the meat is cooling down.

If bitter orange is not available, lemon can be used instead; the difference will be insignificant. Make sure to peel either of them before using.

Estimated time: 2 hours 30 minutes (including marinating and standing time).

3 pounds fresh ham or fresh pork shoulder (gives about 40 pieces of meat)	6 garlic cloves, peeled, and crushed (see note in *More Tips*)
3 bitter oranges, peeled, or 4 lemons*	1 cup chopped shallots
2 teaspoons salt	1 cup vegetable oil
2 habanero chiles**	1/2 cup chopped shallots to garnish chopped parsley to garnish

Express 1/3 cup juice from bitter oranges (or lemons). Strain and set aside.

Rub meat with remaining oranges (or lemons), then rinse with very hot water. Drain. Cut meat into 1 1/2-inch cubes. Marinate in a large bowl with orange juice, salt, two whole chiles, garlic, and shallots for 1 to 2 hours or overnight in the refrigerator.

Heat oil in a heavy lidded 5-quart pan over medium setting and pour in the meat with its marinade. Cook, covered, until meat is tender, about 30 minutes. Poke holes in chiles**, and express some juice into the dish. Transfer meat to a plate, and allow to cool for about 30 minutes. Pour cooking liquid in a bowl and let it rest for a while. Most of the oil will float to the surface.

Take one cup of oil from the cooking liquid and heat it over medium setting. Add 1/4 cup cooking liquid and the meat. Fry until the cooking liquid evaporates completely and the meat reaches a deep reddish brown color, about 20 to 25 minutes. Transfer to a serving dish and toss with chopped shallots. Garnish with chopped parsley. Serve hot with *Sauce Ti Malice for Griyo*.

Serves 4 to 6.

*Read note about bitter orange in the Glossary of this book.

**Learn how to handle habanero chile in *The Cook's Techniques* chapter.

Sauce Ti Malice for Griyo

Sòs Ti Malis pou Griyo
Sauce Ti Malice pour Griyo

Sauce Ti Malice is the partner of *Griyo*. It is then superfluous to say it is a hot sauce. This delicious sauce complements its partner well. It is usually very hot, but as before, the amount of chile can be adjusted, depending on the table companions.

Estimated time: 10 minutes

1/2 cup finely sliced shallots	1 cup cooking liquid from *Griyo*
1/2 teaspoon ground black pepper	1 1/2 tablespoons apple cider vinegar
1/2 tablespoon chopped fresh flat-leaf parsley	1 tablespoon fresh lime juice
	1 habanero chile, cut, and seeded*
1 tablespoon oil (from *Griyo* cooking liquid)	Salt to taste

Put shallots, black pepper, and parsley in a sauce boat. Set aside.

Heat oil over medium setting in a 2-quart saucepan. Add cooking liquid, vinegar, lime juice, and chile. Boil until the sauce thickens. Pour the boiling sauce on the spice and herbs in the sauce boat. Spoon out any excess oil if necessary. Serve hot, with *Griyo*.

Yields about 3/4 cup.

*Wash chile, cut it in half, and remove seeds and membranes. If you wish to have a mild sauce, rub chile gently under fresh running water for 15 seconds.

Honey-Rum Glazed Ham with Pineapple and Prunes

Janbon Prin-Anana ak Sòs Wonm-Myèl
Jambon Glacé à la Sauce Rhum-Miel et Garni à l'Ananas

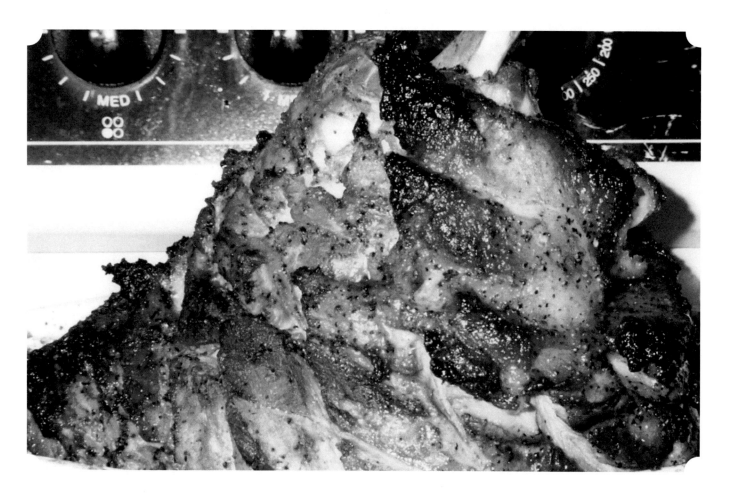

Above all, ham, *Stuffed Turkey*, and *Roast Turkey* are among the meat dishes at Christmas, New-Year's Day, and Easter Sunday in Haiti. They are also invariably served at buffets and banquets.

Estimated time: 3 hours 30 minutes.

one 9-pound (about 4 kilograms) ready to cook smoked bone-in ham
1/2 cup dry white wine
1 1/2 teaspoon black pepper
1 1/2 tablespoons prepared yellow mustard
1/4 cup honey
1/2 teaspoon ground paprika
1/4 teaspoon dry thyme leaves
Pinch of ground cloves
1/4 cup dark Haitian rum (Rhum Barbancourt)

1/4 cup fresh pineapple juice, or fresh orange juice
1/4 cup white balsamic vinegar
1 tablespoon corn starch
1 slice white onion
1 slice red bell pepper
14 slices fresh or canned pineapple, 1/4 inch thick
2 tablespoons brown sugar
14 pitted prunes
7 maraschino cherries, halved
Curly parsley to garnish (optional)

Preheat oven to 325 degrees Fahrenheit.

Remove and discard ham skin, and all but 1/3 inch of the fat coating the ham. Using a sharp knife, slice ham all over 1/4 of an inch deep, making cuts one inch apart in a regular diamond pattern. Put ham in a roasting pan, and pour the white wine over it. Sprinkle with 1/2 teaspoon black pepper. Cover and bake in the middle of preheated oven for 2 hours, basting every 20 minutes with the oil and the juice produced by the ham.

Meanwhile, prepare the honey-rum glaze: In a medium bowl, mix mustard, honey, remaining black pepper, paprika, thyme, cloves, rum, pineapple juice (or orange juice), and vinegar. Set aside.

Remove ham from oven. Transfer ham to a baking pan. Pour pan juice into a 2-quart saucepan, and reserve it. Brush ham with honey-rum glaze. Bake uncovered for one additional hour, brushing with the glaze every 20 minutes. Remove any pan juice and add it to the reserved juice in the saucepan.

Remove and discard excess oil from the pan juice, reserving 2 tablespoons. Mix the cornstarch with 1/4 cup cool boiled water (not hot water). Add it to the pan juice. Reduce over medium heat until it thickens. Add onion and bell pepper slices at the last minute. Remove from heat. Keep hot.

Heat 1 to 2 tablespoons of reserved oil in a large skillet over medium heat. Add the pineapple slices and sauté until their juice evaporates. Sprinkle with brown sugar, and allow them to caramelize. Remove from heat and set aside.

Remove ham from oven. Transfer it to a serving plate. To garnish, cover the ham all over with pineapple slices centered with a prune and a cherry half. Use clean toothpicks to secure the fruits on the ham. Garnish the serving plate all around the ham with curly parsley if desired. Serve ham with the sauce.

Serves 10.

Note. You may also use a fully cooked bone-in ham. In this case, pour the wine over the ham, sprinkle with black pepper, and cook covered for one hour, basting every 20 minutes. Remove the pan juice and bake uncovered for and an additional hour, brushing with the glaze every 20 minutes. Prepare the sauce and garnish the ham as above.

SEAFOOD

Fwidmè
Les Fruits de Mer

Fried Fish

A Fish on My Dish

I wish I had a fish
On my dish.
Do you want some bass?
I wouldn't pass.

Rachel Ménager, 11

Fish in Creole Court-Bouillon

Pwason lan Sòs
Poisson en Court-Bouillon

Among the good choices for Fish in Creole Court-Bouillon are the following fish: Caribbean snapper, Conger eel, Barracuda, King fish, and Swordfish. A fish poacher is very helpful to cook whole fish.

Estimated time: 1 hour (marinating time not included).

2 pounds fresh whole fish (1 or 2 whole fish), fish steak or filet (1 to 1 1/2 inch thick)
3 Persian limes (reserve juice of one lime for marinade)
1/4 teaspoon ground black pepper
1 1/2 teaspoon salt
1 habanero chile (read *Demystifying Habanero Chile*)
1 tablespoon chopped chives, or 1 minced scallion
1/2 teaspoon prepared yellow mustard
1 1/2 tablespoons apple cider vinegar

1/4 cup white onion shavings (see note in *More Tips*)
1/4 cup sliced shallots
1 sprig thyme
1/4 cup vegetable oil
6 garlic cloves, peeled, and crushed (see note in *More Tips*)
1/2 tablespoon tomato paste diluted with 1 cup boiled water
1/2 cup boiled water
1/4 cup sliced shallots (for sauce)

Fish should be dressed, meaning free of scales, gills, and entrails. Read *Cleaning Fish* in *The Cook's Techniques* chapter. Rub fish all over with lime, pressing well to allow the juice to run into fish skin and cuts. Rinse fish under fresh running water. Pat dry. Using a sharp knife, score fish twice diagonally on both sides, 1/4 inch deep. Put in a shallow dish, coat with lime juice, pepper, salt, chile, chives, mustard, vinegar, onion, shallots, and thyme. Cover with plastic wrap, and marinate in a cool place for 1 hour.

Heat oil in a large non-stick pan on medium high setting. Add garlic and sauté for 1 minute. Add diluted tomato paste and boil until no liquid remains, about 20 minutes. Stir-fry for 2 minutes. Add fish marinade (but not fish), and stir-fry for about 5 minutes. Mix in 1/2 cup boiled water. Reduce heat to medium. Add fish and cook until fish is cooked through, about 7 minutes per inch of thickness.

Carefully remove fish and chile from the sauce. Strain the sauce. Discard the residue. Season the sauce with more lime juice if needed. Add fish and reserved chile, reduce over medium heat until sauce thickens, about 3 minutes. Add shallot slices at the last minute. Discard chile. Serve hot. Provide lime wedges separately.

Serves 4.

Fish au Gratin

Pwason Ograten
Poisson au Gratin

Use skinless fish filets that have a tender and fine flesh, such as Caribbean snapper, conger eel, salmon, ... etc. With fish filets you do not have to worry about bones. If you choose to use whole fish, be sure to remove the skin and all bones after the fish is cooked.

This is a very attractive and tasty dish. Not only it is delicious but it can also be prepared in about one hour, which is nothing compared to the result. *Fish in Creole Court-Bouillon* can be prepared one day ahead and kept in the refrigerator, reducing the time to about 30 minutes.

Estimated time: 30 minutes (cooking time for Fish in Creole Court-Bouillon is not included).

1 teaspoon vegetable oil	1 egg yolk
1 cup finely diced white onion	1 egg white
one recipe of *Fish in Creole Court-Bouillon*	1/2 cup freshly grated extra sharp cheddar,
1/3 cup mayonnaise	or freshly grated Parmesan
3 tablespoons milk	1 tablespoon margarine, cut into small pieces
2 chicken bouillon cubes, crushed	

Preheat oven to 500 degrees Fahrenheit. Grease six 8-ounce ramekins with margarine or oil. Set aside.

Heat oil in a medium pan over medium heat. Add onion, and sauté for 3 minutes. Remove from heat and set aside.

Transfer fish to a bowl, reserving the sauce. Mash fish well with a fork. Add sautéed onion, mayonnaise, milk, bouillon cubes, and egg yolk. Mix well.

Beat egg white until foamy (not firm). Add to fish mixture. Mix well. Fill prepared ramekins with fish mixture. Top with grated cheese. Sprinkle with small bits of margarine. Arrange ramekins on a baking sheet and bake in oven for 10 to 15 minutes. Let set for 10 minutes, then unmold and serve with sauce from the Court-Bouillon.

Serves 6.

Note. *Fish au Gratin* can be baked in a stoneware or in a glass baking dish. Make *Crab au Gratin* using 2 pounds of fresh crab meat instead of the fish.

Fish Soufflé

Soufle Pwason
Soufflé de Poisson

Use skinless fish filets that have a tender and fine flesh, such as Caribbean snapper, conger eel, salmon, . . . etc. With fish filets you do not have to worry about bones. If you choose to use whole fish, be sure to remove the skin and all bones after the fish is cooked. Cook the fish following the recipe of *Fish in Creole Court-Bouillon*.

Estimated time: 1 hour (cooking time for Fish in Creole Court-Bouillon is not included).

1 tablespoon butter or margarine (to coat the mold)
1 tablespoon flour (to coat the mold)
2 1/2 tablespoons vegetable oil
3 tablespoons all-purpose flour
1 cup milk
3/4 teaspoon salt, divided (1/2 teaspoon and 1/4 teaspoon)
1/2 teaspoon ground black pepper
1/4 teaspoon ground paprika

3 egg yolks
2/3 cup shredded Parmesan cheese, or 1/3 cup Parmesan plus 1/3 cup extra sharp cheddar
1 1/2 cups well mashed cooked fish (*Fish in Creole Court-Bouillon*)
3 egg whites
1 to 2 tablespoons finely grated Parmesan cheese (to sprinkle on the souffle)

Generously coat a 6-cup soufflé mold with melted butter or margarine. Then coat with the flour. Set aside.

Heat oil over medium setting. Add flour and cook for 1 to 2 minutes, whisking constantly. Whisk in milk, and continue to cook for 1 to 2 minutes until sauce thickens. Remove from heat and stir in 1/2 teaspoon salt, black pepper, and paprika. Let stand to cool a little. Then thoroughly mix in the egg yolks, cheese, and fish.

Meanwhile, preheat oven to 375 degrees Fahrenheit.

Using a hand electric mixer at high speed, beat the egg whites with remaining salt until stiff. Fold beaten egg whites into the cheese-fish mixture. Transfer to the prepared soufflé mold. Sprinkle with finely grated Parmesan cheese, and bake in the middle of preheated oven until golden and puffed, 30 to 35 minutes. Serve immediately with the Court-Bouillon sauce.

Serves 4 to 6.

Note. *Make Crab Soufflé, Lobster Soufflé, Shrimp Soufflé* by replacing the fish with 1 1/2 cups well mashed cooked crab meat, 1 1/2 cups finely minced cooked lobster, or 1 1/2 cups finely minced cooked large shrimp. If possible, use a food processor to mince the seafood.

Fried Fish

Pwason Fri
Poisson Frit

Estimated time: 1 hour (marinating time is not included).

2 pounds fresh whole fish (or fresh fish filets), 1 to 1 1/2 inches thick
3 Persian limes (reserve juice of one lime for marinade)
4 garlic cloves, peeled, and crushed (see note in *More Tips*)
1 1/2 teaspoons salt
1/4 cup chopped fresh flat-leaf parsley
2 tablespoons chopped chives, or 2 minced scallions
1/2 cup finely sliced white onion

1/4 cup chopped shallots
1/4 cup chopped red bell pepper
1 habanero chile, seeded, and washed (read *Demystifying Habanero Chile*)
1/4 teaspoon ground black pepper, or to taste
pinch ground cloves
2 chicken bouillon cubes, crushed
1 1/2 tablespoons apple cider vinegar
1/2 teaspoon prepared yellow mustard
vegetable oil for deep frying

Fish should be dressed, meaning free of scales, entrails, and gills. (Read *Cleaning Fish* in *The Cook's Techniques* chapter.) Rub fish all over with lime, pressing to allow juice to run into cuts. Rinse under fresh running water, and pat dry. With a sharp knife, score fish twice diagonally on both sides, 1/4 inch deep. Put in shallow dish and set aside.

With a blender, purée garlic, salt, parsley, chive, onion, shallots, bell pepper, chile, black pepper, ground cloves, and bouillon cubes with vinegar, mustard, and lime juice. Pour the puréed spices over the fish. Turn to coat. Poke fish with a small fork to allow spices to penetrate it. Cover and marinate in refrigerator for 3 hours, or overnight in the refrigerator.

Remove fish from marinade and use marinade to prepare sauce following the recipe for *Sauce Ti Malice*. Dry fish with a paper towel removing as much liquid as you can.

Heat oil on medium high setting in a large nonstick pan. Add fish and deep-fry until golden on both sides, about 8-10 minutes per inch of thickness, turning once with a spatula. Watch closely to avoid scorching, reducing heat to medium if necessary. Drain on paper towels. Serve hot with the sauce and lime wedges.

Serves 4.

Note. Sometimes, the fish is lightly coated with flour before frying. Personally, I prefer not to use the flour coating.

Fish "Gwo Sèl"

Pwason Gwo Sèl
Poisson Gros Sel

Very popular in "Vallée de l'Artibonite," Haiti, this delicious dish is named after the coarse sea salt (*gwo sèl*) traditionally used to prepare it. *Pwason Gwo Sèl* is usually made with whole fish and served with boiled green plantains or *Twice Fried Pressed Plantains*, boiled name root, avocado slices, watercress, and tomato slices. It is a true delight. Caribbean snapper, conger eel, barracuda, king fish, and swordfish are excellent choices to make this dish. We do not use cod, pollock, or fish of that family to make *Pwason Gwo Sèl*. You may choose to use fish filets or fish steaks. *Pwason Gwo Sèl* is usually a hot dish, but the amount of chile is up to the table companions.

Estimated time: 1 hour (marinating not included).

two 1 1/2-pound fresh whole fish, or 2 pounds fresh fish filets, or fish steak (1 inch thick)

3 Persian limes (reserve juice of one lime, about 1/4 cup lime juice)

1 cup white onion shavings (see note in *More Tips*)

2 chicken bouillon cubes, crushed

1 habanero chile (read *Demystifying Habanero Chile*)

6 garlic cloves, peeled, and crushed (see note in *More Tips*)

1/2 teaspoon ground black pepper

pinch of ground cloves

1 1/2 teaspoons salt

2 tablespoons chopped chives, or 2 minced scallions

1/4 cup chopped fresh flat-leaf parsley

1 cup finely sliced leeks

2 sprigs thyme

1/2 teaspoon prepared yellow mustard

2 tablespoons apple cider vinegar

1/4 cup vegetable oil

1 tablespoon mayonnaise

4 cups boiled water

1/2 cup chopped shallots (for sauce)

3 slices white onion (for sauce)

Fish should be dressed, meaning free of scales, gills, and entrails. Read *Cleaning Fish* in the *Cook's Techniques* chapter.

Rub fish with lime, then rinse under fresh running water. Using a sharp knife, score fish twice diagonally on both sides, 1/4 inch deep. Put in a shallow dish and coat with lime juice, onion, bouillon cubes, chile, garlic, black pepper, ground cloves, salt, chives, parsley, leeks, thyme, mustard, and vinegar. Cover with plastic wrap and marinate in a cool place for 3 hours, or overnight in the refrigerator.

Heat oil in a large nonstick pan on medium setting. Add fish, reserving marinade, and sauté for about 7 minutes per inch of thickness. Transfer fish to a plate. Add marinade, mayonnaise, and 3 cups boiled water to the same pan. Cover, and boil for 25 minutes. Reserving chile, strain sauce, and discard residue. Add fish and reserved chile to sauce. Reduce over medium heat until sauce thickens, about 15 minutes. Poke holes in the chile with tines of a fork, and press gently to express some chile juice into the dish (optional)*. Season with salt and pepper if necessary. Add onion slices and shallots at the last minute. Discard chile. Serve hot. Provide lime wedges separately.

Serves 4.

Note. To cook whole fish, a fish poacher is very helpful.

*Learn how to handle habanero chile in The Cook's Techniques chapter.

Holy Week Cod (Cod in Mustard Sauce)

Mori Semenn Sent (Mori lan Sòs Moutad)
Morue de la Semaine Sainte (Morue à la Sauce Moutarde)

Very much appreciated during Holy Week, this recipe is usually made with dried salt cod. In this recipe, I use fresh cod making it faster and easier, and still very delicious. There is no marinating time. Cod should be 3/4 to 1 inch thick.

Estimated time: 30 minutes.

3 Persian limes
2 1/2 pounds skinless fresh cod filet*
2 tablespoons apple cider vinegar
1/4 cup olive oil
5 garlic cloves, peeled, and finely mashed (see note in *More Tips*)
1 habanero chile (read *Demystifying Habanero Chile*)
1 chicken bouillon cube
1/4 teaspoon ground black pepper

1/4 teaspoon ground cayenne pepper
1 tablespoon chopped chives, or 1 minced scallion
1/4 cup sliced shallots
2 teaspoons prepared yellow mustard
2 tablespoons mayonnaise
1 1/2 teaspoons salt
5 slices white onion, 1/4 inch thick
4 hard-boiled eggs, sliced crosswise or quartered lengthwise

Cut limes into 3 pieces lengthwise. Reserve 2 tablespoons strained lime juice. Rub cod with lime. Rinse well under fresh running water. Pat dry with paper towels. Coat cod with reserved lime juice and vinegar. Set aside.

Heat 2 tablespoons oil in a heavy 12-inch non-stick skillet over medium high setting. Add garlic, and sauté for 1 minute. Add cod and chile. Cook until fish is tender, about 7 minutes turning once. Reduce heat to medium, and add black pepper, cayenne pepper, chives, shallots, mustard, mayonnaise, and salt. Reduce sauce until thickened, about 10 minutes. Add onion slices and remaining olive oil during the last 3 minutes. Discard chile. Garnished with egg pieces. Serve hot, with *Holy Week Salad*. Provide lime wedges separately.

Serves 6.

Notes : Make *Holy Week Herring* by replacing the cod with smoked red herring filets. Soak herring as indicated in *The Cook's Techniques* chapter. Then coat the fish with lime juice and vinegar. Then proceed as above. Work gently so the filets stay whole.

*To use salt cod, first soak it following instructions in *The Cook's Techniques* chapter, then proceed as above.

Cod and Potatoes in Creole Sauce

Mori ak Pomdetè lan Sòs
Morue et Pomme de Terres à la Créole

This recipe can also be made with fresh cod. In this case, soaking is not required, and you will use less water. Cod should be 3/4 to 1 inch thick.

Estimated time: 1 hour 30 minutes (without soaking time).

1 1/2 pounds skinless dried salt cod fillet*, cut into 6 pieces
juice of one Persian lime (about 1/4 cup)
2 tablespoons apple cider vinegar
1/2 teaspoon ground black pepper
1/4 teaspoon ground cayenne pepper
1 tablespoon chopped chives, or 1 minced scallion
1/4 cup sliced shallots
1/2 teaspoon prepared yellow mustard
2 tablespoons mayonnaise

1 habanero chile (read *Demystifying Habanero Chile*)
5 slices white onion, 1/4 inch thick
1/4 cup vegetable oil
4 large potatoes (about 2 1/2 pounds), peeled and cut into small wedges
6 garlic cloves, peeled, and finely mashed (see note in *More Tips*)
1 tablespoon tomato paste diluted with 1 cup boiled water
1 1/2 cups boiled water
salt to taste

Soak salt cod following instructions in *The Cook's Techniques* chapter. Put cod in a shallow dish. Coat with lime juice, vinegar, black pepper, cayenne, chives, shallots, mustard, mayonnaise, habanero chile, and 3 slices of onion. Cover with plastic wrap, and marinate in a cool place for 30 minutes to 1 hour or overnight in the refrigerator.

Heat 2 tablespoons oil in a heavy 8-quart non-stick pan over medium setting. Add potato pieces, and sauté until golden, about 10 to 15 minutes. Transfer potatoes to a plate.

Heat remaining oil over medium high setting in the same pan. Add garlic, and sauté for 1 minute. Add diluted tomato paste. Boil until water evaporates completely, about 15 to 20 minutes. Decrease heat to medium setting, and stir-fry for 2 minutes. Add cod with marinade, and 1/2 cup boiled water. Cover, and cook for about 7 minutes. Transfer fish and chile to a plate. Add 1/2 cup boiled water to sauce, and strain it. Season with salt if necessary. Add fish, reserved chile, sautéed potatoes. Cover and cook until sauce thickens, about 20 minutes. Add remaining onion slices at the last 5 minutes. Discard chile. Serve hot.

Serves 6.

Variation. Carrot slices are often added to the dish. If you wish, peel and cut 3 medium carrots (about 3/4 pound) into 1/2 to 3/4-inch slices and add them at the same time you add the sautéed potatoes.

*Salt cod can be found at Caribbean and Latin-American groceries, and also at specialty Italian import stores. It is called baccala in Italian, and bacalao in Spanish. A recipe to make salt cod is given in this book (*Homemade Salt Cod*).

Grilled Sardines with Hot Sauce

Pimantad (Pwason Boukannen)
Sardines Grillées

Popular in "Vallee de l'Artibonite," Haiti, *Pimentad* takes its name after *Piman* which is a creole word for habanero chile. That tells how hot this dish can be. But again, the amount of hotness depends on the table companions. When grilling, wood charcoal is by far better because it imparts the best extra flavor to grilled food. A greased hinged grilling basket makes the task easier.

Estimated time: 1 hour (marinating time is not included).

16 small fresh sardines, dressed (or other small fish)
4 Persian limes
1 tablespoon apple cider vinegar
1/2 cup finely sliced shallots
4 garlic cloves, peeled, and crushed (see note in *More Tips*)

1 tablespoon chopped chives, or 1 minced scallion
1/2 teaspoon ground black pepper, or to taste
1 habanero chile*
1 teaspoon salt or to taste
1/4 cup olive oil or vegetable oil
1/2 cup boiled water
1/4 cup well sliced shallots (for sauce)

Sardines (or other small fish) should be dressed, meaning free of scales, gills, and entrails. Rub the sardines with three limes, pressing well to allow the juice to run into fish skin and the cuts. Rinse well under fresh running water. Pat dry. Score fish twice diagonally on both sides, 1/4 inch deep. Put fish in a shallow dish and set aside.

Mix juice of remaining lime with vinegar, shallots, garlic, chive, black pepper, chile, and salt. Pour spice mixture on the fish. Cover and marinate for 6 to 7 hours in a cool place.

Remove fish from marinade and use marinade to prepare sauce. Heat oil over medium setting in a heavy 2-quart pan, and pour in marinade and boil down for 7 minutes. Add 1/2 cup boiled water, and reduce for 10 minutes. Remove and reserve chile. Strain the sauce, pressing well on the residue. Discard the residue. Add chile, then reduce slightly over medium setting, 1 to 2 minutes. Season with salt and pepper if necessary. Remove from heat. Add shallot slices immediately.

Get a charcoal grill ready. Remove 2 tablespoons oil from sauce to coat the fish. Grill fish on both sides until cooked through, about 5 to 10 minutes. Transfer to a serving dish. Then reheat sauce quickly over high setting and serve immediately with grilled fish, *Twice Fried Pressed Plantains* or crusty bread, avocado slices, and a green crisp salad. Provide lime wedges separately.

Serves 4.

*Wash chile, cut it in half, and remove seeds and membranes. If you wish to have a mild dish, rub it gently under fresh running water for 15 seconds.

Salt Fish

Pwason Sale
Poisson Salé

Salt fish is eaten particularly during the Lenten season in Haiti. When correctly prepared, it is a true pleasure for the palate. Usually it is served with boiled green plantains, boiled name root, and avocado slices. During Lent, it is served with boiled name root, boiled green plantains, and *Holy Week Salad*. This dish is usually prepared with whole salt fish, but you may use salt fish filets as well.

Estimated time: 1 hour 15 minutes (without soaking time).

2 one-pound whole salt fish (not salt cod)
1/4 cup olive oil or vegetable oil
1/2 cup white onion shavings (see note in *More Tips*)
6 garlic cloves, peeled, and crushed (see note in *More Tips*)
1 habanero chile (read *Demystifying Habanero Chile*)
1 shallot, chopped
1 tablespoon chopped chives, or 1 minced scallion

2 tablespoons chopped flat-leaf parsley
1/4 teaspoon ground black pepper, or to taste
1 large pot of boiled water (reserve 2 cups of water for sauce)
1 tablespoon mayonnaise
1/2 teaspoon prepared yellow mustard
1 tablespoon apple cider vinegar
juice of one Persian lime
4 slices white onion (for sauce)
1 shallot, sliced (for sauce)

Soak fish in a large bowl (or a large pan) filled with hot water for 12 hours, changing water every 4 hours. Drain. Repeat if necessary. Boil in a large pot of water on medium heat for about 15 minutes, or until fish is tender. Do not overcook. Drain and reserve about 1 cup of cooking liquid. Cover fish with hot boiled water. Let soak for 5 to 10 minutes. Drain. Squeeze gently between sheets of paper towels to remove excess water.

Heat half of the oil in a non-stick large pan on medium setting. Add fish, and sauté for 3 minutes on each side. Transfer to a plate.

Heat remaining oil in the same pan. Add onion, garlic, chile, chopped shallot, chives, parsley, black pepper, and sauté for about 5 minutes. Then add 1/2 cup of the fish cooking liquid, 2 cups water, mayonnaise, mustard, vinegar, and lime juice. Boil covered over medium heat for 20 minutes. Remove and reserve chile. Strain sauce, pressing well on the residue. Discard the residue. Add fish and reserved chile. Season with salt if necessary. Reduce over medium high heat until sauce thickens, about 7 minutes. Add onion slices and shallot slices at the last minute. Discard chile. Serve immediately. Provide lime wedges separately.

Serves 4.

Smoked Red Herring in Creole Sauce

Aran Sò lan Sòs
Hareng Saur à la Créole

If you are using herring filets, handle them gently so they hold their shape through the entire process of soaking-draining. Cook gently also for the same reason.

1 pound whole smoked red herring, or smoked red herring filets
1/4 cup vegetable oil
4 garlic cloves, peeled, and crushed (see note in *More Tips*)
2 tablespoons tomato paste diluted with 1 cup of boiled water
1/2 cup finely diced white onion
2 tablespoons chopped chives, or 1 minced scallion

1/4 to 1/2 cup boiled water
2 tablespoons apple cider vinegar
1 teaspoon salt
1/2 teaspoon ground black pepper
Pinch ground cloves
1 habanero chile (read *Demystifying Habanero Chile*)
one 1/4-inch thick white onion slice (for sauce)

Soak herring as indicated in *The Cook's Techniques* chapter.

Heat oil in a heavy 4-quart pan over medium high setting. Add garlic and sauté for 1 minute. Add diluted tomato paste and boil uncovered until all liquid evaporates, 15 to 20 minutes. Stir-fry for about 1 minute. Add onion, and chives, and continue to sauté for 3 to 4 minutes, stirring often. Add soaked herring, and sauté for 3 minutes. Add water, vinegar, salt, black pepper, ground cloves, and chile. Reduce briefly over medium heat. Sauce should be thick. Add onion slice at the last minute. Serve hot with avocado slices, watercress, boiled green plantains or boiled name root.

Serves 4.

Conch in Creole Sauce

Lambi lan Sòs
Conque à La Créole

Conch is a tropical marine mollusk, found mainly in the Caribbean Sea. It tastes a lot like clams, although much stronger. When properly cooked, it is very delicious. It should never be cleaned or boiled with lime, which we believe toughens its flesh. We add lime juice after conch is cooked.

Estimated time: 2 hours 30 minutes to 3 hours.

2 pounds fresh or frozen conch
3 bitter oranges, peeled* (reserve 1/4 cup juice for cooking)
1/4 cup vegetable oil
a large pot of boiled water
1/2 cup white onion shavings (see note in *More Tips*)
1/2 cup minced shallots
1 tablespoon chopped fresh flat-leaf parsley
1 sprig thyme
1 cup finely sliced leeks
2 tablespoons chopped chives, or 2 minced scallions

1 habanero chile (read *Demystifying Habanero Chile*)
1/2 teaspoon ground black pepper, or to taste
2 tablespoons fresh lime juice
2 chicken bouillon cubes, crushed
1/4 teaspoon salt or to taste
2 tablespoons apple cider vinegar
5 garlic cloves, peeled, and crushed (see note in *More Tips*)
1/2 to 1 tablespoon tomato paste, diluted with 1 cup boiled water
1 tablespoon brown sugar**
1/4 cup sliced shallots (for sauce)
1 slice white onion (for sauce)
1 slice red bell pepper (for sauce)

Remove and discard any black and pink skin from the conch. Rub conch all over with orange, pressing well. Rinse them under fresh running water. Squeeze them between sheets of paper towels to remove excess water. Open conch flat by slicing 3/4 of the way through the thicker parts of the flesh. Then pound it with a meat tenderizer (meat hammer). Cut conch into 2 to 3 pieces each.

Heat 2 tablespoons of oil in a pressure cooker***, over medium high setting. Add conch, and sauté until golden, about 10 minutes. Add 7 cups of boiled water to the pressure cooker. Add reserved orange juice, then cook under pressure for 1 hour 30 minutes over medium heat. Conch should be tender. If not, add more boiled water if necessary and cook under pressure for an additional 30 minutes or so, until conch is very tender. Transfer conch to a bowl, reserving cooking liquid. Reduce cooking liquid to 3 cups by boiling, or add boiled water to cooking liquid to obtain 3 cups. Set aside.

Coat cooked conch with onion, shallots, parsley, thyme, leeks, chives, chile, black pepper, lime juice, chicken bouillon cubes, salt, and vinegar. Set aside.

Heat remaining oil in a non-stick heavy lidded 5-quart pan over medium setting. Add garlic and sauté for 1 minute. Add diluted tomato paste and boil until all liquid evaporates, 15 to 20 minutes. Stir-fry for about 2 minutes. Add conch and sugar, and sauté until conch is golden. Then add marinade, and sauté for a few minutes until no liquid remains. Add 2 cups of the reserved cooking liquid. Cover and boil for about 30 minutes. Remove conch and chile from sauce. Add remaining cooking liquid to the sauce and strain, pressing well on the residue. Add conch and reserved chile to sauce. Season with salt and pepper if necessary. Reduce on medium heat until sauce thickens, about 15 minutes. Add shallots, and onion, and bell pepper slices during the last minutes of cooking. Discard chile. Serve hot with *Twice Fried Pressed Plantains* and a crisp green salad. Provide lime wedges separately.

Serves 6.

* Read about bitter orange in the Glossary of the book.

**Fresh conch flesh has a subtle sweet taste. When the conch is not freshly caught, people add a little bit of sugar to recreate this delicate flavor. We do not do that in Haiti where the freshest seafood is available.

***You may also cook conch in a heavy pan fitted with a heavy lid. It will take lots and lots of water and more than 6 hours of boiling to become tender. If you plan to do that, start early.

Spiny Lobster in Creole Sauce

Woma lan Sòs
Langouste à la Créole

Spiny lobster is the only lobster available in Haiti, but this recipe can be made with other lobsters or even with jumbo shrimp. Spiny lobster has no claws.

Estimated time: 1 hour 30 minutes.

6 spiny lobster tails
3 Persian limes (reserve juice of one lime for marinade)
1 cup finely sliced shallots
1 tablespoon chopped chives, or 1 minced scallion
1 habanero chile (read *Demystifying Habanero Chile*)
1 tablespoon chopped fresh flat-leaf parsley
1/2 teaspoon salt or to taste
2 chicken bouillon cubes, crushed
pinch ground cloves

1/4 teaspoon ground black pepper, or to taste
2 tablespoons white wine vinegar
1/2 teaspoon prepared yellow mustard
1/4 cup vegetable oil
6 garlic cloves, peeled, and crushed (see note in *More Tips*)
1 Roma tomato, chopped
1 tablespoon mayonnaise
3 cups boiled water
1/4 cup sliced shallots (for sauce)
1 slice white onion (for sauce)

Cut lobster shells with kitchen shears on both sides, open and detach flesh. Discard shells and tail fans, or boil them for 2 minutes and reserve for garnishing. Devein lobster and rub with 2 limes. Rinse quickly under fresh running water. Squeeze gently in paper towel to remove excess water. Transfer to bowl, and coat with lime juice, shallots, chives, habanero chile, parsley, salt, bouillon cubes, cloves, black pepper, vinegar, and mustard. Cover and marinate in a cool place for 1 hour.

Heat 3 tablespoons oil in a 5-quart heavy pan on medium high setting. Add lobster, reserving its marinade, and sauté until no liquid remains, about 10 minutes. Transfer lobster to a plate.

In the same pan, heat remaining oil. Add garlic, and sauté for 1 minute, add tomato and sauté for about 10 minutes. Add marinade, mayonnaise, and lobster and stir-fry until no liquid remains. Transfer lobster to plate. Add 3 cups boiled water in the pan. Boil covered over medium high heat for about 15 minutes. Remove and reserve chile. Strain. Season with additional salt and pepper if desired. Add reserved chile, and reduce sauce until thickened, about 10 to 15 minutes. Add lobster, shallot slices and onion slice during the last minute. Discard chile. Serve hot.

Serves 3 to 6.

Note. Follow this recipe to make Shrimp in Creole Sauce. Use 2 pounds of the biggest shrimps available to you. Shell the shrimps, marinate them, sauté for 6 to 8 minutes, and then proceed as above.

Grilled Spiny Lobster

Woma Griye (Woma Boukannen)
Langouste Grillée

When grilling, wood charcoal is better by far because it imparts the best flavor to food. A greased hinged grilling basket makes the task easier.

Estimated time: 45 minutes.

3 Persian limes
6 lobster tails in their shells*
1/4 cup vegetable oil
6 garlic cloves, peeled, and crushed (see note in *More Tips*)
1/2 cup white onion shavings (see note in *More Tips*)
1/2 cup finely minced shallots

1 tablespoon chopped chives, or 1 minced scallion
1/4 teaspoon ground black pepper, or to taste
2 tablespoons apple cider vinegar
1 1/2 cups boiled water
1/2 teaspoon salt
1 habanero chile**
2 tablespoons butter or margarine
1/2 cup finely sliced shallots (for sauce)

Reserve juice of one lime (about 1/4 cup). Rub lobster tails with remaining lime and rinse quickly under fresh running water. Pat dry.

Have a charcoal grill ready. Brush lobster tails with 2 tablespoons of oil. Grill lobster tails in shells for 15 to 20 minutes, turning once. Transfer lobster tails to a plate. Keep warm.

While lobster is grilling, heat remaining oil in a 2-quart heavy saucepan over medium setting. Add garlic, and sauté for 1 to 2 minutes. Add onion, shallots, chives, and black pepper. Increase heat to medium high, and sauté for about 4 minutes. Add vinegar, 1 1/2 cups boiled water, salt, and chile, then boil over medium heat for about 10 minutes. Remove and reserve chile. Strain sauce, pressing well on the residue. Discard the residue. Add reserved chile, and reduce slightly for 2 minutes or so. Season with salt and pepper if desired. Gently stir butter in the sauce until melted. Put shallots for sauce in a sauce boat. Pour the hot sauce over the shallots in the sauce boat. Keep hot.

Cut each lobster tail in half, remove and discard intestines. Collect any juice that comes from the lobster and add it to the sauce. Put lobster halves on the grill, shell down. Brush each lobster half with oil scooped from the sauce. Lightly grease a small grill and heat it as much as possible. Place it on the lobster flesh for a few seconds, to add visual interest. Remove from heat. Serve hot, in the shells, with the sauce. Provide lime wedges separately.

Serves 6.

*If you are using whole lobster, sauté the tomalley with the spices and boil it in the sauce before straining it.

**Wash chile, cut it in half, and remove seeds and membranes. Rub it gently under fresh running water for 15 seconds. Read *Demystifying Habanero Chile*.

Sautéed Spiny Lobster

Woma Sote
Langouste Sautée

Estimated time: 20 minutes.

3 Persian limes
6 lobster tails in their shells
6 garlic cloves, peeled and sliced
1/2 cup finely sliced white onions
1/2 cup minced shallots
1 tablespoon chopped chives, or 1 minced scallion
1/4 teaspoon ground black pepper, or to taste
2 tablespoons apple cider vinegar
1/4 cup vegetable oil

2 tablespoons dark Haitian rum (Rhum Barbancourt)
Salt to taste
1/2 cup sliced shallots
1/2 cup boiled water
1 habanero chile, seeded, and washed (read *Demystifying Habanero Chile*)
2 tablespoons butter or margarine
1/4 cup sliced shallots (for sauce)

Reserve 1 tablespoon of lime juice. Remove lobster flesh from the shells as directed in *The Cook's Techniques* chapter. Rub lobster flesh with remaining lime and rinse quickly under fresh running water. Pat dry. Slice tails crosswise into about 1 1/2-inch pieces. Set aside.

Purée garlic, onions, shallots, chives, black pepper, vinegar, and reserved lime juice in a blender until smooth.

Heat oil over medium high setting in a large skillet. Add the puréed spices-herb mixture, and sauté until golden, lowering the heat down to medium toward the end to avoid scorching, about 10 minutes. Increase heat to medium high. Add lobster pieces and rum to the sautéed spices, then sauté until the meat is opaque and the rum evaporates, about 7 minutes. Sprinkle with salt and additional pepper. Add shallot slices during the last 3 minutes. Transfer to a hot serving dish and serve with the following sauce.

Pour boiled water in the skillet and scrape every brown bit from it. Strain into a small pan. Add remaining oil and reduce until thickened, 2 to 3 minutes. Add chile, then gently stir butter into sauce until melted. Season with additional salt and lime juice if necessary. Add shallot slices at the last minutes. Discard chile. Pour the sauce over the lobster pieces.

Serves 6.

Note. You can sauté large shrimp following the same recipe (*Sautéed Shrimp*).

Fried Shrimp Creole with Sauce Ti Malice

Kribich Fri ak Sòs Ti Malice
Crevettes Frites et Sauce Ti Malice

This is a street dish in Port-au-Prince, Haiti. It also makes good finger food. These shrimp are excellent, particularly when dipped in the sauce.

Devein the shrimp, leaving the shells on. This is what will give them their pleasing crispiness. You will eat even the tails! Popularly, the shrimp are eaten unpeeled, but you may choose to peel them before eating. Shell-on deveined shrimp are available at some groceries and supermarkets.

4 garlic cloves, unpeeled (see note in *More Tips*)
1 pound medium shrimp, shells on, deveined*
3 Persian limes
1/2 teaspoon salt
1 teaspoon prepared yellow mustard
1/4 cup white onion shavings (see note in *More Tips*)

2 tablespoons finely sliced shallots
1 teaspoon ground black pepper
2 tablespoons apple cider vinegar, or 2 tablespoons *Pikliz*
1 habanero chile, seeded, washed, and finely minced (read *Demystifying Habanero Chile*)
vegetable oil for deep-frying

Bring 3 cups of water to a boil in a small saucepan. Add unpeeled garlic cloves, cover, and boil for 7 minutes. Drain. Peel garlic cloves, then mash them in a small plate with the back of a spoon until pasty. Set aside.

Put shrimp, shells on, in a large bowl. Express the juice of two limes over them. Toss to coat. Rinse them twice with fresh running water. Drain well. Put the shrimp in a large bowl, and coat them with the juice of the remaining lime. Mix in mashed garlic, salt, mustard, onion, shallot, black pepper, vinegar, and chile. Cover and marinate in a cool place for one hour at least, or overnight in the refrigerator.

Remove the shrimp from the marinade. Prepare the sauce with the marinade following *Sauce Ti Malice* recipe. Set aside

Heat oil in a 5-quart heavy pan over high setting. Add half of the shrimp and deep-fry them until crispy, about 5 minutes. Remove from the oil with a slotted spoon. Drain on paper towels. Repeat with the remaining shrimp. Serve hot with the sauce and *Twice Fried Pressed Plantains*.

Serves 4.

*With a sharp paring knife, slit the shell lengthwise on the middle of the back. Do not incise the last segment, or cut the tail off. Gently, push the shell aside. Do not remove the shell. Hold shrimp with its back facing you, slide the tip of the knife lengthwise along the black vein on the back to make a small slit, and carefully remove and discard the vein.

Seafood au Gratin

Fwidmè Ograten
Gratin de Fruits de Mer

Estimated time: 1 hour (cooking time for seafood is not included).

1 tablespoon vegetable oil
1/2 cup finely diced white onion
1/2 cup sliced shallots
one recipe of *Fish in Creole Court-Bouillon*
1/2 pound conch*, cut into 1/2-inch pieces
and boiled in plain water until tender
2 lobster tails
1/2 pound medium shrimp

1/3 cup mayonnaise
1/4 teaspoon Tabasco sauce
1/4 teaspoon black pepper
1 egg yolk
1 egg white
1/2 cup freshly grated extra sharp cheddar,
or freshly grated Parmesan
1 tablespoon margarine, cut into small pieces

Preheat oven to 500 degrees Fahrenheit. Grease a 2 1/2-quart stoneware or glass baking dish with margarine or oil. Set aside.

Heat oil in a medium pan over medium heat. Add onion and shallots and sauté for 3 minutes. Set aside.

Transfer fish to a bowl, reserving sauce. Mash fish with a fork. Add sautéed onion and shallots. Mix well. Mix in conch. Set aside.

Boil lobster tails in a large pot of water for 5 minutes. Remove lobster from water. Blanch shrimp in the same boiling water for 1 minute. Remove lobster meat from shell, and cut it into 1/2- inch pieces. Shell, devein, and cut shrimp crosswise into 2 to 3 portions. Mix lobster and shrimp pieces with fish mixture. Mix in mayonnaise, Tabasco sauce, egg yolk, black pepper, and 3 tablespoons of sauce from the fish court-bouillon. Season with salt to taste. Set aside.

Beat egg white until foamy. Add to seafood mixture. Mix well, then pour into prepared baking dish. Top with grated cheese. Sprinkle with small bits of margarine, and bake in preheated oven until golden, 10 to 15 minutes. Serve hot with the fish sauce.

Serves 8 to 10.

Note. Mix the conch cooking water and the lobster blanching water. Pour in a covered container and freeze. You can use this to cook rice, or to add in other dishes that contain seafood.

* Where conch is not available, use canned clams in juice.

POULTRY AND RABBIT

Poul, Lot Bèt Volay, ak Lapen
La Volaille et le Lapin

Chicken with Vegetables

INTRODUCTION

The recipes in this section are for already plucked and ready-to-cook poultry. However, just before cooking, we always "clean" the plucked bird with limes and hot water. This way, we wash away any blood that can give an unfresh taste to the bird when it is cooked.

To clean a bird, we proceed the same way whether the bird is whole or cut up: bring a large pot of water to boil, or close to a boil. Cut sufficient limes lengthwise in 3 portions. Usually two to three Persian limes, or five to six key limes, are enough for one 4-pound bird. Plug the kitchen sink and place the bird in it. If the bird is whole, remove and discard any blood clots from the cavity. Rub the bird inside and out with lime pulp, allowing the juice to run freely over it. Pour boiling (or almost boiling water) on the bird. Turn with a strong spoon to rinse it well inside and out. Do not let it soak in the water. Drain carefully and pat dry. The bird is now ready to be seasoned. When rinsing a bird that will be stuffed, the water should be only warm. This will preserve the integrity of the skin, thus allowing it to withstand sewing if necessary.

When cooking cut-up poultry in sauce, do not discard the back bones, or the feet (if you happen to have them). They add flavor to the sauce and are good thickening agents. Once the bird is cooked and the sauce ready, you may discard them, or use them again for stock or broth.

To add flavor to any poultry or rabbit recipe, replace at least half of the cooking water by the same amount of dark Haitian rum (Rhum Barbancourt) or the same amount of dry white or dry red wine.

Chicken in Creole Sauce

Poul lan Sòs
Poulet à la Créole

Estimated time: 1 hour 40 minutes (including marinating time).

one 4-pound frying chicken, cut up (2 breast halves, 2 thighs, 2 drumsticks, 2 wings, 2 backbone pieces)
2 Persian limes (reserve 2 tablespoons juice)
1 1/2 teaspoons salt
1 chicken bouillon cube, crushed
1 habanero chile (read *Demystifying Habanero Chile*)
1 tablespoon chopped chives, or 1 minced scallion
2 tablespoons apple cider vinegar
1 cup white onion shavings (see note in *More Tips*)

1/4 cup chopped fresh flat-leaf parsley
pinch ground cloves
1/4 teaspoon ground black pepper, or to taste
1 sprig thyme
3 tablespoons vegetable oil
6 garlic cloves, peeled, and crushed (see note in *More Tips*)
1 tablespoon tomato paste, diluted with 1 cup of boiled water
1 1/2 cups or so boiled water
1 slice white onion (for sauce)
1 slice red bell pepper (for sauce)

Trim excess fat from chicken, and rub with lime, then rinse well with very hot (almost boiling) water. Drain. Transfer chicken to a bowl. Coat chicken with reserved lime juice, salt, bouillon cube, chile, chives, vinegar, onion, parsley, ground cloves, black pepper, and thyme. Cover, and marinate in a cool place for 30 minutes or overnight in the refrigerator.

Heat 2 tablespoons oil in a heavy lidded 5-quart nonstick pan over medium high setting. Add chicken, reserving marinade. Brown chicken pieces on all sides, about 15 minutes. Transfer to a plate.

Heat remaining oil over medium high heat in the same pan, add garlic and sauté for 1 minute. Add diluted tomato paste and cook until all liquid evaporates, about 15 to 20 minutes. Stir-fry for 1 minute. Add chicken with marinade, and 1/2 cup boiled water. Cover and cook over medium heat, scraping the bottom of the pan occasionally to avoid scorching, until sauce thickens and chicken is cooked through, about 30 minutes.

Meanwhile, preheat oven to broil. Lightly grease a large baking dish, and set aside.

Transfer chicken and chile to a plate. Remove excess oil. Add 1/2 cup boiled water to the sauce. Strain the sauce, pressing on the spice residue. Discard the residue. Season with additional salt and pepper if desired. Add chicken and reserved chile. Reduce sauce uncovered until sauce thickens, about 7 to 10 minutes. Add onion and bell pepper slices at the last minute.

Discard chile. Remove chicken from sauce, transfer to the prepared baking dish, and quickly brown chicken under the broiler for 3 to 4 minutes before serving. Serve hot.

Serves 4 to 6.

Variation. *Chicken with Dumplings*. To make dumplings, follow the recipe for dumplings in *Vegetable Stew*. Roll them smaller, and add them to the strained sauce. They will cook while the sauce is reducing.

Note. *Rabbit* is very delicious. It tastes a lot like chicken breast, and is more tender. You may follow the same recipe to cook rabbit. Make a delicious *Rabbit in Rum and Wine Sauce* by substituting 1/4 cup of dry white wine and 1/4 cup of Rhum Barbancourt for the water. Rabbit can be cooked following all the chicken recipes. You can make *Rabbit in Creole Sauce*, *Rabbit with Cashew Nuts*, *Roast Rabbit*, . . . etc.

Usually rabbit is available ready-to-cook at butcher shops. You may need to cut it up. To do so, put the rabbit on a large cutting board, backside up. Using a strong knife and cutting across the spine, cut off the front legs just below the shoulders. Still cutting across the spine, cut off the back legs where they are attached to the body. Detach the legs one from the other by cutting along their portion of the spine. Cut the back in two portions, crosswise. You will get six portions in all.

Chicken with Cashew Nuts

Poul ak Nwa
Poulet aux Noix de Cajou

Roasted cashew nuts are a popular snack in Haiti. We also use cashew nuts to make *Cashew Candy*, and we add them to meat dishes to which they add a very interesting twist. *Poulet aux Noix de Cajou* is a speciality of the North of Haiti.

Estimated time: 1 hour 40 minutes (including marinating time).

2 Persian limes (reserve 2 tablespoons juice) one 4-pound frying chicken, (2 breast halves, 2 thighs, 2 drumsticks, 2 wings, 2 backbone pieces)
1 1/2 teaspoons salt
1 chicken bouillon cube, crushed
1 habanero chile (read *Demystifying Habanero Chile*)
1 tablespoon chopped chives, or 1 minced scallion
2 tablespoons apple cider vinegar
1 cup white onion shavings (see note in *More Tips*)

2 tablespoons chopped fresh flat-leaf parsley
pinch ground cloves
1/4 teaspoon ground black pepper, or to taste
2 small sprigs thyme
1 cup unsalted roasted cashew nuts
3 tablespoons vegetable oil
6 garlic cloves, peeled, and crushed (see note in *More Tips*)
1 tablespoon tomato paste diluted with 1 cup boiled water
1 1/2 cups or so boiled water
1 slice white onion (for sauce)
1 slice red bell pepper (for sauce)

Cut limes and express 2 tablespoons of juice. Strain and reserve.

Trim excess fat from chicken, and rub with remaining lime and rinse with very hot water. Drain. Transfer chicken to a bowl. Coat chicken with salt, bouillon cube, chile, chives, vinegar, reserved lime juice, onion, parsley, ground cloves, black pepper, and thyme. Cover, and marinate in refrigerator 30 minutes or overnight in the refrigerator.

Bring 3 cups of water to a boil in a small saucepan over medium heat, add the nuts, and boil until tender, about 15 minutes. Cover and set aside. Drain just before adding them to the chicken.

Heat 2 tablespoons oil in a heavy lidded 5-quart nonstick pan over medium-high setting. Add chicken, reserving marinade. Brown chicken on all sides, about 15 minutes. Transfer chicken to a plate.

Heat remaining oil over medium high heat in the same pan, add garlic and sauté for 1 minute. Add diluted tomato paste and cook until all liquid evaporates, about 15 to 20 minutes. Stir-fry for 1 minute. Add chicken, marinade, and 1/2 cup boiled water. Cover, and cook over medium heat until sauce thickens and chicken is cooked through, about 30 minutes. Scrape the bottom of the pan occasionally to avoid scorching. Transfer chicken and chile to a plate. Remove excess oil. Mix 1/2 cup of boiled water with the sauce. Strain, pressing on the spice residue. Season with additional salt and pepper if desired. Add chicken, reserved chile, and drained cashew nuts. Reduce on medium-high heat until sauce thickens, about 7 to 10 minutes. Add onion slice and bell pepper slice at the last minute. Discard chile. Serve hot.

Serves 4 to 6.

Variation. Replace the boiled water by 1/2 cup of dark Haitian rum, or 1/2 cup of dry white wine.

Make a delicious *Chicken with Almonds* by using sliced blanched almonds instead of the cashews.

Make a very delicious *Chicken with Chestnuts* by using boiled chestnuts instead of the cashew nuts. Boil the chestnuts, peel them, cut them into small wedges, then add them to the dish as with the cashew nuts. Read about chestnuts in the Glossary. Chestnuts take a long time to cook.

Black Haitian Chicken (Chicken with Haitian Mushrooms)

Poul ak Djondjon
Poulet aux Champignons Haïtiens

This chicken dish is amazingly black and delicious. This black coloration is due to the presence of small mushrooms that also impart a delicious flavor and add sophistication to the dish.

Estimated time: 1 hour 40 minutes (including marinating time).

1/2 cup Haitian mushrooms
one 4-pound frying chicken, cut up (2 breast halves, 2 thighs, 2 drumsticks, 2 wings, 2 backbone pieces)
2 Persian limes (reserve 2 tablespoons juice)
1 1/2 teaspoons salt
1 chicken bouillon cube, crushed
1 habanero chile (read *Demystifying Habanero Chile*)
1 tablespoon chopped chives, or 1 minced scallion
2 tablespoons apple cider vinegar

1 cup white onion shavings (see note in *More Tips*)
1/4 cup chopped fresh flat-leaf parsley
pinch of ground cloves
1/4 teaspoon ground black pepper, or to taste
1 sprig thyme
3 tablespoons vegetable oil
6 garlic cloves, peeled, and crushed (see note in *More Tips*)
1/2 tablespoon tomato paste, diluted with 1 cup boiled water
1 1/2 cups or so boiled water
1 slice white onion (for sauce)
1 slice red bell pepper (for sauce)

Boil mushrooms in 1/2 cup of water for 1 minute. Remove from heat, cover, and allow the mushrooms to steep in the hot water until ready to use.

Trim excess fat from chicken, and rub with remaining lime, then rinse well with very hot (almost boiling) water. Drain. Transfer chicken to a bowl. Coat chicken with reserved lime juice, salt, bouillon cube, chile, chives, vinegar, onion, parsley, ground cloves, black pepper, and thyme. Cover, and marinate in a cool place for 30 minutes or overnight in the refrigerator.

Heat 2 tablespoons oil in a heavy 5-quart non-stick pan on medium-high setting. Add chicken, reserving marinade. Brown chicken on all sides, about 15 minutes. Transfer to a plate.

Heat remaining oil over medium high heat in the same pan, add garlic and sauté for 1 minute. Add diluted tomato paste and cook until all liquid evaporates, about 15 to 20 minutes. Stir-fry for 1 minute. Add chicken and marinade. Strain mushrooms over the chicken. Add 1/2 cup of boiled water to the residue, and reserve.

Cover chicken and cook over medium heat, scraping the bottom of the pan occasionally to avoid scorching, until the sauce thickens and chicken is cooked through, about 30 minutes. Transfer chicken and chile to a plate. Strain the reserved mushroom residue over the sauce. Strain sauce, pressing on the spice residue. Discard all residues. Season with additional salt and pepper if desired. Add chicken and reserved chile. Reduce sauce uncovered until sauce thickens, about 7 to 10 minutes. Add onion and bell pepper slices at the last minute. Discard chile. Serve hot.

Serves 4 to 6.

Note. To make "Black Haitian Chicken with Okra", sauté 2 cups of sliced okra in a separate skillet until slightly golden; add the sautéed okra slices to the dish before reducing the sauce at the end of the recipe. This is usually eaten with white rice.

Chicken with Green Peas

Poul ak Pwa Frans
Poulet aux Petits Pois

Estimated time: 1 hour 40 minutes (including marinating time).

one 4-pound frying chicken, (2 breast halves, 2 thighs, 2 drumsticks, 2 wings, 2 backbone pieces)
2 Persian limes (reserve 2 tablespoons juice)
1 1/2 teaspoons salt
1 chicken bouillon cube, crushed
1 habanero chile (read *Demystifying Habanero Chile*)
1/4 cup chopped leeks
2 tablespoons apple cider vinegar
1 cup white onion shavings (see note in *More Tips*)

2 tablespoons chopped fresh flat-leaf parsley
pinch ground cloves
1/4 teaspoon ground black pepper, or to taste
2 small sprigs thyme
3 tablespoons vegetable oil
6 garlic cloves, peeled, and crushed (see note in *More Tips*)
1 tablespoon tomato paste diluted with 1 cup boiled water
2 cups frozen green peas, thawed
1 1/2 cups or so boiled water
1 slice white onion (for sauce)
1 slice red bell pepper (for sauce)

Trim excess fat from chicken, and rub chicken with lime, then rinse well with very hot water. Drain. Transfer chicken to a bowl. Coat chicken with salt, bouillon cube, chile, leeks, vinegar, reserved lime juice, onion, parsley, ground cloves, black pepper, and thyme. Cover and marinate in a cool place for 30 minutes or overnight in the refrigerator.

Heat 2 tablespoons oil in a heavy lidded 5-quart nonstick pan over medium-high setting. Add chicken, reserving marinade. Brown chicken on all sides, about 15 minutes. Transfer to a plate.

Heat remaining oil in the same pan over medium high heat, add garlic and sauté for 1 minute. Add diluted tomato paste and cook until all liquid evaporates, about 15 to 20 minutes. Stir-fry for 1 minute. Add chicken, marinade, 1/2 cup green peas, and 1/2 cup boiled water. Cover and cook, scraping the bottom of the pan occasionally to avoid scorching, until sauce thickens and chicken is cooked through, about 30 minutes. Transfer chicken and chile to a plate. Remove excess oil. Mash peas with a fork in the sauce and add 1/2 cup of boiled water. Strain, pressing well on the residue. Discard the residue. Season with pepper, and salt if necessary. Add remaining peas, bring to a boil. Add chicken and reserved chile. Reduce uncovered until sauce thickens, about 15 minutes. Add onion and bell pepper slices at the last 3 minutes. Discard chile. Serve hot.

Serves 4 to 6.

Chicken with Vegetables

Poul ak Pomdetè ak Pwa Frans
Poulet aux Légumes

Estimated time: 1 hour 40 minutes (including marinating time).

one 4-pound frying chicken, (2 breast halves, 2 thighs, 2 drumsticks, 2 wings, 2 backbone pieces)
2 Persian limes (reserve 2 tablespoons juice for marinating)
2 tablespoons apple cider vinegar
1 1/2 teaspoons salt
2 chicken bouillon cubes, crushed
1 habanero chile (read *Demystifying Habanero Chile*)
1/4 medium leek, chopped
1 cup white onion shavings (see note in *More Tips*)
2 tablespoons chopped fresh flat-leaf parsley

pinch ground cloves
1/4 teaspoon black pepper, or to taste
1 sprig thyme
1/4 cup vegetable oil
3 large baking potatoes, peeled, and cut into wedges
6 garlic cloves, peeled, and crushed (see note in *More Tips*)
1 tablespoon tomato paste, diluted with 1 cup boiled water
1 1/2 cups or so boiled water
1 1/2 cups frozen green peas, thawed
1 slice white onion (for sauce)
1 slice red bell pepper (for sauce)

Trim excess fat from chicken, and rub with lime, then rinse well with very hot (almost boiling) water. Drain. Transfer chicken to a bowl. Coat with reserved lime juice, vinegar, salt, bouillon cubes, chile, leek, onion, parsley, cloves, black pepper, and thyme. Cover, and marinate in a cool place for 30 minutes or overnight in the refrigerator.

Heat 2 tablespoons of oil over medium setting, in a large non-stick frying pan. Add potato wedges, and sauté until golden on all sides, about 10 to 15 minutes. Transfer potatoes to plate and set aside. Then add 1 tablespoon of oil into the same pan, add chicken and sauté until golden.

Heat remaining oil in a heavy lidded 8-quart round pan (12 x 4 inches) over medium high heat. Add garlic and sauté for 1 minute. Add diluted tomato paste and boil until all liquid evaporates, about 15 to 20 minutes. Reduce heat to medium and stir-fry for 1 minute. Add chicken and marinade and 1/2 cup of boiled water. Cover and cook until sauce thickens and chicken is cooked through, about 30 minutes. Transfer chicken and chile to plate. Remove excess oil. Add 1/2 cup of boiled water to the sauce. Strain the sauce. Season with additional salt and pepper if desired. Add potato wedges, peas, reserved chile and chicken. Reduce on medium high heat until sauce thickens, about 10 minutes. Add onion and bell pepper slices during the last 2 minutes. Discard chile. Serve hot.

Serves 4 to 6.

Note. To make "Chicken with Okra", use 1/2 cup sliced okra instead of the potato and peas.

Roast Chicken

Poulè Woti
Poulet Rôti

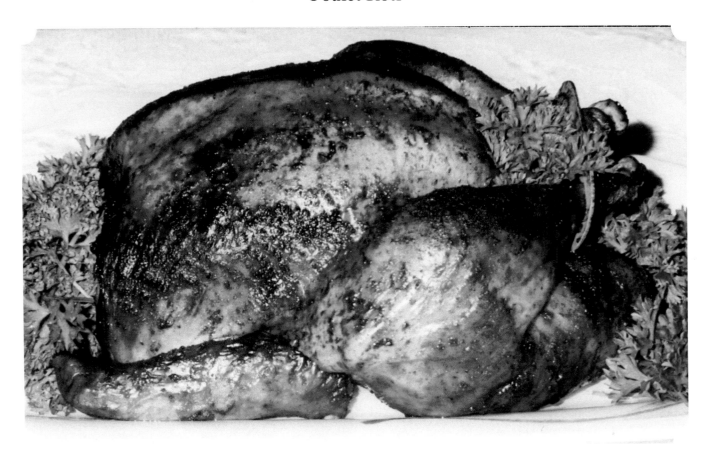

Estimated time: 2 hours 15 minutes (including 2 hours roasting time).

1/4 cup chopped white onion
1 habanero chile, seeded, and washed (read *Demystifying Habanero Chile*)
1/4 cup chopped red bell pepper
2 garlic cloves, peeled (see note in *More Tips*)
pinch ground cloves
2 tablespoons chopped fresh flat-leaf parsley
1 tablespoon chopped chives, or 1 minced scallion

1 sprig thyme (leaves only)
1 chicken bouillon cube, crushed
1 teaspoon salt
1/4 teaspoon ground black pepper
1 tablespoon apple cider vinegar
2 Persian limes (reserve 1 tablespoon juice for spice mixture)
one 4-pound roasting chicken
1/2 stick butter or margarine, melted
1 1/2 cups boiled water

Preheat oven to 350 degrees Fahrenheit. With a blender, purée onion, chile, bell pepper, garlic, cloves, parsley, chives, and thyme with bouillon cube, salt, black pepper, vinegar, and lime juice. Set the purée aside.

Remove and discard large blobs of fat from both openings of chicken. Rub chicken inside and out with lime and rinse with very hot (almost boiling) water. Pat dry. Coat chicken with 1 tablespoon of melted margarine (or butter), then inside and out with spice mixture. Mix any remaining spice mixture with 1 cup boiled water and pour into a roasting pan. Truss and place chicken, breast side up, on a rack in the roasting pan, so that chicken does not touch the water. Roast for 2 hours (30 minutes per pound) in the middle of the oven. After the first hour of roasting, baste every 20 minutes with remaining melted butter. When the butter runs out, baste with drippings. Add remaining boiled water to roasting pan if necessary. Twenty minutes before the end of cooking, poke chicken in the thigh-back junction with the tines of a fork to allow the juice to drip, and stop basting. Let stand for about 20 minutes before carving. Serve with baked potatoes, potatoes sautéed in butter with a dash of garlic, *Mashed Potato au Gratin*, or *Scalloped Potatoes*. Prepare sauce with the drippings during the standing time. The recipe for the sauce follows.

Serves 4.

Note. To prevent the chicken from browning too quickly, tent it with a sheet of aluminum foil during the first hour of roasting.

Roast Turkey: For a 10 to 12-pound turkey, double the ingredients except for the habanero chile, then roast at 325 degrees Fahrenheit for 3 to 3 hours 45 minutes, basting as above.

Roast Turkey

Sauce for Roast Chicken

Sòs pou Poulè Woti
Sauce pour Poulet Rôti

This is quite simple, delicious, and easy to prepare. It has a beautiful reddish brown color.

Estimated time: 20 minutes.

Drippings from *Roast Chicken*
1/2 tablespoon tomato paste diluted with 1 cup boiled water
1 slice of white onion
1 slice of red bell pepper

Skim excess fat from drippings. Discard the fat, reserving 1 tablespoon. Put the reserved fat in a 2-quart pan, add the diluted tomato paste, and boil over medium heat until water evaporates completely, about 15 to 20 minutes. Stir-fry for 1 to 2 minutes. While the chicken is roasting, you can start the preparation of the sauce up to this point using vegetable oil.

Mix in the drippings and reduce until the sauce thickens, about 8 to 10 minutes. Add onion and red bell pepper slices at the last minute. Serve hot.

Yields enough sauce to serve with one roast chicken.

Fried Chicken

Poul Fri
Poulet Frit

Estimated time: 40 minutes (marinating not included)

1/4 cup minced white onion
1 habanero chile, seeded, and washed (read *Demystifying Habanero Chile*)
1/4 cup chopped red bell pepper
3 garlic cloves, peeled, and crushed (see note in *More Tips*)
pinch ground cloves
2 tablespoons chopped fresh flat-leaf parsley
1 tablespoon chopped chives, or 1 minced scallion
1 chicken bouillon cube, crushed

1/4 teaspoon ground black pepper, or to taste
1 teaspoon salt
1 tablespoon apple cider vinegar
2 Persian limes (reserve 2 tablespoons for spice mixture)
one 4-pound frying chicken, cut-up (2 breast halves, 2 thighs, 2 drumsticks, 2 wings, 2 backbone pieces), or 8 chicken drumsticks, or 8 chicken thighs
vegetable oil for frying

With a blender, purée onion, chile, bell pepper, garlic, cloves, parsley, chives, bouillon cubes, black pepper, salt, vinegar and lime juice. Set aside.

Trim excess fat from chicken pieces. Rub chicken pieces well with limes, then rinse them with very hot water. Drain. Transfer chicken to a large bowl and coat with the spice mixture. Poke chicken with the tines of a fork to allow the flavor to penetrate the meat. Cover and marinate in a cool place for 5 to 7 hours or overnight in the refrigerator.

Heat oil in a large non-stick skillet over high setting. Add chicken, reserving marinade. Sauté on high heat for the first minute or so, to trap the juice inside the meat. Then reduce heat to medium. Cook until chicken is tender, golden brown, and the juice runs clear, about 30 minutes. Watch closely to avoid burning, reducing and increasing the heat as necessary. Drain on paper towels. Serve hot. Use marinade to prepare sauce following *Sauce Ti Malice* recipe.

Serves 4.

Note. Sometimes, the chicken pieces are lightly coated with flour before frying. Personally, I prefer not to use the flour coating.

Hen in Creole Sauce

Poul Di lan Sos
Poule à la Créole

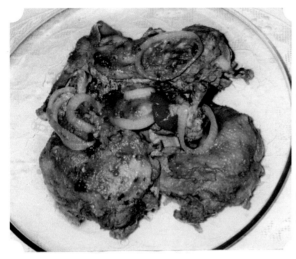

Many Haitians living in the USA call hen *poul di* in reference to the toughness of its meat. It is comparable to what we call *poul peyi* in Haiti. Because of its toughness, hen is suitable only for stewing and braising. There is no need for marinating, but you can if you wish. This takes more than three hours to cook, but it is worth the time. It can be prepared with cashew nuts, chestnuts, green peas, and vegetables. You will need a large, heavy lidded round pan (about 8 quarts, 12 x 4 inches).

Estimated time: 3 hours.

one 6-pound hen, cut up (2 breast halves, 2 thighs, 2 drumsticks, 2 wings, 2 backbone pieces)
3 Persian limes (reserve 2 tablespoons of juice)
3 tablespoons vegetable oil
6 garlic cloves, peeled, and crushed (see note in *More Tips*)
1 tablespoon tomato paste diluted in 1 cup of boiled water
7 cups boiled water
1 tablespoon granulated garlic
1 tablespoon apple cider vinegar
1 tablespoon white balsamic vinegar

1 1/2 cups white onion shavings (see note in *More Tips*)
1/4 cup chopped fresh flat-leaf parsley
1/8 teaspoon ground cloves
1/4 heaping teaspoon ground black pepper
2 tablespoons chopped chives, or 2 minced scallions
1 teaspoon salt
2 chicken bouillon cubes, crushed
2 sprigs thyme
1/2 teaspoon ground cayenne pepper
1 habanero chile (read *Demystifying Habanero Chile*)
1 slice white onion (for sauce)
1 slice red bell pepper (for sauce)

Trim as much excess fat from hen as you can. Discard wing tips if you wish. Cut limes and rub hen vigorously with their pulp. Rinse with very hot, almost boiling, water. Drain.

Heat 2 tablespoons oil in a heavy lidded round 8-quart pan (12 x 4 inches) over medium high setting. Add hen and brown on all sides, about 15 minutes. Transfer hen to a plate.

Heat remaining oil in the same pan over medium high setting. Add garlic and sauté for 1 minute. Add diluted tomato paste and boil until no liquid remains, about 15 to 20 minutes. Stir-fry for 2 minutes. Add hen, 6 cups of boiled water, reserved lime juice, granulated garlic, vinegars, onion, parsley, cloves, black pepper, chives, salt, bouillon cubes, thyme, cayenne pepper, and habanero chile. Cover and cook over medium heat until meat is tender, about 3 hours, scraping the bottom of the pan occasionally to avoid scorching. Sauce should be thick. Remove hen from sauce. Discard excess fat from the sauce. Add 1/3 to 1/2 cup boiled water to the sauce. Discard chile. Strain sauce, pressing well on the residue. Pour sauce into the same pan. Season with additional salt and pepper if desired. Add hen to sauce, and reduce until sauce thickens, about 5 to 7 minutes. Add onion and red pepper slices at the last minute. Serve hot.

Serves 6.

Note. You may follow the same recipe to cook duck and guinea fowl. You will need less water and less cooking time (about one hour). *Guinea Fowl with Green Peas* is particularly delicious.

You may substitute 1 cup of dry red wine for 1 cup of boiled water.

Chicken Au Gratin

Poulè Ograten
Gratin de Poulet

Estimated time: 1 hour.

2 cups whole milk

2 chicken bouillon cubes, crushed

1 1/2 pounds boneless chicken breast, cubed into 1/2-inch pieces

1/4 cup vegetable oil

1 cup finely diced white onion

1/4 cup all-purpose flour

3/4 cup freshly grated Parmesan cheese

1/4 teaspoon ground black pepper

1 egg yolk

1/4 teaspoon salt

1 egg white, beaten until foamy

1 tablespoon butter or margarine

Preheat oven to 375 degrees Fahrenheit. Lightly grease a 10-inch quiche dish or a 8x8x2 inch stoneware or glass baking dish with butter or margarine, and set aside.

Mix milk and bouillon cubes in a 12-inch skillet, add chicken cubes, cover (lid slightly ajar), and cook over medium heat until chicken is tender, 10 minutes. The milk will curdle. Remove from heat, and strain, reserving the cooking milk. Set aside until ready to use.

Heat 1 tablespoon oil over medium heat in a heavy 3-quart pan. Add onion, and sauté for 3 minutes. Transfer onion to a plate. Heat remaining oil over medium setting in the same pan. Add flour and cook for 3 minutes whisking often. Remove from heat. Using a wire whisk, vigorously whisk in reserved chicken cooking milk until mixture becomes creamy and homogeneous. Reduce for 2 to 3 minutes over medium heat to thicken, whisking constantly. Remove from heat. Mix in sautéed onion, 1/2 cup Parmesan, black pepper, egg yolk, salt, and cooked chicken. Then mix in beaten egg white. Mix well. Pour into prepared dish. Sprinkle with remaining Parmesan and bits of butter or margarine. Bake in the middle of preheated oven until golden, 30 to 35 minutes. Serve hot.

Yields 6 servings.

Turkey in Creole Sauce

Kodenn lan Sòs
Dinde à la Créole

Turkey is very often served along with other meat (ham, rabbit, . . .) at Christmas, New-Year's Day, and Easter Sunday dinners in Haiti. It is roasted with or without stuffing, or cut up and braised.

This delicious recipe is for cut-up turkey. It's a long process and that is mainly why it is reserved for special occasions. But it is worth the time. You will have to plan and organize your work. The cutting and cleaning of the turkey for this recipe takes more than 30 minutes, and turkey is cooked in 3 batches. It takes time, so take your time to prepare it. Also take the time to read the recipe. To shorten the preparation, ask the butcher to cut up the turkey for you. Watch chile closely or preferably cut, seed, wash, and mince chile to avoid its bursting in the pan.

Two large basins and two large ordinary shallow serving dishes will be helpful. You will also need a 12-inch non-stick frying pan, a heavy lidded 8-quart round pan (12 x 4 inches), and a 15 x 10 x 2-inch baking dish or 2 smaller baking dishes.

one 10 to 12 pound whole turkey, cut- up (2 breast halves, 2 drumsticks, 2 thighs, 2 wings, 2 back bones pieces)
4 Persian limes, cut lengthwise in 3 pieces each
2 tablespoons apple cider vinegar
4 tablespoons white balsamic vinegar
1/4 cup fresh lime juice
1/4 teaspoon ground cloves
1/2 teaspoon ground black pepper
2 cups white onion shavings (see note in *More Tips*)
1/2 cup finely chopped fresh flat-leaf parsley
2 tablespoons chopped chives, or 2 minced scallions

1/2 cup sliced leeks
1/2 tablespoon salt
2 chicken bouillon cubes, crushed
2 sprigs thyme
1/2 teaspoon ground cayenne pepper
2 habanero chiles (read *Demystifying Habanero Chile*)
1/3 cup vegetable oil
12 garlic cloves, peeled, and crushed (see note in *More Tips*)
1 tablespoon tomato paste diluted with 1 cup boiled water
2 cups boiled water
2 slices white onion (for sauce)
2 slices red bell pepper (for sauce)

Have on hand a 15 x 10 x 2-inch baking dish, or two smaller baking dishes. Bring a large pot of water to a boil.

Meanwhile mix vinegar, lime juice, cloves, black pepper, onion, chives, leeks, salt, bouillon cubes, thyme, cayenne pepper, and chile in a bowl.

Remove and discard excess fat from the turkey pieces. Plug the kitchen sink and place the turkey into it. Rub turkey pieces with the limes. Quickly rinse turkey with very hot water. Drain, and pat dry. Place turkey in two large basins. Pour half of the spice mixture over the turkey in each basin. Turn turkey pieces to coat them well with the mixture. Cover with plastic wrap and let marinate in a cool place for 1 to 2 hours, or overnight in the refrigerator.

Heat 3 tablespoons oil over medium high setting in a 12-inch non-stick frying pan. Add turkey pieces, reserving the marinade. Sauté until golden. Transfer turkey to a large shallow dish as they are browned. This takes about 20 minutes, or so.

Heat remaining oil over medium high setting in a heavy lidded 8-quart round pan (12 x 4 inches). Add garlic, and sauté for 1 minute. Add diluted tomato paste and boil until liquid evaporates completely, about 15 to 20 minutes. Stir-fry for 2 minutes. Remove from heat, add 1 cup of boiled water to tomato paste-garlic mixture. Mix well. Transfer half of the tomato paste mixture into a bowl. Add half of the turkey and marinade into the pan containing the other half of the tomato paste mixture. Cover and cook until turkey is tender, about 45 minutes, scraping bottom of the pan often to avoid scorching. Transfer turkey and chile to a shallow dish, transfer sauce to a bowl. Scrape and clean the pan if necessary. Put reserved tomato paste mixture, remaining turkey and marinade into the pan. Cover and cook over medium heat until turkey is tender, about 45 minutes, scraping bottom of the pan often to avoid scorching. Transfer turkey and chile to the shallow dish with the first portion of the turkey. Mix both sauces in the pan, add 1 cup boiled water to it, and strain pressing well on the residue. Add turkey and reserved chile. Reduce in the heavy 8-quart round pan over medium heat until sauce thickens, about 10 minutes. Add onion slices and bell pepper slices at the last minute. Discard chile.

Meanwhile, heat oven to the maximum. Place turkey in prepared baking dishes. Drizzle with some of the sauce, and brown quickly under the broiler until golden, 2 minutes. Serve hot with the sauce.

Serves 8 to 10.

Note. In Haiti the turkey breast is always halved lengthwise in two. In Haiti, local turkey is not as big as that carried by American groceries, thus its breast as not as large as its American counterpart. You may cut each turkey breast half crosswise in two, making four breast portions in total.

As I said in the introduction of this chapter, the backbones are important for the sauce. Once the turkey and the sauce are ready, you may discard them, or use them to make broth or stock.

Variation. You can make a delicious *Turkey with Cashew Nuts*, *Turkey with Chestnuts*, or *Turkey with Almonds* by adding 1 cup of cashew nuts, 1 cup of chestnuts, or 1 cup of blanched sliced almonds (See *Chicken with Cashew Nuts*).

Turkey Drumsticks in Creole Sauce

Kuis Kodenn lan Sòs
Pilon de Dinde à la Creole

This dish is made with sliced turkey drumsticks, and needs a large heavy covered pan (about 8 quarts) to cook it in. You can cut the drumsticks yourself or ask the butcher to slice them for you, so you have neater cuts. Do not throw away the meatless tips of the drumsticks; they are important for the sauce. Once the sauce is ready, you may discard them, or use them to make broth or stock.

Estimated time: 1 hour 30 minutes (marinating time is not included).

4 turkey drumsticks (about 5 pounds), sliced crosswise into 2-inch pieces
4 Persian limes, cut lengthwise in 3 pieces
2 tablespoons apple cider vinegar
2 tablespoons white balsamic vinegar
1/8 teaspoon ground cloves
1/4 heaping teaspoon ground black pepper
1 1/2 cups white onion shavings (see note in *More Tips*)
1/4 cup chopped fresh flat-leaf parsley
2 tablespoons chopped chives, or 2 minced scallions
1/2 tablespoon salt

2 chicken bouillon cubes
2 sprigs thyme
1/2 teaspoon ground cayenne pepper
1 habanero chile, seeded, and washed (read *Demystifying Habanero Chile*)
1/4 cup vegetable oil
10 garlic cloves, peeled, and crushed (see note in *More Tips*)
1 tablespoon tomato paste diluted with 1 cup of boiled water
1 slice white onion
1 slice red bell pepper

Use 3 limes to rub turkey slices. Rinse well with very hot (almost boiling) water. Drain carefully. Transfer turkey to a large bowl. Coat with juice of remaining lime (about 1/4 cup), vinegar, cloves, black pepper, onion, parsley, chives, salt, bouillon cubes, thyme, cayenne pepper, and chile. Cover with plastic wrap and marinate in a cool place for one to two hours, or overnight in the refrigerator.

Heat 3 tablespoons oil in a large, heavy, covered 8-quart round pan (12 x 4 inches) over medium high setting. Add turkey, reserving marinade. Brown turkey on all sides, about 15 minutes. Transfer turkey to a plate.

Heat remaining oil in the same pan over medium heat. Add crushed garlic and sauté for 1 minute. Add diluted tomato paste, and boil over medium high heat until all liquid evaporates, about 15 to 20 minutes. Stir-fry for 1 to 2 minutes. Add turkey, marinade, and 1 1/2 cups of boiled water. Cover, and cook over medium heat until turkey is tender, about 45 minutes. Scrape the bottom of the pan occasionally to avoid scorching.

Meanwhile, preheat oven to broil. Grease a 11 x 7 x 1 1/2-inch glass baking dish with vegetable oil. Set aside.

Remove turkey and chile from sauce. Strain sauce. Add reserved chile to sauce. Reduce uncovered over medium heat for about 8 minutes. Add onion slice and bell pepper slice at the last minute. Discard chile. Arrange turkey pieces in the prepared dish. Drizzle turkey with some of the sauce. Brown shortly under the broiler until golden, about 5 minutes. Serve hot, with the sauce. The turkey drumsticks are also delicious with *Sauce Ti Malice*.

Serves 4.

Sautéed Chicken Livers with Onion

Fwa Poul Sote ak Zonyon
Foie de Poulet Sauté à l'Oignon

Quick, easy, and quite delicious, these sautéed chicken livers are often served with fried eggs and toasted bread for a copious breakfast, or they can be chopped, mixed with finely chopped and sautéed white mushrooms, and served on canapés.

Estimated time: 30 minutes.

Juice of 3 Persian limes
1/4 cup finely chopped white onion
1 habanero chile, seeded, washed, and chopped (read *Demystifying Habanero Chile*)
1/4 cup finely chopped red bell pepper
2 garlic cloves, peeled, and chopped (see note in *More Tips*)
pinch ground cloves
2 tablespoons finely chopped fresh flat-leaf parsley

1 tablespoon chopped chives, or 1 minced scallion
1 sprig thyme (leaves only)
1 chicken bouillon cube, crushed
1/4 teaspoon ground black pepper
1 1/2 pounds chicken livers
1/4 cup vegetable oil
2 tablespoons apple cider vinegar
1/2 teaspoon salt or to taste
4 thin white onion slices

With a blender, purée onion, chile, bell pepper, garlic, cloves, parsley, chives, and thyme with the bouillon cube, black pepper, and 2 tablespoons of lime juice. Set the purée aside.

Put livers in a large bowl and pour the remaining lime juice on them. Toss to coat the livers with juice. Rinse with very hot water, then drain well through a strainer. Set the strainer aside over a bowl.

Heat oil in a large skillet over medium setting. Add the puréed spices-herbs mixture and sauté until golden, lowering the heat toward the end to avoid scorching, about 5 minutes. Increase heat to medium high. Add chicken livers and vinegar to pan, and sauté until livers are golden and no juice remains, about 10 minutes, lowering the heat to medium toward the end to avoid scorching. Add onion slices during the last 3 minutes. Sprinkle with salt and additional pepper. Serve hot with avocado slices and crusty bread.

Serves 6.

Cooked Stuffing for Poultry, Rabbit, Beef, and Pork

Fas Kuit pou Poul, Kodenn, Lapen, Bèf ak Kochon
Farce Cuite pour Volaille, Lapin, Boeuf et Porc

This preparation can be made one day ahead. Work raw ground beef with a large spoon to break up the pieces of meat, so it cooks evenly. Stuff meat just before roasting. Otherwise juice from the raw meat will spoil the stuffing. Chicken, turkey and rabbit can be boned before stuffing. Boning is quite a delicate operation. If you prefer, ask the butcher to do it for you. The cavity will shrink somewhat during cooking. Do not pack stuffing, even if the bird is not boned. Boned poultry needs less stuffing. As a general rule, use 1/2 cup of stuffing for every pound of chicken or turkey with bone, and 1/4 cup of stuffing per pound of boned chicken or turkey. This stuffing can be used also to make turnovers. In this case do not use the green peas.

Estimated time: 1 hour.

1/4 cup vegetable oil
1/2 cup minced white onion
1/4 cup minced red bell pepper
1 habanero chile, seeded, carefully washed, and minced*
1/4 cup finely sliced leeks (white part only)
1/2 cup packed chopped or sliced white mushroom caps
1/4 cup frozen green peas, thawed
1/4 teaspoon prepared yellow mustard
2 tablespoons mayonnaise
6 garlic cloves, peeled, and crushed (see note in *More Tips*)
3 tablespoons tomato paste diluted in 1 cup water
1/2 cup minced white onion
1 habanero chile, seeded, and washed*

1 tablespoon chopped chives, or 1 minced scallion
1/4 cup chopped fresh flat-leaf parsley
3 chicken livers, coated with lime juice, then rinsed with hot water
1/2 pound ground beef (preferably extra-lean)**
pinch ground cloves
1/4 teaspoon ground black pepper
1/2 teaspoon salt
1 tablespoon apple cider vinegar
1 tablespoon fresh bitter orange juice*, or fresh lemon juice
1 tablespoon ketchup
1/4 cup *Fresh Bread Crumbs*
1 egg, beaten just to mix the yolk and the white

Heat 1 1/2 tablespoons oil in a 2-quart pan on medium setting, add onion, bell pepper, chile, and leeks and sauté for 3 minutes. Add mushrooms, and sauté for 5 additional minutes. Add green peas, and sauté for 3 additional minutes. Transfer to a bowl using a slotted spoon. Cool. Mix in mustard and mayonnaise. Set aside.

Heat remaining oil in the same pan over medium high. Add garlic and sauté for 1 minute. Add diluted tomato paste, and boil until water evaporates completely, about 15 to 20 minutes. Reduce heat to medium and stir-fry for 2 minutes. Add onion, chile, chives, and parsley. Sauté for 3 additional minutes. Add chicken livers, and, sauté until cooked through, about 5 minutes. With the back of a strong spoon mash chicken livers, then add ground beef, stirring constantly to avoid lumps, until meat is no longer pink. Add ground cloves, black pepper, salt, vinegar, orange juice (or lemon juice). Cover and cook over medium heat until all liquid evaporates, stirring occasionally, about 10-15 minutes. Season with additional salt and pepper if needed. Remove and discard chile. Mix in ketchup, and bread crumbs. Cool. Add onion mixture. Combine well. The mixture should hold together***. Mix in egg. Cool completely at room temperature before using. This recipe can be doubled.

Yields about 2 1/2 cups.

Note: You may decide to serve the stuffing on the side as it is often done with turkey in the USA. If you do it, omit the eggs. When a stuffing that is to be served on the side is prepared in advance, mix the mayonnaise at the very last minute. After reheating, allow the stuffing to cool down for a short while then mix in the mayonnaise. Serve immediately with the turkey.

*Read *Demystifying Habanero Chile* in *The Cook's Techniques* chapter. Read note about bitter orange in the Glossary of this book.

**You can also use 1/4 pound of ground beef plus 1/4 pound of ground pork instead of the 1/2 pound of ground beef.

***The stuffing can be prepared up to this point, and stored in a covered container in the refrigerator for up to 2 days. Before using, bring it to room temperature, then mix in the beaten egg.

RICE AND CORNMEAL

Diri ak Mayi Moulen
Le Riz et le Maïs Moulu

Rice with Green Peas and Carrots

Cornmeal or rice

Cornmeal or rice?
They both sound nice.
Both if you could.
They both sound good.

Rachel Ménager, 11

INTRODUCTION

There is simply no Haitian dinner without a dish of rice. Usually we prefer the long grain varieties for savory dishes, and we reserve the short grain rices to prepare desserts and fresh baby foods.

Most of the rice we buy in Haiti comes from the open-air market. Thus we always sort and wash any rice before cooking it. This not only cleans it, but also eliminates most of the fine starch coating the grains, helping to keep the grains separated after cooking. To wash two to four cups of rice, fill a very large basin with fresh water. Add the rice, then take it between your palms and rub firmly up and down as you would do if you were washing your hands. Drain carefully through a large and fine strainer. Repeat until water runs clear, 3 to 4 times. Act quickly. Do not let rice stand in water and soak it. Otherwise, it will become mushy when cooked. Once the rice is washed and drained, it must be cooked; in other words, rice must only be washed just before adding it to the pan. Use a heavy round flat-bottom pan with a tight-fitting heavy lid (Dutch oven type) to cook rice. There is little liquid in the rice before putting the lid on. To know if rice is ready to cover, insert a spatula in the middle of the cooking rice and push gently on one side to see the bottom of the pan. Rice is ready to cover if the water has almost completely evaporated. The rice will be moist with very little water at the bottom of the pan. If the lid is light or does not fit properly, cover the pan with a piece of aluminum foil, then cover with the lid.

Rice is best when it is cooked just before serving. If you have leftover rice, transfer it promptly to a bowl, cover, and refrigerate. To reheat, bring it to room temperature, and use a fork to gently break up lumps if there are any. Smear 1 tablespoon of oil in a heavy lidded heavy pan over medium low heat. Add the rice, sprinkle it with a little water, toss it, cover tightly, and reheat for about 25 minutes.

You can make a **rice ring** with any rice recipe in this book; transfer the rice once it is cooked to a bundt pan or any other tube pan. Press it gently with the back of a spoon. Cover with foil. Set the pan over a small pan of simmering water for 20 to 30 minutes. The tube pan should not touch the water. Leave the rice in the tube pan on a rack for 5 to 10 minutes, then overturn on a serving dish to unmold. If you wish, fill the ring with whatever appeals to you. *Black Haitian Rice*, filled with sautéed seafood, makes a very attractive and amazing rice ring.

All the rice recipes in this chapter can be doubled. To do so, use a heavy 8-quart round pan (12 x 4 inches) with a tight-fitting heavy lid. Watch closely to avoid scorching. For the garlic, use the given amount plus half of that; for example, if the recipe asks for 4 garlic cloves, use 6 garlic cloves for the doubled recipe. Cooking time remains the same.

In Haiti, most (if not all) of the cornmeal we buy comes also from the open-air market. Thus, cornmeal is also washed with fresh water before cooking. This eliminates the dirt from the meal, and unfortunately also part of the starch in the meal. The starch helps the meal to stick together. The stickiness is desirable for cornmeal dishes, contrary to most rice recipes. If cornmeal is properly bagged, there is no need to wash it to prepare the recipes in this book, unless it contains too much starch. Some cornmeal is indeed overloaded with starch and flour. It needs to be sifted and/or washed to eliminate the excess starch and flour. To protect from burns, I would suggest long gloves to stir and beat the cornmeal, as it bubbles and splatters when cooking.

White Rice

Diri Blan
Riz Blanc

Everyone in Haiti knows how to cook plain white rice. White rice goes well with a lot of dishes, and leftover white rice is very convenient for preparing a rice salad or fried rice. Following is the most popular way we cook plain rice in Haiti. The amount of water that remains in the rice before putting the lid on determines whether the grains will separate or not. If too much water is left, the rice will be mushy. This recipe gives a delicious rice with perfectly separated grains.

Wild rice and Basmati rice can be found in some supermarkets in Haiti, but they are not truly known in our country. Wild rice cannot be accommodated following this recipe. Some Basmati rice needs more water and more time to cook. Brown rice needs also more water and more time.

Estimated time: 40 minutes

3 tablespoons vegetable oil
3 cups water
1 teaspoon salt
2 cups long grain white rice

Heat 1 tablespoon oil on high setting in a heavy 4-quart round pan. Do not let it smoke. Add water, salt, and bring to a boil.

When water starts bubbling, wash rice with lots of fresh water 3 to 4 times, or until water runs clear. Drain well through a large strainer. Add rice to boiling water and spread evenly with a spoon. Do not stir. Cook uncovered until water evaporates, scraping bottom of the pan once or twice, about 10 minutes. Reduce heat to medium low, cover the pan tightly, and cook undisturbed for 20 minutes. Uncover, drizzle with remaining oil. Cover and cook for 5 additional minutes. Serve hot.

Yields 8 servings.

Rice Pilaf (Rice Pilau)

Diri Fri
Riz Pilaf

Rice Pilaf is a true pleasure; it is light and grains are well separated. To make pilaf, the rice should be dry. If the rice has been washed, dry it thoroughly with kitchen towels. If the rice is properly bagged, there is no need to wash it. I use *Rice Pilaf* as a base for almost all the rice recipes in this book.

Estimated time: 40 minutes

2 cups long grain white rice
3 tablespoons vegetable oil
3 cups boiling water
1 teaspoon salt

Wash rice with fresh water 3 to 4 times, or until water runs clear. Drain carefully, and dry with kitchen towel. Heat oil in a heavy 4-quart round pan on medium high setting. Do not let it smoke. Add rice, and sauté for about 3 minutes, stirring constantly. Rice should not brown. Add boiling water, and salt. Boil over medium high until water evaporates completely, about 10 minutes. Reduce heat to medium low. Cover tightly, and cook undisturbed for 25 minutes. Serve hot.

Yields 8 servings.

Rice and Beans

Diri Kole ak Pwa Wouj (Diri Nasiyonal)
Riz aux Haricots Rouges (Riz et Pois National)

    Diri Kole ak Pwa Wouj is our national dish. It is a delicious dish made of rice cooked with red beans, spices, and herbs. Parboiled long grain rice, called *diri jonn* in Haitian Creole, makes the best *Rice and Beans*. When sorting the beans, make sure to remove split beans as they cook faster. Once rice is cooked, serve it immediately. Otherwise it will taste a bit off.

Estimated time: 2 hours (including 1 hour boiling time for the beans).

1/2 cup dry red beans or red kidney beans*
2 pieces of *Cured Pork*, washed (optional)**
1/3 cup vegetable oil, plus 1 tablespoon vegetable oil to add into the boiling beans
1/4 heaping teaspoon finely ground black pepper
1/8 teaspoon ground cloves
3 garlic cloves, peeled, and crushed (see note)
1 tablespoon minced chives, or 1 minced scallion
1/2 cup finely diced white onion
1/2 cup minced shallots

1 habanero chile, seeded, washed, and minced (read *Demystifying Habanero Chile*)
1/4 cup finely diced red bell pepper
2 chicken bouillon cubes, crushed
1/8 teaspoon ground cayenne pepper
1/2 teaspoon ground paprika
3 cups bean cooking liquid (if necessary add water to bean cooking liquid to obtain 3 cups)
1 to 2 sprigs thyme (leaves only)
1 1/2 teaspoons salt
1 sprig parsley
2 cups parboiled long grain rice

In a large pot, bring 8 cups of water to a boil. Sort, then wash beans 3 to 4 times with fresh water. Drain. Add beans, cured pork (if using), and 1 tablespoon of oil to the boiling water. Cover and cook over medium heat, with lid ajar, until beans are cooked through, 45 minutes to 1 hour. The beans should hold their shape. Drain, reserving cooking liquid.

Heat 2 tablespoons oil in a heavy 4-quart round pan, over medium heat. Add beans and cured pork, and sauté until beans are crispy, stirring occasionally, about 7 minutes. Add black pepper and ground cloves to the beans at the last minute. Transfer beans and pork to a plate.

Heat 2 tablespoons oil in the same pan over medium setting. Add garlic and chives, and sauté until slightly golden, about 1 to 2 minutes. Add onion, shallots, chile, and red bell pepper, and sauté for 3 to 5 additional minutes stirring constantly. Add bouillon cubes, cayenne pepper, paprika, bean cooking liquid, thyme, salt, and parsley, then bring to a boil over high heat.

When the liquid starts bubbling, wash rice with lots of fresh water 3 to 4 times, or until water runs clear. Drain carefully. Add rice, beans, and pork to boiling liquid. Spread rice evenly with a spoon. Do not stir. When boiling restarts, lower heat to medium high and cook uncovered until liquid evaporates, scraping bottom of the pan once or twice, about 7 to 8 minutes. Lower heat to medium low setting. Cover the pan tightly, and cook undisturbed for 20 minutes. Uncover, drizzle with remaining 2 tablespoons oil, then cover, and cook for 5 additional minutes. Discard parsley. Serve immediately. To double the recipe, use an 8-quart heavy pan with a tight-fitting lid.

Yields 8 servings.

Note. Sometimes we add coconut milk to the rice and beans for a delicious variation. If you wish to do so, add 2 tablespoons of fresh coconut milk, or 2 tablespoons of canned coconut milk into the boiling bean liquid before adding the rice. Be sure that the coconut is very fresh. Otherwise the rice will taste unpleasantly rancid. To learn how to make fresh coconut milk, read *About Coconut*, in *The Cook's Techniques* chapter. Canned coconut milk is available in Caribbean, Latin-American, and Asian markets and groceries, and the ethnic section of most supermarkets and groceries.

*Pinto beans make an excellent *Diri Kole ak Pwa Wouj*. Their taste is very similar to the taste of the red beans we have in Haiti. When making this dish in the USA, pinto beans are my choice.

**Read about *Cured Pork* in the *Special Condiments* chapter. If *Cured Pork* is not readily available, use 4 ounces of the salt pork belly available at many groceries and supermarkets.

Rice with Green Peas and Carrots

Diri Kole ak Pwa Frans ak Kawot
Riz aux Petits Pois et Carottes

To make this dish in Haiti we use fresh peas and fresh carrots. The peas are very mature; they are boiled first until tender, then they are sautéed. Frozen vegetables can be used as well, as it is the case in this recipe. They do not need much boiling.

Estimated time: 1 hour.

1/4 cup vegetable oil
3 garlic cloves, peeled, and crushed (see note in *More Tips*)
1 cup finely diced white onion
1 tablespoon chopped chives, or 1 minced scallion
1/4 cup finely diced red bell pepper
2 cups long grain white rice
3 cups water

1 1/2 cups frozen mixed green peas and carrots, thawed
2 chicken bouillon cubes, crushed
1 teaspoon ground paprika (optional)
1/8 teaspoon ground cayenne pepper (optional)
1/4 cup finely chopped fresh flat-leaf parsley
1/4 teaspoon black pepper
1 1/2 teaspoons salt

Heat 2 tablespoons of oil in a 4-quart heavy pan over medium high setting. Add garlic, onion, chives, red bell pepper, and sauté for about 5 minutes, stirring often.

Wash rice with lots of fresh water 3 to 4 times, or until water runs clear.* Drain carefully, and dry thoroughly with kitchen towels. Add rice to pan, and sauté for 3 additional minutes, stirring constantly. Rice should not brown.

Meanwhile, bring the water to a boil in a 2-quart saucepan. Add frozen vegetables. When boiling restarts, pour over the rice. Add bouillon cubes, paprika, cayenne pepper, parsley, black pepper, and salt. Spread rice evenly with a spoon. Do not stir. Boil uncovered over medium high heat until liquid evaporates, scraping bottom of the pan once or twice, about 8 minutes. Lower heat to medium low. Cover the pan tightly, and cook undisturbed for 20 minutes. Uncover, drizzle with remaining oil. Cover, and cook for 5 additional minutes. Serve hot.

Yields 8 servings.

Variation. Make *Rice with Mixed Vegetables* by using 1 1/2 cup of mixed vegetables. Use a mix of frozen green peas, lima beans, corn kernels, green beans, and diced carrots.

*If the rice is properly bagged, there is no need to wash it.

Black Haitian Rice (Rice with Haitian Mushrooms)

Diri ak Djondjon
Riz aux Champignons Haïtiens

This rice is black and very delicious. Its amazing color comes from a variety of little sun-dried mushrooms, very popular in Haiti. As far as I know, there is only one variety of local mushroom eaten in Haiti. These mushrooms give the rice a very delicious flavor and its surprising black color. Shrimp, lobster, and green peas are often added to this dish. *Black Haitian Rice* can make a very attractive *Black Haitian Rice Ring* filled with sautéed seafood and/or sautéed vegetables.

Estimated time: 1 hour.

4 cups of water
1/2 pound medium shrimp
1 cup Haitian mushrooms*
1/4 cup vegetable oil
3 garlic cloves, peeled, and crushed (see note in *More Tips*)
1 cup finely diced white onion
1 habanero chile, seeded, washed, and minced (read *Demystifying Habanero Chile*)

1/4 cup finely diced red bell pepper
1/4 teaspoon finely ground black pepper
1/4 cup finely chopped fresh flat-leaf parsley
1 sprig thyme, leaves only
2 chicken bouillon cubes
1 1/2 teaspoons salt
1 1/2 cups frozen green peas, thawed
2 cups parboiled long grain rice, or 2 cups long grain white rice

Bring 4 cups of water to a boil in a large pot and blanch shrimp for 1 minute. Use a slotted spoon to transfer shrimp to a plate. Reserve blanching water. Shell and devein shrimps. Do not discard the shells.

In the reserved blanching water, boil mushrooms with shrimp shells for 20 minutes. Then cover and let steep for at least 15 minutes. Strain "black water." If the black water does not yield 3 cups, add hot water to the residue and strain again. Then add enough to the black water to obtain 3 cups. Discard mushrooms and shrimp shell residue.

Heat 2 tablespoons of oil in a 4-quart heavy pan over medium high setting. Add garlic and sauté for 1 minute. Add onion, chile, red pepper, and sauté for about 3 additional minutes. Add shrimp, black pepper, parsley, thyme, and bouillon cubes, and stir-fry for 2 additional minutes. Add 3 cups of black water, salt, and peas, then bring to a boil over high heat.

When the liquid starts bubbling, wash rice with lots of fresh water 3 to 4 times, or until water runs clear. Drain carefully and add it to the boiling liquid. Spread rice evenly with a spoon. Do not stir. When boiling restarts, lower heat to medium high and cook uncovered until liquid evaporates, scraping bottom of the pan once or twice, about 8 to 10 minutes. Lower heat to medium low. Cover the pan tightly, and cook undisturbed for 20 minutes. Uncover, drizzle with remaining oil. Then cover, and cook for 5 additional minutes. Serve hot.

Yields 8 servings.

Variation. To make *Black Haitian Rice Ring*, transfer the rice once it is cooked to a bundt pan, or any other tube pan or ring mold. Press it gently with the back of a spoon. Cover with foil. Set the pan over a small pan of simmering water for 20 to 30 minutes. The tube pan should not touch the water. Then remove the tube pan from the simmering water and place it on a rack for 5 minutes or so, then overturn on a serving dish to unmold. Fill the rice ring with whatever you please (sautéed seafood and/or sautéed vegetables).

Black Haitian Rice can be prepared like a pilaf. I prefer long grain white rice for the pilaf.

*Read note about Haitian mushrooms in the Glossary of this book.

Rice with Seafood

Diri ak Fwidmè
Riz aux Fruits De Mer

Estimated time: 1 hour 20 minutes.

1/4 pound conch*
1 bitter orange
1/4 pound shrimp
1/4 pound crab legs
1/3 cup vegetable oil
1 cup frozen green peas, thawed (optional)
3 Roma tomatoes, peeled, seeded, and chopped**
1/4 pound lobster flesh, cut into 1/2-inch pieces
1/4 pound sea scallops
3 garlic cloves, peeled, and crushed (see note in *More Tips*)

1 tablespoon chopped chives, or 1 minced scallion
1 cup diced white onion
1 habanero chile, seeded, washed, and minced (read *Demystifying Habanero Chile*)
1/4 cup diced red bell pepper
2 cups long grain white rice
2 chicken bouillon cubes
1/4 cup finely chopped fresh flat-leaf parsley
1 1/2 teaspoons salt
1/4 teaspoon finely ground black pepper, or to taste

Remove gray and pink skin from conch. Rub with bitter orange, then rinse with hot water. Cut conch into about 1/2-inch pieces, and boil covered in 6 cups of unsalted water until tender, about 1 hour, or more if necessary. Drain, reserving cooking liquid.

Blanch shrimp and crab in 2 cups of boiling water on medium heat for 1 minute. Drain, reserving blanching liquid. Shell shrimp and crab. Reserve. Add shrimp-crab liquid to conch liquid. Add water if necessary or reduce to obtain 3 1/2 cups of liquid. Keep liquid simmering.

Heat 2 tablespoons oil in a heavy 5-quart round pan over medium heat. Add peas and sauté for 5 to 10 minutes. Using a slotted spoon, transfer peas to a plate and reserve.

Heat 2 tablespoons oil in the same pan over medium high setting. Add tomato and sauté for 10 minutes, stirring often. Add lobster, scallops, shrimp, crab, conch, and sauté for 3 additional minutes. Transfer sautéed tomato-seafood mixture to a plate. Set aside.

Heat 1 tablespoon of oil in the same pan over medium high heat. Add garlic, chives, onion, chile, red bell pepper, and sauté for about 5 minutes, stirring often.

Meanwhile, wash rice with lots of fresh water 3 to 4 times, or until water runs clear***. Drain carefully, and dry thoroughly with kitchen towels. Add rice to pan, and sauté for 3 additional minutes, stirring constantly. Rice should not brown. Add 3 cups of reserved seafood liquid, bouillon cubes, parsley, salt, and black pepper. Spread rice evenly with a spoon. Do not stir. Cook uncovered until liquid evaporates, scraping bottom of the pan once or twice, about 8 minutes. Reduce heat to medium-low, and quickly fold in the green peas and the seafood. Do not stir. Cover the pan tightly, and cook undisturbed for 20 minutes. Uncover, drizzle with remaining oil, then cover, and cook for 5 additional minutes. Serve hot.

Yields 8 servings.

*Where conch is not available, use two 6 1/2-ounce cans of chopped clams in juice.

**Bring a large pot of water to a boil, add tomatoes and blanch for 1 minute. Drain, and put the hot tomatoes in a large pot of cold water for 1 minute. Drain. Peel off the skin which should come off very easily. Halve tomatoes crosswise, then seed, and chop them.

***If the rice is properly bagged, there is no need to wash it.

Rice with Cod and Carrots

Diri ak Mori ak Kawòt
Riz à la Morue et aux Carottes

The nice light orange color of this delectable dish is due to the carrots and the bell pepper

1/2 pound skinless dried salt cod fillet*
1/4 cup vegetable oil
3 garlic cloves, peeled, and crushed (see note in *More Tips*)
1 tablespoon chopped chives, or 1 minced scallion
1 cup finely chopped white onion
1 habanero chile, seeded, washed, and minced (read *Demystifying Habanero Chile*)

1/4 cup finely diced red bell pepper
2 cups long grain white rice
3 cups boiling water
2 chicken bouillon cubes, crushed
1/4 cup finely chopped fresh flat-leaf parsley
1 1/2 teaspoons salt
1/4 teaspoon finely ground black pepper
1 1/2 cups diced carrots (about 3 medium carrots, peeled, and cut into 1/2-inch cubes)

Soak cod in a large pot of hot water for 12 hours, changing water three times (every 4 hours). Check for saltiness. Repeat the process if necessary. Drain carefully. Squeeze cod between paper towels to remove excess of water. Cut cod into about 1/2-inch pieces with kitchen shears or a sharp knife.

Heat 2 tablespoons oil in a heavy 4-quart round pan over medium high heat. Add garlic, chive, onion, chile, red bell pepper, and sauté for about 5 minutes, stirring often.

Meanwhile, wash rice with lots of fresh water 3 to 4 times, or until water runs clear**. Drain carefully, and dry thoroughly with kitchen towels. Add rice and soaked cod to pan, and sauté for 3 additional minutes, stirring constantly. Rice should not brown. Add boiling water, bouillon cubes, parsley, salt, and black pepper. Spread rice evenly with a spoon. Do not stir. Cook uncovered until liquid evaporates, scrapping bottom of the pan once or twice, about 8 minutes. Then reduce heat to medium-low, and quickly fold in carrots (do not stir). Cover the pan tightly, and cook undisturbed for 20 minutes. Uncover, drizzle with remaining oil, then cover, and cook for 5 additional minutes. Serve hot.

Yields 8 servings.

*Salt cod can be found at Caribbean and Latin-American groceries, and also at speciality Italian import stores. It is called baccala in Italian, and bacalao in Spanish. A recipe to make salt cod is given in the *Special Condiments* chapter. A method of soaking is given in *The Cook's Techniques* chapter.

**If the rice is properly bagged, there is no need to wash it.

Rice with Cod and Okra

Diri ak Mori ak Kalalou
Riz à la Morue et aux Gombos

This rice is surprisingly good. Okra must be fried at medium low heat until golden.

1/2 pound skinless dried salt cod fillet*
1/2 pound okra pods (yields slightly more than
2 cups sliced okra)
1/3 cup vegetable oil
3 garlic cloves, peeled, and crushed (see
note in *More Tips*)
1 cup finely chopped white onion
1 habanero chile, seeded, washed, and
minced (read *Demystifying Habanero Chile*)

1 tablespoon chopped chives, or 1 minced
scallion
2 cups long grain white rice
3 cups boiling water
2 chicken bouillon cubes, crushed
1/4 cup finely chopped fresh flat-leaf parsley
1 1/2 teaspoons salt
1/4 teaspoon finely ground black pepper

Soak cod in a large pot of hot water for 12 hours, changing water three times, every 4 hours. Check for saltiness. Repeat the process if necessary. Drain carefully. Squeeze cod between paper towels to remove excess water. Cut cod into about 1/2-inch pieces with kitchen shears or a sharp knife.

Wash okra pods under fresh running water. Trim and discard both ends of okra. Cut them into 1/4-inch slices. Heat 1/4 cup (4 tablespoons) oil over medium setting in a heavy 4-quart round pan. Add okra slices and sauté for 10 minutes, stirring carefully and often. Reduce heat to medium low, cover leaving lid ajar, and continue to cook until okra becomes golden, 15 to 20 minutes. Using a slotted spoon, transfer okra to a plate.

Add 1 tablespoon oil to the same pan over medium high heat. Add garlic, onion, chile, chives, and sauté for about 5 minutes, stirring often.

Meanwhile, wash rice with lots of fresh water 3 to 4 times, or until water runs clear**. Drain carefully, and dry thoroughly with kitchen towels. Add rice and soaked cod to pan, and sauté for 3 additional minutes, stirring constantly. Rice should not brown. Add boiling water, bouillon cubes, parsley, salt, black pepper, and fried okra. Spread rice evenly with a spoon. Do not stir. Cook uncovered until liquid evaporates, scraping bottom of the pan once or twice, about 8 minutes. Then reduce heat to medium-low setting. Cover the pan tightly, and cook undisturbed for 20 minutes. Uncover, drizzle with remaining oil, then cover, and cook for 5 additional minutes. Serve hot.

Yields 8 servings.

*Read the note about salt cod in the Glossary of this book. Use smoked red herring instead of cod to make *Rice with Herring and Okra*. Read the note about smoked red herring also in the Glossary.

**If the rice is properly bagged, there is no need to wash it.

Rice with Green Peas

Diri Kole ak Pwa Frans
Riz aux Petits Pois

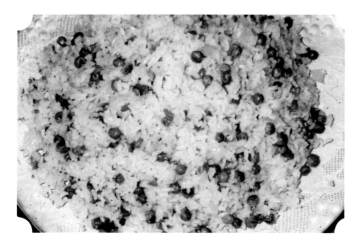

The green peas sold in Haiti's open-air markets are called "*Pwa Frans*" in Haitian Creole. They are very mature, thus very firm. They are boiled until tender, then they are sautéed. In this recipe I use frozen green peas, which are much more tender and do not require much boiling.

Estimated time: 1 hour.

1/4 cup vegetable oil
3 garlic cloves, peeled, and crushed (see note in *More Tips*)
1 cup finely diced white onion
1 tablespoon chopped chives, or 1 minced scallion
1/4 cup finely diced red bell pepper
2 cups long grain white rice
3 cups water
1 1/2 cups frozen green peas
2 chicken bouillon cubes, crushed
1/4 cup finely chopped fresh flat-leaf parsley
1/4 teaspoon black pepper
1 1/2 teaspoons salt

Heat 2 tablespoons of oil in a 4-quart heavy pan over medium high setting. Add garlic, onion, chives, red bell pepper, and sauté for about 5 minutes, stirring often.

Wash rice with lots of fresh water 3 to 4 times, or until water runs clear*. Drain carefully, and dry thoroughly with kitchen towels. Add rice to pan, and sauté for 3 additional minutes, stirring constantly. Rice should not brown.

Meanwhile, bring the water to a boil in a 2-quart saucepan. Add frozen peas. When boiling restarts, pour over the rice. Add bouillon cubes, parsley, black pepper, and salt. Spread rice evenly with a spoon. Do not stir. Boil uncovered over medium high heat until liquid evaporates, scraping bottom of the pan once or twice, about 8 minutes. Lower heat to medium low setting. Cover the pan tightly, and cook undisturbed for 20 minutes. Uncover, drizzle with remaining oil. Cover, and cook for 5 additional minutes. Serve hot.

Yields 8 servings.

Note. Use lima beans instead of the green peas to make *Rice with Lima Beans*. Lima beans are called *Pwa souch* in Haitian Creole. Use fresh or frozen Congo peas instead of the green peas to make *Rice with Congo Peas*.

*If the rice is properly bagged, there is no need to wash it.

Basic Cornmeal Recipe

Mayi Moulen
Maïs Moulu

Haitians eat cornmeal just as they eat rice. We eat it plain along with *Bean Purée*, gratinéed, cooked with red beans, black beans, Haitian mushrooms, smoked red herring . . . etc.

Use a heavy lidded 8-quart round pan because cornmeal expands considerably when it cooks, and you will need room to beat the cooking cornmeal. As I said earlier, it would be a good idea to wear long gloves to stir and beat the cornmeal, as it bubbles and pops when cooking. Here is the Haitian basic recipe for plain cornmeal.

Estimated time: 40 minutes
2 tablespoons vegetable oil
8 cups water
1 tablespoon salt
2 cups coarse yellow cornmeal*
1 cup fresh coconut milk**

Heat oil in a heavy 8-quart round pan (12 x 4 inches) over medium setting. Add water and salt. Bring to a boil.

When liquid just starts boiling, wash cornmeal with fresh running water 2 to 3 times. Add it to the boiling liquid. Stir often to avoid lumps. When boiling restarts, reduce heat to medium and cook uncovered, stirring constantly with a strong wooden spoon, until it forms a thick mixture, about 8 to 10 minutes. Reduce heat to medium low, mix in coconut milk. Cover the pan tightly and cook undisturbed for 30 minutes. Uncover and stir cornmeal vigorously (beat) with wooden spoon for 2 minutes or until smooth. Cornmeal should be thick and creamy. Serve hot.

Yields 8 servings.
Note. If you wish, you may sauté one crushed garlic clove and 1/4 cup finely diced white onion in the oil before adding the water. This gives a tastier cornmeal dish.

*Coarse cornmeal is available in Caribbean, African, and Italian markets, natural food stores, and some supermarkets. See the note about cornmeal in the Introduction of this chapter.

**To make fresh coconut milk, put 1 cup thinly chopped fresh coconut in a blender with 1 cup of hot water. Process on high speed for 2 minutes. Coconut will look as if it has been grated. Press coconut through a fine strainer to collect the milk. Strain again. It might yield a little more than 1 cup, but it will not make any difference. You can also grate coconut with a fine grater. Then add 1 cup of hot water, mix thoroughly, and press through a fine strainer as above. Make sure that the coconut is fresh and does not taste rancid.

Cornmeal with Cheese

Mayi Moulen ak Fwomaj
Maïs à la Bonne Femme

Estimated time: 1 hour 30 minutes.

2 tablespoons vegetable oil
2 tablespoons tomato paste diluted with
1 cup of boiled water
1 cup minced white onion
8 cups water
2 teaspoons salt
2 cups coarse yellow cornmeal*
1 cup fresh coconut milk**

1 1/2 cups evaporated milk
2 cups freshly grated extra sharp cheddar cheese or Parmesan cheese
2 chicken bouillon cubes, crushed
1/2 tablespoon granulated garlic
1/4 cup mayonnaise
freshly grated Parmesan cheese (optional)

Heat vegetable oil in an 8-quart heavy pan over medium high setting. Add diluted tomato paste and cook until liquid evaporates completely, about 15 to 20 minutes. Stir-fry for 2 minutes. Add onion and sauté for 3 to 5 minutes. Add water, and salt. Bring to a boil.

When liquid just starts boiling, wash cornmeal with fresh running water 2 to 3 times. Add it to the boiling liquid. Stir often to avoid formation of lumps. When boiling restarts, reduce heat to medium high and cook uncovered, stirring constantly with a strong wooden spoon, until it forms a thick mixture, about 8 to 10 minutes. Reduce heat to medium low, mix in coconut milk. Cover the pan tightly, and cook undisturbed for about 30 minutes. Uncover, add evaporated milk, cheddar, bouillon cubes, granulated garlic, and mayonnaise. Stir vigorously (beat) with wooden spoon for 2 minutes or until smooth. Cornmeal should be thick and creamy. Serve hot. Serve additional grated Parmesan separately if you wish.

Yields 8 servings.

*Coarse cornmeal is available in Caribbean, African, and Italian markets, natural food stores, and some supermarkets. See the note about cornmeal in the Introduction of this chapter.

**To make fresh coconut milk, put 1 cup thinly chopped fresh coconut in a blender with 1 cup of hot water. Process on high speed for 2 minutes. Coconut will look as if it has been grated. Press coconut through a fine strainer to collect the milk. Strain again. It might yield a little more than 1 cup, but it will not make any difference. You can also grate coconut with a fine grater. Then thoroughly mix in 1 cup of hot water, and press through a fine strainer as above. Make sure that the coconut is fresh and does not taste rancid.

Cornmeal with Smoked Red Herring

Mayi Moulen ak Aran Sò
Maïs à l'Hareng Saur

Estimated time: 1hour 30 minutes (herring soaking time is not included)

1/4 pound smoked red herring filets
1/4 cup vegetable oil
3 garlic cloves, peeled, and crushed (see note in *More Tips*)
2 tablespoons tomato paste, diluted with 1 cup of water
1 cup finely minced white onion
1/2 teaspoon finely ground black pepper

1/4 cup finely chopped fresh flat-leaf parsley
8 cups water
1 habanero chile, seeded, and washed (read *Demystifying Habanero Chile*)
1 tablespoon salt, or to taste
2 cups coarse yellow cornmeal*
1 cup fresh coconut milk**

Bring a large pot of water to a boil. Remove from heat. Add herring and soak for 4 hours. Drain carefully. Set aside.

Heat oil in a heavy lidded 8-quart round pan (12 x 4 inches) on medium setting. Add garlic and sauté for 2 minutes. Add diluted tomato paste and boil over medium high setting until no liquid remains, about 15 to 20 minutes. Reduce heat to medium and stir-fry for about 2 minutes. Add onion, herring, black pepper, and parsley, and sauté for 3 minutes. Add water, habanero chile, and salt. Bring to a boil.

When liquid just starts boiling, wash cornmeal with fresh running water 2 to 3 times. Add it to the boiling liquid. Stir often to avoid lumps. When boiling restarts, reduce heat to medium high and cook uncovered, stirring constantly with a strong wooden spoon, until it forms a thick mixture, about 8 to 10 minutes. Reduce heat to medium low, mix in coconut milk. Cover the pan tightly and cook undisturbed for about 30 minutes. Uncover, discard chile, and stir cornmeal vigorously (beat) with wooden spoon for 2 minutes or until smooth. Cornmeal should be thick and creamy. Serve hot with avocado slices.

Yields 8 servings.

*Coarse cornmeal is available in Caribbean, African, and Italian markets, natural food stores, and some supermarkets. See the note about cornmeal in the Introduction of this chapter.

**To make fresh coconut milk, put 1 cup of thinly chopped fresh coconut flesh in a blender with 1 cup of hot water. Process on high speed for 2 minutes. Coconut will look as if it has been grated. Press coconut through a fine strainer to collect the milk. Strain again. It might yield a little more than 1 cup, but it will not make any difference.

You can also grate coconut with a fine grater. Then thoroughly mix in 1 cup of hot water, and press through a fine strainer as above. Make sure that the coconut is fresh and does not taste rancid.

Cornmeal and Beans

Mayi Kole ak Pwa Wouj
Maïs Moulu aux Haricots Rouges

1 cup dry beans (red beans or red kidney beans)
1/2 pound *Cured Pork*, carefully washed to remove excess salt*
2 tablespoons vegetable oil
3 garlic cloves (see note in *More Tips*)
1 cup finely diced white onion
1 habanero chile, seeded, carefully washed, and minced (read *Demystifying Habanero Chile*)

2 tablespoons minced chives, or 2 minced scallions
2 sprigs thyme, leaves only
Pinch of ground cloves
1/2 teaspoon ground black pepper
2 cups coarse yellow cornmeal**
Salt to taste (about 1 tablespoon)
1 cup fresh coconut milk***

Sort and wash beans under fresh running water. Bring 10 cups of water to a boil in a large pot. Add beans and pork. Cover and cook over medium heat, with lid ajar, until beans are cooked through, 1 hour. Drain and reserve cooking liquid. Add water to cooking liquid to obtain 8 cups.

Heat oil over medium setting in a heavy lidded 8-quart round pan. Add garlic, and sauté for 1 to 2 minutes. Add onion, chile, and scallion, and sauté for 5 additional minutes. Add pork, beans, thyme, cloves, and pepper. Sauté for 5 more minutes. Add cooking liquid and bring to a boil over high heat.

When liquid starts bubbling, wash cornmeal with fresh running water 2 to 3 times. Add it to the boiling liquid. Lower heat to medium high and cook, uncovered, stirring constantly, about 8 minutes. Cornmeal should be thick. Season with salt to taste. Mix in coconut milk. Lower heat to medium low. Cover tightly and cook for 30 minutes. Uncover, stir cornmeal vigorously (beat) until thick and creamy about 2 minutes. Serve hot.

Yields 8 servings.

*If *Cured Pork* is not readily available, use 4 ounces of the salt pork available at many groceries and supermarkets.

**Coarse cornmeal is available in Caribbean, African, and Italian markets, natural food stores, and some supermarkets. See the note about cornmeal in the Introduction of this chapter.

***To make fresh coconut milk, put 1 cup of thinly chopped fresh coconut flesh in a blender with 1 cup of hot water. Process on high speed for 2 minutes. Coconut will look as if it has been grated. Press coconut through a fine strainer to collect the milk. Strain again. It might yield a little more than 1 cup, but it will not make any difference. You can also grate coconut with a fine grater. Then thoroughly mix in 1 cup of hot water, and press through a fine strainer as above. Make sure that the coconut is fresh and does not taste rancid.

Mayi Tyaka

Mayi Tyaka is a popular Haitian dish made with dry beans, broken dry corn kernels, and *Cured Pork* cooked together. Use a heavy 8-quart pan with a tight heavy lid to make it.

Estimated time: 2 hours 20 minutes.

2 tablespoons vegetable oil
5 garlic cloves, peeled, and crushed (see note   in *More Tips*)
1 1/4 cups cubed white onion
2 tablespoons minced chives, or 2 minced scallions
1 habanero chile, seeded, carefully washed, and minced (read *Demystifying Habanero Chile*)

3/4 to 1 pound *Cured Pork*, carefully washed to remove excess salt*
2 chicken bouillon cubes
pinch of ground cloves
1/2 teaspoon ground black pepper
1 to 2 sprigs thyme, leaves only
1 1/2 cups dry beans (pinto, red kidney, or red beans)
2 cups broken yellow hominy (samp)**
salt to taste
1 cup fresh coconut milk

Heat oil over medium setting in a heavy lidded 8-quart round pan. Add garlic and sauté for 1 to 2 minutes. Increase heat to medium high, then add onion and scallions, and continue to sauté for 2 additional minutes. Add chile, *Cured Pork*, bouillon cubes, cloves, black pepper, and thyme. Continue to sauté until the onion is very soft, about 5 to 7 minutes. Add 14 cups of water to the pan, and bring to a boil.

Sort and wash beans and hominy under fresh running water. Add these to the boiling liquid. Cook over medium high heat, covered with lid slightly ajar, for 1 hour and 30 minutes, stirring and scraping the bottom of the pan often to prevent beans and hominy from sticking and scorching. At this point, *tyaka* should already be creamy. Taste, add additional salt if necessary. Mix in coconut milk. Reduce heat to medium low, cover the pan tightly, and continue to cook for 30 minutes. The beans and hominy should be tender and in a thick and creamy sauce. If too thick, add a small amount of boiled water, and bring to a short boil. Tyaka must be thick and creamy, not thin. Serve hot.

Yields 6 servings.

*If *Cured Pork* is not readily available, use the salt pork available at many groceries and supermarkets. You may use a whole 12-ounce package.

**Broken hominy is made from dry corn kernels that have been hulled, degerminated, and broken. It is available at Caribbean, Latin-American groceries and supermarkets, and natural food stores.

Haitian Style Spaghetti

Espageti
Spaghetti à l'Haïenne

Estimated time: 30 minutes.

1 pound spaghetti
3 tablespoons vegetable oil
3 tablespoons tomato paste
4 garlic cloves, peeled, and crushed (see *More Tips*), or 1/2 tablespoon granulated garlic

3 chicken bouillon cubes, crushed
1/4 teaspoon finely ground black pepper
1/4 cup heavy whipping cream
1 cup freshly shredded Edam 40+ cheese, or Parmesan cheese (see note in *More Tips*)

Cook spaghetti in a large pot of boiling salted water as directed on the package. Do not overcook. Remove spaghetti from heat. Drain carefully, reserving about 2 cups of cooking liquid.

Heat the oil over medium setting. Add tomato paste, garlic, and 1 cup of the reserved cooking liquid and boil until liquid evaporates completely, about 8 minutes. Stir-fry for 2 minutes. Mix in crushed bouillon cubes, black pepper, 1/2 cup of the remaining cooking liquid, cream, then the cooked spaghetti. Using two serving forks, mix spaghetti carefully with the sauce. Cook for 1 to 2 minutes. Then mix in the cheese. Remove from heat. Serve immediately.

Yields 6 servings.

BEANS AND PEAS

Pwa Sèch ak Pwa Vèt
Les Haricots Secs et les Pois Frais

Green Pea Purée

Beans and Peas

I love beans and peas.
They make me healthy,
But don't make me wealthy.
I just love beans and peas!

Rachel Ménager, 11

Bean Purée

Sòs Pwa
Purée de Haricots Secs

In Haiti, we serve this smooth purée with white rice, cornmeal, and other cereals. I also use it to make my own very delicious and smooth version of Chili con Carne. This recipe can be made with almost any kind of dry beans (kidney beans, black beans, pinto beans, red beans, ...), or some combinations of dry beans, called *pwa mele* in Haitian Creole. Usually, we do not combine beans in Haiti, but if you wish to do so, one of the best combinations is made with 2 parts kidney beans, 1 part black beans, and 1 part pinto beans. In the traditional Haitian kitchen, a food mill or a pestle and a large round heavy pan are used to purée the beans.

Estimated time: 2 hours 20 minutes (including 1 hour 55 minutes boiling time).

1 1/2 cups dry beans (read the above introduction)
1/4 cup vegetable oil
4 garlic cloves, peeled and coarsely chopped (see note in *More Tips*)
1/2 cup coarsely chopped white onion, plus 2 tablespoons thinly diced white onion
1 habanero chile, seeded, carefully washed, and minced (read *Demystifying Habanero Chile*)

1 tablespoon chopped chives, or 1 minced scallion
2 pieces of *Cured Pork*, washed (optional)* (See the *Special Condiments* chapter.)
Pinch of ground cloves
1 sprig thyme (optional)
4 coarsely crushed black peppercorns (or 1/8 teaspoon ground black pepper)
1 1/2 teaspoons salt or to taste
1/8 teaspoon finely ground black pepper

Carefully sort and wash beans with fresh water. Drain well.

Heat 2 tablespoons oil in a heavy 5-quart pan over medium heat. Add garlic and sauté for 2 minutes. Then add 1/2 cup chopped onion, chile, and chives. Sauté for 1 to 2 additional minutes. Add 12 cups of water, beans, cured pork, ground cloves, thyme, and crushed black pepper. Cook covered over medium heat, with lid slightly ajar. After 45 minutes of cooking, remove one cup cooked beans, and reserve until ready to use (optional). Continue to boil the remaining beans for 45 minutes. The beans must be cooked for 1 hour 30 minutes, and they should be mushy.

Reserving the cured pork, purée mixture of beans and spices with the cooking liquid using a blender at moderate speed for 7 to 10 seconds. Strain twice, being sure to use a fine strainer the second time. Discard the residue.

Heat remaining oil in a heavy 4-quart pan. Add diced onion, and sauté for 1 minute. Add bean purée, reserved cooked beans, reserved pork, salt, and ground black pepper. Reduce bean purée, uncovered, over medium heat until smooth, 30 to 40 minutes. Scrape bottom of the pan often, so purée does not stick to it, preventing burning. Bean purée should have the same consistency as a thick gravy. Serve hot with white rice.

Yields 8 servings.

*If *Cured Pork* is not readily available, use 4 ounces of the salt pork available at many groceries.

White Bean Purée

Sòs Pwa Blan
Purée de Haricots Blancs

We serve this smooth purée with white rice.

Estimated time: 2 hours 25 minutes (including 2 hour 10 minutes boiling time).

1 1/2 cups dry navy beans
1/4 cup vegetable oil
4 garlic cloves, peeled and coarsely chopped (see note in *More Tips*)
1/2 cup coarsely chopped white onion
1 tablespoon chopped chives, or 1 minced scallion

1 slice red bell pepper (about 1/2 inch thick)
3 coarsely crushed black peppercorns (or 1/8 teaspoon ground black pepper)
1 1/2 teaspoons salt
1 chicken bouillon cube, crushed
1 tablespoon sugar

Carefully sort and wash beans with fresh water. Drain well.

Heat 2 tablespoons oil in a heavy 5-quart pan over medium heat. Add garlic and sauté for 2 minutes. Then add onion, chives, and bell pepper, and sauté for 1 to 2 additional minutes. Add 10 cups of water, beans, and black pepper to spices, and bring to a boil. Cook covered, with lid slightly ajar, over medium heat. After one hour of cooking, remove one cup cooked beans, and reserve (optional). Continue to boil the remaining beans for 30 minutes. Beans must be cooked for 1 hour 30 minutes, and they should be mushy.

Purée mixture of beans and spices with cooking liquid using a blender at moderate speed for 7 to 10 seconds. Strain twice, being sure to use a fine strainer the second time. Discard the residue. Transfer purée to a heavy 4-quart pan. Add reserved cooked beans, salt, remaining oil, bouillon cube, and sugar. Reduce bean purée, uncovered, over medium heat until smooth, about 40 minutes. Scrape bottom of the pan often, so purée does not stick to it, preventing burning. Bean purée should have the same consistency as a thick gravy. Serve hot over white rice.

Yields 8 servings.

Green Pea Purée

Sòs Pwa Frans
Purée de Petits Pois

When the green peas are not freshly picked from the vine, sometimes we add a dash of sugar to recreate the taste of fresh peas. In this recipe I use frozen peas.

Although very close to a soup, we do not serve this as a soup, but rather as an accompaniment for white rice.

Estimated time: 1 hour.

1 1/2 pounds (3 cups) frozen green peas
1/2 cup chopped white onion
4 garlic cloves, peeled and coarsely chopped (see note in *More Tips*)

1/4 teaspoon ground black pepper
1/2 tablespoon salt
1/4 cup vegetable oil
1 tablespoon sugar (optional)

Bring 7 cups of water to boil in a heavy 3-quart pan with peas, onion, garlic, and black pepper. Cook covered, with lid slightly ajar, over medium heat for about 30 minutes or until peas are tender.

Reserve 3/4 cup cooked peas (optional). Purée (remaining) mixture of peas and spices with cooking liquid in a blender at low speed for 7 seconds. Strain twice, the second time through a fine strainer. Discard the residue. Transfer purée to a heavy 3-quart pan and add salt, oil, and sugar if using. Stirring often, reduce purée, uncovered, over medium heat until smooth, about 30 to 40 minutes. The purée should have the same consistency as a thick gravy. If you choose to reserve cooked peas, add them during the last 5 minutes. Serve hot.

Serves 6.

Note. Use lima beans (*pwa souch* in Haitian Creole), to make *Lima Bean Purée*.

Pigeon Pea Purée

Sòs Pwa Congo
Purée de Pois Congo

In Haiti we also serve this purée with white rice or with plain millet (*pitimi* in Haitian Creole). When the peas are not freshly picked, people often add a dash of sugar to recreate the taste of fresh peas.

Estimated time: 1 hour.

1 1/2 pounds (3 cups) fresh or frozen pigeon peas (Congo peas)
1/2 cup chopped white onion
4 garlic cloves, peeled and coarsely chopped (see note in *More Tips*)
1 1/2 cups peeled and chopped West Indian pumpkin or acorn squash

1/4 teaspoon ground black pepper
1/2 tablespoon salt
1/4 cup vegetable oil
2 tablespoons sugar

Bring 7 cups of water to boil in a heavy 5-quart pan with peas, onion, garlic, pumpkin and black pepper. Cook covered, with lid slightly ajar, over medium heat for 30 minutes, or until peas are very tender.

Reserve 3/4 cup cooked peas (optional). Purée (remaining) mixture of peas and spices with cooking liquid in a blender at low speed for 7 seconds. Strain twice, the second time through a fine strainer. Discard the residue. Transfer purée to a heavy 4-quart pan and add salt, oil, and sugar. Stirring often, reduce purée, uncovered, over medium heat until smooth, about 30 to 40 minutes. If you choose to reserve cooked peas, add them during the last 5 minutes. Serve hot, with additional sugar if desired.

Serves 6.

Note. This *Pigeon Pea Purée* can also be done with dry pigeon peas, but the fresh peas taste much better. It will take more water and more time. Do not use the canned pigeon peas; they are not good.

Bean Soup with Dumplings

Pwa nan Sòs ak Donmbrèy
Soupe de Haricots Secs aux Boulettes de Farine

In Haiti, this popular soup is served with white rice, or other plain cereals like cornmeal. Made with the same ingredients as *Bean Purée*, it differs because most of the beans are not puréed and by the addition of dumplings.

Estimated time: 2 hours.

1 1/2 cups dry beans (red, kidney, black, pinto)
1/4 cup vegetable oil
3 garlic cloves, peeled and crushed (see note in *More Tips*)
1/2 cup finely diced white onion
1 habanero chile, seeded, carefully washed, and finely minced*
1 tablespoon finely chopped chives, or 1 finely chopped scallion
1/4 teaspoon ground black pepper
small pinch of ground cloves
1 sprig thyme, leaves only
2 pieces of *Cured Pork*, washed (optional)**
2 1/2 teaspoons salt or to taste
1/2 cup water (for the dumplings)
1 1/4 cups all-purpose flour (for the dumplings)

Carefully sort and wash beans with fresh water. Drain well.

Heat oil in a heavy 5-quart pan over medium heat. Add garlic and sauté for 1 minute. Then add onion, minced chile, and chopped chives, and sauté for 1 to 2 additional minutes. Add 12 cups of water, beans, black pepper, cloves, thyme, and cured pork (if using). Cover and cook over medium heat for 1 hour 30 minutes, with lid slightly ajar.

Meanwhile, make the dumplings: Dissolve 1 teaspoon of salt in the water. Gradually add to the flour to form a smooth dough. Sprinkle palms of both hands with flour and roll dough to form 1 1/2-inch balls. Cover and set aside.

After 1 hour 30 minutes of cooking, purée 1 cup of cooked beans with some cooking liquid. Strain this into the remaining bean mixture; add the dumplings and the remaining salt. If the purée is too thick, mix in some boiled water before reducing. Then reduce, uncovered, over medium heat until fairly thick, about 20 to 30 minutes. Scrape bottom of the pan often, so purée does not stick, preventing burning. Serve hot with white rice.

Yields 8 servings.

*Read *Demystifying Habanero Chile* in *The Cook's Techniques* chapter.

**Read about *Cured Pork* in the *Special Condiments* chapter. If cured pork is not readily available, use 4 ounces of the salt pork available at many groceries and supermarkets.

GRATINS

Graten
Les Gratins

Creamy Corn au Gratin

Gratin

I'd rather make some gratin,
Than hang curtains made of satin.
It's easy to bake;
It doesn't give an ache.

Rachel Ménager, 11

Macaroni au Gratin

Makawoni Ograten
Macaroni au Gratin

Macaroni au Gratin is among our favorite side dishes for Sunday dinner in Haiti. It is also often present on the New Year's dinner table.

Estimated time: 1 hour.

1 pound (slightly more than 5 cups) large tube-shaped macaroni (rigatoni, penne rigate)
1 tablespoon margarine
1 1/2 cups finely diced white onion
1/2 cup whipping cream
1/2 teaspoon prepared yellow mustard
1/3 cup mayonnaise
2 teaspoons soy sauce
2 chicken bouillon cubes, crushed

1 teaspoon granulated garlic
2 cups evaporated milk, or whole milk
1/4 teaspoon finely ground black pepper
1 1/2 cups freshly grated Parmesan cheese*
1 1/2 cups freshly grated extra sharp cheddar cheese*
salt to taste**
1/3 cup freshly grated Parmesan cheese (to sprinkle)
1 tablespoon margarine, cut into small pieces

Preheat oven to 400 degrees Fahrenheit. Grease a 2 1/2-quart x 2 inch deep glass or stoneware baking dish with oil or margarine. Set aside.

Bring a large pot of salted water to a boil. Add macaroni and cook uncovered for 18 minutes for rigatoni and 12 minutes for penne rigate. Drain well.

While macaroni is boiling, heat margarine over medium setting. Add onion and sauté until translucent and tender, about 3 minutes. Set aside.

In a large bowl, whip cream, mustard, and mayonnaise until a homogeneous mixture is formed. Add soy sauce, bouillon cubes, garlic, and milk. Season with pepper. Add Parmesan cheese, cheddar cheese, and sautéed onion. Mix in cooked macaroni. Mix well. Season with salt to taste. Transfer mixture to the prepared dish. Sprinkle with grated Parmesan cheese and bits of margarine. Bake in the middle of preheated oven for 35 to 40 minutes, until golden. Allow to set for about 15 minutes at room temperature before serving. Serve warm.

Yields 8 to 10 servings.

*Instead of the combination of the two cheeses, use 2 cups of freshly grated Edam 40+ if available. See the note about cheese in *More Tips*.

**Take the high salt content of cheese into account before adding salt.

Scalloped Potatoes

Pomdetè Tranche Ograten
Gratin Dauphinois

Estimated time: 2 hours 20 minutes.

2 cups whole milk
1 teaspoon granulated garlic
2 chicken bouillon cubes, crushed
2 cups heavy whipping cream
1/2 tablespoon soy sauce
1/4 teaspoon finely ground black pepper
1 teaspoon salt

1 cup freshly shredded extra sharp cheddar cheese
1 cup freshly shredded Parmesan cheese
2 1/2 pounds baking potatoes
1/4 cup freshly shredded Parmesan cheese (to sprinkle)

Preheat oven to 400 degrees Fahrenheit. Grease a 2 1/2-quart x 2 inch-deep glass or stoneware baking dish with oil or margarine. Set aside.

In a large pitcher mix milk, garlic, bouillon cubes, whipping cream, soy sauce, pepper and salt. Set aside.

Mix the Parmesan and the cheddar in a medium bowl. Set aside.

Peel, then thinly slice the potatoes crosswise. Alternate potato slices with cheese in the prepared dish, ending with potato slices. You should have 3 layers of potato slices, and 2 layers of cheese. Pour the milk mixture over the potatoes. Cover with a sheet of aluminum foil. Place the dish on a jelly roll pan, and bake in the middle of preheated oven for 1 hour 30 minutes. Then uncover the dish, sprinkle with Permesan cheese, and bake uncovered until golden, about 30 additional minutes. Allow to set at room temperature for 15 minutes or so before serving. Serve warm.

Yields 8 to10 servings.

Note. Use a mandolin slicer to rapidly obtain really thin potato slices.

Mashed Potatoes au Gratin, Mashed Breadfruit au Gratin

Pomdetè Ograten, Veritab Ograten
Pommes de Terre au Gratin, Véritable au Gratin

Estimated time: 1 hour.

6 large baking potatoes (about 3 pounds)
2 tablespoons margarine or vegetable oil
1 1/2 cups finely chopped white onion
3/4 cup evaporated milk
1/4 cup whipping cream
2 chicken bouillon cubes, crushed
3 tablespoons mayonnaise
1/4 teaspoon finely ground black pepper, or to taste
1/2 teaspoon granulated garlic

1 teaspoon soy sauce
1 1/2 cups freshly grated Parmesan cheese
1 1/2 cups freshly grated extra sharp cheddar cheese
1/2 teaspoon salt or to taste
1 egg yolk
1 egg white, beaten
1/4 cup freshly grated Parmesan cheese (to sprinkle)
1 tablespoon margarine, cut into small pieces

Preheat oven to 500 degrees Fahrenheit. Grease a 2-quart x 2 inch deep glass or stoneware baking dish with margarine or oil. Set aside.

Boil potatoes in a large pot of water until cooked through, about 30 minutes.

Meanwhile, heat margarine or oil over medium setting. Add onion and sauté for about 3 minutes. Set aside.

Peel and mash potatoes with a potato ricer, a food mill, or a fork. Add onion, milk, cream, bouillon cubes, mayonnaise, black pepper, granulated garlic, soy sauce, Parmesan cheese, cheddar cheese, salt, and egg yolk. Mix well. Fold in beaten egg white. Mix quickly. Transfer to the prepared dish. Sprinkle with Parmesan and margarine. Bake in the center of preheated oven until golden, about 20 minutes. Allow to set at room temperature for 15 minutes or so before serving. Serve warm.

Serves 8.

Notes : Make an exquisite *Breadfruit au Gratin* using mashed breadfruit instead of the mashed potatoes. Flake 1/4 pound soaked salt cod filets. Sauté it with the onion, mix it with the mashed breadfruit, then proceed as above. The breadfruit must be firm, ripe and green but not ripe and sweet. Learn how to soak salt cod in *The Cook's Techniques* chapter. To make a *Potato Soufflé* or a *Breadfruit Soufflé*, see the *Eggs and Soufflés* chapter.

Stuffed Mashed Potatoes au Gratin

Pomdetè Fasi Ograten
Pommes de Terre Farcies au Gratin

Ground beef can be prepared one day ahead and stored in the refrigerator.

Estimated time: 1 hour 10 minutes.

1 recipe of *Ground Beef*
5 large baking potatoes (about 2 1/2 pounds)
1/2 tablespoon margarine
1 1/2 cups finely chopped white onion
3/4 cup evaporated milk
2 chicken bouillon cubes, crushed
3 tablespoons mayonnaise
1/4 teaspoon finely ground black pepper, or to taste
1/2 teaspoon granulated garlic

1 teaspoon soy sauce
1 1/2 cups freshly grated Parmesan cheese
1 1/2 cups freshly grated extra sharp cheddar cheese
1/4 teaspoon salt or to taste
1 egg, beaten
two 16-ounce cans of corn kernels, drained
1/4 cup freshly grated Parmesan cheese (to sprinkle)
1 tablespoon margarine, cut into small pieces

Preheat oven to 500 degree Fahrenheit. Grease a 2 1/2-quart x 2 inch deep glass or stoneware baking dish with oil or margarine. Set aside.

Boil potatoes in a large pot of water until cooked through, about 30 minutes.

Meanwhile, heat margarine in a heavy 3-quart pan over medium setting. Add onion and sauté for about 3 minutes. Set aside.

Peel and mash potatoes with a fork, a food mill, or a potato ricer. Add sautéed onion, milk, bouillon cubes, mayonnaise, black pepper, granulated garlic, soy sauce, Parmesan cheese, cheddar cheese, salt, and beaten egg. Combine well. Season with salt if necessary.

Layer the prepared dish with half of the mashed potato mixture, then half of the corn, then the ground beef, then the remaining corn, then the remaining mashed potato mixture. Sprinkle with Parmesan cheese, and pieces of margarine. Bake in the center of preheated oven until golden, about 20 minutes. Allow to set at room temperature for 15 minutes or so before serving. Serve warm.

Serves 8 to 10.

Creamy Carrot au Gratin

Kawòt Blanchi
Gratin de Carottes à la Crème

Estimated time: 1 hour.

1 1/2 to 2 pounds carrots (about 9 to 12 medium carrots), peeled, and halved crosswise
6 tablespoons vegetable oil
2 cups finely diced white onion
1/2 cup all-purpose flour
2 cups whole milk

1 cup heavy whipping cream
1 1/2 teaspoons salt
1/2 teaspoon finely ground black pepper
1 tablespoon butter or margarine, cut into small pieces

Steam carrots covered over medium heat until tender, about 10 to 12 minutes. Cut cooked carrots crosswise into very thin slices (about 1/16-inch thick). Set aside.

Heat 2 tablespoons oil in a 3-quart heavy pan over medium setting. Add onion and sauté for 2 minutes. Onion should become translucent and tender but not brown. Using a slotted spoon, transfer onion to a plate. Set aside.

Heat oven to broil. Grease lightly a 2-quart x 2 inch deep glass or stoneware baking dish. Set aside.

Heat remaining oil in the same pan over medium setting. Add flour, and cook for 5 minutes, stirring constantly with a wire whisk. Flour should not brown. Remove from heat, add milk while whisking vigorously until flour dissolves completely. Whisk over medium heat to thicken a little bit, 6 to 7 minutes. Remove from heat. Mix in whipping cream, salt, black pepper, and sautéed onion. The sauce should be thick, creamy, and easily spreadable.

Mix some of the white sauce with the carrot slices, then arrange carrot slices in the prepared dish. Pour the remaining white sauce over the carrots. Distribute bits of butter over the sauce, then brown shortly under the broiler, 3 to 4 minutes. Allow to set at room temperature for 15 minutes or so before serving. Serve warm.

Serves 6 to 8.

Creamy Spinach au Gratin

Zepina Ograten
Gratin d'Epinard à la Crème

5 pounds fresh spinach (about 7 bundles of spinach)*
1/4 cup vegetable oil
2 cups finely diced white onion
4 ounces cream cheese, softened
1 cup freshly grated Parmesan cheese
1 cup freshly grated extra sharp cheddar cheese

1 teaspoon salt
1/4 teaspoon black pepper
1/4 cup all-purpose flour
2 cups whole milk
1/4 cup freshly grated Parmesan cheese (to sprinkle)
1 tablespoon butter or margarine, cut into small bits

Preheat oven to 375 degrees Fahrenheit. Grease a 2 quart x 2 inch deep glass or stoneware baking dish with oil or margarine. Set aside.

Trim and discard roots and lower stems of spinach, then wash under fresh running water to remove all the dirt. Blanch spinach for 1 to 2 minutes in a large pot of boiling water. Drain, and discard water. Transfer spinach to a large plate. With a sharp knife, slice the spinach into small pieces.

Heat 1 tablespoon oil over medium setting in a heavy pan. Add onion and sauté until tender and translucent, about 2 minutes. Transfer to a large bowl. Mix in softened cream cheese, cheese, salt, and pepper. Set aside.

Heat remaining oil over medium setting in the same pan. Add flour and sauté for 2 to 3 minutes, stirring constantly with a wire whisk. Flour should not brown. Remove from heat. Immediately whisk in milk until flour dissolves completely. Reduce over medium heat to thicken a little bit, about 4 to 5 minutes. Remove from heat. Pour into cheese mixture. Mix well. Fold in spinach. Season with additional salt and pepper if necessary. Pour in prepared dish. Sprinkle with grated Parmesan and bits of butter or margarine. Bake in the middle of preheated oven until golden, about 35 to 40 minutes. Allow to set at room temperature for 15 minutes or so before serving. Serve warm.

Serves 6 to 8.

Note. To make *Spinach Soufflé*, add 4 egg yolks before adding the spinach. Add the spinach, then fold in 4 stiffly beaten egg whites. Pour in an 8-cup soufflé mold generously coated with butter and flour. Sprinkle with grated Parmesan. Bake at 375 degrees Fahrenheit until puffed and golden, 30 to 35 minutes. Serve immediately.

*You may as well use ready-to-use fresh bagged spinach. This is available in the vegetable section of groceries and supermarkets.

Creamy Cabbage au Gratin

Chou Ograten
Gratin de Chou à la Crème

one 3-pound cabbage
5 tablespoons vegetable oil
2 cups finely diced white onion
4 ounces cream cheese, softened
1/2 cup freshly grated Parmesan cheese
1 cup freshly grated extra sharp cheddar cheese
1 1/2 teaspoons salt
2 chicken bouillon cubes, crushed

1/4 teaspoon black pepper
1/4 cup all-purpose flour
2 cups whole milk
1/2 cup heavy whipping cream
1/4 cup freshly grated Parmesan cheese (to sprinkle)
1 tablespoon butter or margarine, cut into small bits

Preheat oven to 375 degrees Fahrenheit. Grease a 2 quart x 2 inch deep glass or stoneware baking dish with oil or margarine. Set aside.

Wash cabbage then cut it lengthwise into 8 pieces. Remove and discard the core. Steam cabbage wedges over medium heat until tender, about 15 minutes. Transfer cabbage to a large plate. With a sharp knife, slice the cabbage wedges into small pieces. Heat 1 tablespoon oil over medium setting in a heavy 8-quart round pan (12 x 4 inches). Add cabbage, and stir-fry for 10 minutes. This will help the cabbage lose some moisture. Remove from heat, and set aside.

Heat 1 tablespoon oil over medium setting in a heavy 3-quart pan. Add onion and sauté until tender and translucent, about 2 minutes. Transfer to a large bowl. Mix in softened cream cheese, cheese, salt, chicken bouillon cubes, and pepper. Mix with cabbage. Set aside.

Heat remaining oil over medium setting in the same 3-quart pan. Add flour and sauté for 2 to 3 minutes, stirring constantly with a wire whisk. Flour should not brown. Remove from heat. Immediately whisk in milk until flour dissolves completely. Reduce over medium heat to thicken, about 4 minutes. Remove from heat. Pour into cheese-cabbage mixture. Add cream. Mix well. Season with additional salt and pepper if necessary. Pour in the prepared dish. Sprinkle with grated Parmesan and bits of butter or margarine. Bake in the middle of preheated oven until golden, about 45 minutes. Allow to set at room temperature for 20 minutes or so before serving. Serve warm.

Serves 6 to 8.

Note. Make *Cauliflower au Gratin* and *Broccoli au Gratin* following the same recipe. Cauliflower and broccoli must be cut into bite-size pieces, then steamed.

Creamy Corn au Gratin

Mayi Ograten
Gratin de Maïs à la Crème

1/4 cup vegetable oil
1 1/2 cups diced white onion
2 pounds (two 16-ounce packages) frozen corn kernels*, thawed
2 ounces cream cheese, softened
1/2 cup heavy whipping cream
1 cup freshly grated Parmesan cheese
1 cup freshly grated extra sharp cheddar cheese

1 teaspoon salt
1/4 teaspoon black pepper
1/4 cup all-purpose flour
1 1/2 cups whole milk
1/4 cup freshly grated Parmesan cheese (to sprinkle)
1 tablespoon butter or margarine, cut into small bits

Preheat oven to 375 degrees Fahrenheit. Grease a 2 1/2 quart x 2 inch deep glass or stoneware baking dish with oil or margarine. Set aside.

Heat 1 tablespoon oil over medium high setting in a heavy 5-quart pan. Add onion and sauté until tender and translucent, about 2 minutes. Steam corn over medium heat until tender, about 15 minutes. Transfer to plate and set aside.

In a large bowl, mix cream cheese with cream, cheese, salt, and pepper. Stir in corn and onion. Set aside.

Heat remaining oil in a 3-quart heavy pan over medium setting. Add flour and sauté for 2 to 3 minutes, stirring constantly. Flour should not brown. Remove from heat. Using a wire whisk, immediately whisk in milk until flour dissolves completely. Whisk over medium heat to thicken a little bit, about 4 minutes. Remove it from heat, and pour into cheese-corn mixture. Mix well. Pour into the prepared dish. Sprinkle with Parmesan and bits of butter or margarine. Bake in the middle of preheated oven until golden, about 35 to 40 minutes. Allow to set at room temperature for 15 minutes or so before serving. Serve warm.

Serves 6 to 8.

Note. To make *Corn Soufflé*, add 4 egg yolks before adding the corn mixture. Add the corn mixture, then fold in 4 stiffly beaten egg whites. Pour in an 8-cup soufflé mold generously coated with butter and flour. Sprinkle with grated Parmesan. Bake at 375 degrees Fahrenheit until puffed and golden, 30 to 35 minutes. Serve immediately.

*You may use two 15 1/4-ounce cans of corn kernels instead of the frozen corn. Drain the kernels and discard the liquid. It is not necessary to steam the canned corn.

Creamy Leeks au Gratin

Powo Ograten
Gratin de Poireau à la Crème

6 cups 1/2-inch leek slices, white parts only (about 14 large leeks)*
1 cup heavy whipping cream
1 1/2 teaspoons salt
1/4 teaspoon finely ground black pepper
1 cup freshly grated Parmesan cheese
1 cup freshly grated extra sharp cheddar cheese

1/3 cup vegetable oil
1/2 cup all-purpose flour
2 cups whole milk
1/4 cup freshly grated Parmesan cheese (to sprinkle)
1 tablespoon butter or margarine, cut into small bits

Preheat oven to 375 degrees Fahrenheit. Grease a 2 quart x 2-inch deep glass or stoneware baking dish with oil or margarine. Set aside.

Steam leek slices over medium heat until tender, about 15 minutes. Arrange them carefully in the prepared dish. Set aside.

In a large bowl, mix cream, salt, pepper, Parmesan, and cheddar. Set aside.

Heat oil in a heavy 4-quart pan over medium setting. Add flour and sauté for 2 to 3 minutes, stirring constantly with a wire whisk. Flour should not brown. Remove from heat. Immediately whisk in milk until flour dissolves completely. Whisk over medium heat to thicken a little bit, about 4 minutes. Pour into cheese mixture. Mix well. Pour over steamed leek slices. Sprinkle with Parmesan and bits of butter or margarine. Bake in the middle of preheated oven until golden, about 40 to 45 minutes. Allow to set at room temperature for 15 minutes or so before serving. Serve warm.

Serves 6 to 8.

*Reserve the green parts of the leeks to use in soups, stews, broths, . . . etc.

Cornmeal au Gratin

Mayi Moulen Ograten
Mais Moulu au Gratin

Estimated time: 1 hour 30 minutes, if meat is prepared one day in advance.

1 tablespoon vegetable oil	1/2 tablespoon granulated garlic
1 cup diced white onion	1/4 cup mayonnaise
1/2 recipe of *Basic Cornmeal Recipe*	1 recipe of *Ground Beef*
1 1/4 cups evaporated milk	1/4 cup freshly grated Parmesan cheese (to
2 cups freshly grated extra sharp cheddar	sprinkle)
cheese	1 tablespoon margarine, cut into small pieces
2 chicken bouillon cubes, crushed	

Preheat oven to 425 degrees Fahrenheit. Grease a 2 1/2 quart x 2 inch deep glass or stoneware baking dish with margarine or vegetable oil. Set aside.

Heat 1 tablespoon vegetable oil over medium setting. Add onion and sauté for 3 to 5 minutes.

In a large bowl, mix cooked cornmeal with milk, cheddar, sautéed onion, bouillon cubes, garlic, and mayonnaise until a homogeneous mixture is formed. Layer the prepared dish in the following order: Spread half of the cornmeal mixture, then the meat, and last the remaining cornmeal mixture. Sprinkle with Parmesan and bits of margarine. Bake in the middle of preheated oven until golden, about 30 minutes. Allow to set at room temperature for 15 minutes or so before serving. Serve warm.

Yields 8 servings.

Chayote Squash au Gratin

Militon Ograten
Mirliton au Gratin

In markets in the United States, the chayote squash are often not fully mature. I use the chayote squash commonly available here; they are close to ripe. If the chayote squash are very ripe, they will yield more mash, thus you will not need as many to make the dish. The gratin made with mature chayote squash tastes undeniably better.

Estimated time: 1 hour 40 minutes.

8 pounds chayote squash
1 tablespoon margarine
1 cup finely diced white onion
1 cup whole milk
2 chicken bouillon cubes, crushed
2 tablespoons mayonnaise
1/2 cup freshly grated Parmesan cheese

1/2 cup freshly grated extra sharp cheddar cheese
salt to taste
3 tablespoons freshly grated Parmesan cheese (to sprinkle)
1 tablespoon margarine, cut into small bits

Cut, peel, and seed squash. Cut each squash into four pieces. Boil in a large pot of water over medium setting until cooked through, 25 minutes. Drain and discard water. Mash squash with a fork, discarding all fiber, if any. Set aside. Squash will release a lot of liquid.

Preheat oven to 425 degrees Fahrenheit. Grease a 2 quart x 2 inch deep glass or stoneware baking dish with margarine or oil. Set aside.

Heat margarine over medium setting. Add onion and sauté for about 3 minutes. Add mashed squash and reduce over medium high heat until all liquid evaporates, about 30 minutes. Add milk and reduce for 15 minutes, stirring constantly. Remove from heat. Add bouillon cubes, mayonnaise, Parmesan cheese, and cheddar cheese. Mix well. Season with salt. Transfer to the prepared dish. Sprinkle with grated Parmesan and bits of margarine. Bake in preheated oven until golden, about 30 minutes. Allow to set at room temperature for 15 minutes or so before serving. Serve warm.

Serves 6.

DESSERTS

Desè
Les Desserts

Butter Cake

Sweets

I love the taste of sweets.
They cheer me up when I am sad,
They cheer me up when I am mad.
No matter what, they taste so good.
I'd make so many if I could.

Rachel Ménager, 11

Butter Cake with Guava Filling

Gato Obè ak Ganiti Gwayav
Gateau au Beurre Fourré à la Goyave

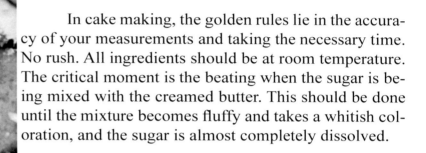

This delicious cake is quite popular in Haiti when it comes time to make a birthday cake or any celebration cake.

In cake making, the golden rules lie in the accuracy of your measurements and taking the necessary time. No rush. All ingredients should be at room temperature. The critical moment is the beating when the sugar is being mixed with the creamed butter. This should be done until the mixture becomes fluffy and takes a whitish coloration, and the sugar is almost completely dissolved.

Once the baking powder is mixed with the batter, work quickly and bake the cake promptly. When it comes to baking cakes, my preference goes to the aluminum pans. They work perfectly well, giving uniform cooking and a cake with an even light golden surface.

An easy and delicious butter cream frosting recipe is also given. If you do not wish to use rum in the filling, plain water will do.

Cake

2 cups (4 sticks) margarine or butter, at room temperature
2 cups sifted granulated sugar
4 large egg yolks
freshly grated zest of one Persian lime
1 teaspoon pure vanilla extract

1/4 teaspoon salt
4 large egg whites
3 cups sifted cake flour (not self rising flour)
1 cup milk
4 teaspoons double-acting baking powder

Preheat oven to 350 degrees Fahrenheit. Grease two 9-inch cake pans. Line the bottom of the pans with wax paper. Grease wax paper. Flour lined pans. Set aside.

Using a hand electric mixer on high speed, beat the butter in a large bowl until creamy. Beat in sugar in four additions. Beat until creamy and sugar is almost completely dissolved. This should take about 15 minutes, and the mixture should be fluffy and yellowish white. Beat in egg yolks, lime zest, vanilla extract, and salt just to blend. You may use a stand mixer to cream the butter-sugar mixture. The time will then be less.

Beat egg whites until firm but not stiff, using an electric hand mixer at high speed. Set aside.

Using a strong wooden spoon, alternately mix the flour and the milk into the butter-sugar mixture, starting and ending with the flour. Mix the baking powder with the last portion of flour before adding it to the batter. Fold in the beaten egg whites. Divide the batter between the prepared cake pans. Bake in the middle of preheated oven for 30 to 35 minutes, until a clean wooden toothpick inserted in the middle of the cake comes out clean. Cool for 15 minutes in the pan before removing from pan. Peel off wax paper and cool completely on a rack before frosting.

Guava Filling

1/2 recipe of *Guava Jelly* (recipe in this book)
2 to 3 tablespoons dark Haitian rum (Rhum Barbancourt)

Mix guava jelly with rum in a heavy 2-quart pan. Stir gently over low heat for 1 minute. Cool completely before using. Filling should be spreadable, but not runny. Add more or less rum, or reduce a little longer if necessary. If you prefer, use water instead of the rum. Yields about 3/4 cup.

Butter Cream Lime Frosting

1 cup unsalted butter or margarine, at room temperature
4 cups sifted powdered sugar
1 to 2 teaspoons pure vanilla extract
1 tablespoon milk

2 tablespoons fresh lime juice
pinch of salt
food coloring, if desired
icing decorations

In a large bowl, mix margarine, sugar, and vanilla extract. Beat with a hand electric mixer at high speed until light and fluffy, about 3 to 4 minutes. Add milk, and beat for 1 to 2 minutes. Add lime juice and salt while beating, 2 minutes. Mix in food coloring if desired. If necessary, cover with plastic wrap, and chill until ready to use. Before using, allow to stand at room temperature until spreadable. Yields about 4 cups.

Assembling the cake

Put one cake layer upside down on the cake platter. Brush lightly with a pastry brush to remove all crumbs. Spread the top (which was the bottom) with the filling. Top with the other layer upside down. Spread frosting on top and sides of cake. Garnish with decorations or as you wish. Cover cake with a cake dome, and store in the refrigerator. To get perfect slices, cut the cake while still cold. Allow the slices to come to room temperature for a few minutes before serving.

Yields 16 to 18 servings.

Variation. Use this *Prune Marmalade* as filling: put 20 pitted prunes in a medium bowl and add hot water to just cover them. Soak for about 2 hours. Then mix in 1/4 cup granulated sugar, 1 teaspoon vanilla extract, 1/2 teaspoon ground cinnamon. Cover and cook over medium-low heat for 15 minutes. Purée in a blender, then reduce marmalade over medium low heat until spreadable.

Orange Cake

Gato Aloranj
Gateau à l'Orange

This is also a delicious and very flavorful cake that follows the same rules as the *Butter Cake with Guava Filling*. There is also a recipe for filling and frosting.

1 1/2 cups (3 sticks) margarine or butter, at room temperature	1/4 teaspoon salt
1 1/2 cups sifted granulated sugar	4 large egg whites
4 large egg yolks	3 cups sifted cake flour (not self rising flour)
freshly grated zest of one orange (about 1 tablespoon)	1 cup strained fresh orange juice
	3 teaspoons double acting baking powder

Preheat oven to 350 degrees Fahrenheit. Grease two 9-inch cake pans. Line the bottom of the pans with wax paper. Grease wax paper. Flour lined pans. Set aside.

With a hand electric mixer on high speed, beat the butter in a large bowl until creamy. Beat in sugar gradually. Beat until creamy and sugar is almost completely dissolved. This should take about 15 minutes, and the mixture should be fluffy and yellowish white. Beat in egg yolks, orange zest, and salt just to blend. You may use a stand mixer to cream the butter-sugar mixture. The time will then be less.

Beat egg whites until firm but not stiff, using an electric hand mixer at high speed. Set aside.

Using a strong wooden spoon, alternately mix the flour and the orange juice into the butter-sugar mixture, starting and ending with the flour. Mix the baking powder with the last portion of flour before adding it to the batter. Fold in the beaten egg whites. Pour the batter into the prepared cake pans. Bake in the middle of preheated oven for 30 to 35 minutes, until a clean wooden toothpick inserted in the middle of the cake comes out clean. Cool for 15 minutes in the pan before removing. Peel off wax paper and cool completely on a rack before frosting.

For filling, you may use strained orange marmalade, or use any filling that suits your taste. For the **frosting**, make *Butter Cream Lime Frosting* using 2 tablespoons of fresh orange juice instead of the lime juice. Then assemble as for *Butter Cake with Guava Filling*, and garnish with orange sections and candied orange peel if desired.

Yields 16 to 18 servings.

Pineapple-Rum Cake with Rum-Raisin Sabayon

Gato Wonm-Anana ak Sòs Wonm-Rezen
Gateau au Rhum et à l'Ananas avec Sabayon au Rhum et aux Raisins

1 cup (2 sticks) margarine or butter, at room temperature
2/3 cup sifted granulated sugar
3 large egg yolks
freshly grated zest of one orange (about 1 tablespoon)
1/4 teaspoon salt

3 large egg whites
1/2 cup strained fresh pineapple juice
1/4 cup dark Haitian rum (Rhum Barbancourt)
2 cups sifted cake flour (not self rising flour)
2 teaspoons double acting baking powder
1 1/2 cups raisins, coated with flour*

Preheat oven to 350 degrees Fahrenheit. Grease and flour a medium tube pan with butter or margarine. Set aside. A 6-cup bundt pan will do.

With a hand electric mixer on high speed, beat the butter in a large bowl until creamy. Gradually beat in sugar until almost completely dissolved. This should take about 15 minutes and the mixture should be fluffy and yellowish white. Beat in egg yolks, orange zest, and salt just to blend. You may use a stand mixer to cream the butter-sugar mixture. The time will then be less.

Beat egg whites until firm but not stiff, using an electric hand mixer at high speed. Set aside.

Mix the pineapple juice with the rum. Using a strong wooden spoon, alternately mix the flour and the juice and rum into the butter-sugar mixture, starting and ending with the flour. Mix the baking powder with the last portion of flour before adding it to the batter. Fold in the beaten egg whites and the raisins. Pour the batter into the prepared pan. Bake in the middle of preheated oven for 40 to 45 minutes, or until a clean wooden toothpick inserted in the middle of the cake comes out clean. Cool for 15 minutes in the pan before removing. Unmold, and cool completely on a rack before slicing.

Quick Rum-Raisin Sabayon.

Make this sauce while the cake is baking.
1/2 cup raisins
3 tablespoons dark Haitian rum (Rhum Barbancourt)
One 4-serving package instant vanilla pudding and pie filling (see below for preparation)

Put the raisins in a small bowl. Sprinkle the rum over them, and allow to soak for at least 20 minutes to soften them, turning occasionally.

Replacing half of the milk with heavy whipping cream, prepare the pudding as directed for pie filling on the package. Then add in the rum-raisin mixture. To serve, spoon the sabayon on top of the cake before slicing or on top of each slice of cake.

*Roll the raisins in flour to just coat them so they do not sink to the bottom of the cake.

Baba au Rhum

Baba Owonm
Baba au Rhum

For the babas

2 tablespoons granulated sugar
2/3 cup lukewarm milk   4 large eggs
two 1/4 ounce packages active dry yeast   1/2 teaspoon salt
10 tablespoons butter or margarine, softened   2 1/2 cups all-purpose flour

For the rum syrup

1 cup granulated sugar
1 cup water
1 cup dark Haitian rum (Rhum Barbancourt)

To finish

1/4 cup pineapple syrup to brush the babas (see *Fresh Fruit Syrup*)

Generously grease eight baba molds, or eight 5-ounce ramekins, with butter or margarine.

Mix sugar and the warm milk in a small bowl, then mix in the yeast. Let stand for 20 minutes. Mix. Then whisk in butter, egg, and salt until well blended.

Put flour in a large mixing bowl. Pour the egg-yeast mixture on it. Mix with a strong wooden spoon until a homogeneous, smooth, and fairly thick batter is formed. Fill the greased molds half-way with the batter, set in a warm place and let rise until doubled, about 1 hour.

Meanwhile, preheat oven to 375 degrees Fahrenheit. Then prepare the rum syrup as follows: Dissolve the sugar completely in the water. Mix in 1/2 cup rum, then boil over medium high heat until a light syrup is formed, about 15 minutes. Remove from heat. Keep hot. Add the remaining rum just before using. This yields about 2 tablespoons of rum per baba.

After the dough has risen for about 1 hour, bake in the middle of preheated oven until the babas are golden, 15 to 17 minutes.

When babas are done, let them stand in the molds for 5 to 10 minutes, then unmold them. Transfer the babas onto a serving plate. Pick them several times with a toothpick or the tines of a fork. Gradually, pour the hot rum syrup over the babas while still hot, so the babas soak up the syrup. Be sure not to overdo it to prevent the babas from falling apart. To finish, brush the babas with the pineapple syrup.

Yields 8 babas.

Chocolate Cake

Gato Ochokola
Gateau au Chocolat

1 cup (2 sticks) butter or margarine, at room temperature
2 cups granulated sugar
2 large eggs
2 teaspoons pure vanilla extract
1/4 teaspoon salt

2 cups sifted cake flour (not self rising flour)
1 teaspoon baking soda
1/2 teaspoon baking powder
1/2 cup unsweetened cocoa powder
1 cup milk

Preheat oven to 350 degrees Fahrenheit. Grease two 9-inch cake pans. Line the bottom of the pans with wax paper. Grease wax paper. Flour lined pans. Set aside.

With a hand electric mixer on high speed in a large bowl, beat the butter, sugar, eggs, vanilla extract, and salt until the mixture becomes fluffy, about 7 minutes. You may use a stand mixer to cream the butter-sugar mixture. The time will then be less.

Mix flour, baking soda, baking powder, and cocoa powder in a bowl. Using a strong wooden spoon, alternately mix the flour mixture and the milk into the butter-sugar mixture, starting and ending with the flour. Pour the batter into the prepared cake pans. Bake in the middle of preheated oven for 30 to 35 minutes, or until a clean wooden toothpick inserted in the middle of the cake comes out clean. Cool for 15 minutes in the pan before removing. Peel off wax paper, and cool completely on a rack before frosting.

Chocolate filling and Frosting

1 cup unsalted butter or margarine, at room temperature
4 cups sifted powdered sugar
1 to 2 teaspoons pure vanilla extract

3 tablespoons milk
1/2 cup unsweetened cocoa powder
pinch of salt

In a large bowl, mix margarine, sugar, and vanilla extract. Beat with a hand electric mixer at high speed until light and fluffy, about 3 to 4 minutes. Add milk, and beat for 1 to 2 minutes. Add cocoa powder and salt, beating for 2 minutes. If necessary, cover with plastic wrap, and chill until ready to use. Bring to a spreadable consistency at room temperature before using.

Yields about 4 cups.

Assembling the cake

Put one cake layer upside down on the cake platter. Brush lightly with a pastry brush to remove small particles. Spread the top (which was the bottom) with part of the frosting. Top with the other cake upside down. Spread frosting on top and sides of cake. Garnish as desired. Cover with cake dome, and store in the refrigerator. Let stand at room temperature for 20 to 30 minutes before serving.

Yields 16 servings.

Christmas Log

Gato Nwèl
Buche de Noël

A Christmas favorite of all time, this cake is impressive once garnished. Despite its sophisticated appearance, it is very easy to make. The filling must be prepared in advance. It may be made one day ahead and stored in the refrigerator. You may use the frosting to fill the cake as well.

Filling
1/2 cup heavy whipping cream
1/2 recipe of *Pastry Cream*, flavored with 4 tablespoons unswetened cocoa powder and one tablespoon dark Haitian rum (Rhum Barbancourt).

Using an electric hand mixer at medium speed, whip the cream until stiff peaks form. Fold the whipped cream into the *Pastry Cream*. Refrigerate until ready to use. This can be prepared one day ahead. See *Pastry Cream* recipe in the *Bread and Pastry* chapter.

Cake.

1 1/2 cups sifted cake flour (not self rising flour)	2 tablespoons dark Haitian rum (Rhum Barbancourt)
2 teaspoons double acting baking powder	1 teaspoon pure vanilla extract
1/4 teaspoon salt	1/2 cup butter or margarine, at room temperature
6 large egg yolks	6 large egg whites
2/3 cup sifted granulated sugar	

Preheat oven to 350 degrees Fahrenheit. Grease a 17 x 11-inch jelly roll pan. Line the bottom of the pan with wax paper. Grease and flour the lined pan. Set aside.

Mix flour, baking powder, and salt in a large bowl. Set aside.

With a hand electric mixer on high speed, beat the egg yolks until creamy. Gradually beat in sugar. Then beat in rum, vanilla extract, and butter until the batter becomes creamy. Gradually beat in the flour mixture.

Beat egg whites until firm but not stiff, using an electric hand mixer at high speed. Add these to the batter, and mix thoroughly. Transfer the batter into the prepared pan and bake in the middle of the preheated oven for 10 to 12 minutes. A clean wooden toothpick inserted in the middle of the cake should come out clean. Ummold immediately on a slightly damp kitchen towel.

Unpeel the wax paper, and quickly spread 1/2 cup of filling over the cake. Immediately, using the towel as a guide, roll up the cake tightly over the filling as for a jelly roll, starting with the shorter side. Transfer the cake onto a platter, seam side down. Refrigerate to cool down completely.

Mocha Frosting

1/2 cup butter or margarine, at room temperature
2 cups powdered sugar
1/2 teaspoon pure vanilla extract
1/2 tablespoon dark Haitian rum
(Rhum Barbancourt)

1 tablespoon strong brewed coffee
1/4 cup unsweetened cocoa powder
pinch of salt

In a large bowl, mix butter, sugar, and vanilla extract. Beat with an electric mixer at high speed until light and fluffy, about 3 to 4 minutes. Add rum and coffee, and beat for 1 to 2 minutes. Add cocoa powder and salt, beating for 2 minutes. This can be used as filling as well.

Finishing the cake

Carefully unroll the cake just enough to be able to work with it. Do not unroll it all the way; the cake should somewhat retain it shape. Spread the remaining filling, and then roll up the cake over the filling to recreate the log. Transfer the cake to a serving platter seam side down.

Cut off both ends of the rolled cake. If you wish to make a "branch", cut one of the ends a little longer and fix it to the side of the cake with a small amount of frosting.

Spread the frosting on the rolled cake, top and sides. Use the tip of a clean toothpick to draw lines on it, mimicking the bark of a tree. Garnish with Christmas cake decorations, and red-coated chocolate candies or candied cherries. Cover with a cake dome, and store in the refrigerator. Let stand at room temperature for 20 minutes before serving.

Serves 10 to 12.

Gingerbread

Bonbon Siwo II
Pain d'Epices à la Mélasse

Bonbon Siwo is the common Haitian snack. It is made by practically every bakery in the country. The typical ingredient is the molasses. The recipe can vary slightly from bakery to bakery. *Bonbon Siwo* is served warm or at room temperature, with or without a glass of milk. Either way, it is very enjoyable.

Estimated time: 1 hour 15 minutes.

3 1/2 cups sifted all purpose flour
2 teaspoons double acting baking powder
1 teaspoon baking soda
1/2 cup vegetable shortening
1/2 cup dark brown sugar
1 cup dark unsulphured molasses

1/2 teaspoon salt
2 teaspons ground cinnamon
1 teaspon ground ginger
1 cup milk
2 large eggs, beaten just to mix

Preheat oven to 325 degrees Fahrenheit. Grease and flour a 11x 7-inch or a 9 x 9- inch brownie pan.

Mix flour with baking powder and baking soda. Set aside. Cream shortening with brown sugar in a large bowl. Mix in molasses, salt, cinnamon, and ginger until creamy. Set aside.

Bring milk to a boil, then pour it into the creamed shortening mixture. Mix. Whisk in the flour mixture, then the eggs. Transfer to the prepared brownie pan. Bake in the center of the preheated oven until a clean wooden toothpick inserted in the middle of the cake comes out clean, about 45 to 50 minutes. Cool for 10 minutes in the pan, then unmold. Cool on a rack. Cut into lozenges or square shapes. Serve warm or at room temperature.

Yields about 18 to 20 pieces.

Sugar Cookies

Bonbon Sik
Sablés

This cookie dough is perfect for small cookies (about 2 inches in diameter and 1/6 inch thick before baking). The dough will be soft. You will need to refrigerate it for about 20 minutes, or to put it in the freezer for 5 to 10 minutes, to firm it. This will make it easier to handle.

Estimated time: 50 minutes.

1 1/2 cups all purpose flour
1 teaspoon baking powder
1/4 teaspon salt
1/2 cup (1 stick) butter or margarine
1/2 cup granulated sugar
1/2 teaspoon pure vanilla extract
1 egg yolk, slightly beaten
2 tablespoons milk

Preheat oven to 375 degrees Fahrenheit. Have a round 2-inch cookie cutter* and 2 large ungreased cookie sheets on hand.

Mix flour with baking powder, and salt. Set aside.

Cream butter in a large mixing bowl with a strong wooden spoon. Mix in sugar and vanilla extract. Mix in egg yolk, then flour mixture alternately with milk. Do not overwork the dough because it will toughen. Form a ball with the cookie dough. Then flatten it on a lightly floured surface. Place in a small tray, cover with a piece of wax paper, and refrigerate for 20 minutes. Then roll the flattened dough ball into a 1/6-inch thick circle with a lightly floured rolling pin. Cut with the cookie cutter. Using a spatula, carefully transfer the cookies onto the ungreased cookie sheet, 1/2 inch apart. Bake in the middle of preheated oven until slightly golden, about 10 minutes. Cool on the cookie sheet for 3 minutes, then transfer to a rack to cool completely. This recipe can be doubled.

Yields about 30 to 35 small cookies.

*Any shape cookie cutter can be used.

Coconut Cookies

Kokonèt
Petits Gateaux à la Noix de Coco

The Haitian Creole word *kokonèt* seems to come from the English word "coconut." These cookies are light and delicious.

Estimated time: 30 minutes.

2 cups all-purpose flour
1 1/2 teaspoons double acting baking powder
1/4 teaspoon salt
1/2 cup (1 stick) butter or margarine, at room temperature
3/4 cup granulated sugar

1 large egg, slightly beaten
1/4 cup fresh coconut milk, or canned coconut milk
1/2 teaspoon pure vanilla extract
2 1/2 cups packed freshly grated coconut*

Preheat oven to 350 degrees Fahrenheit. Have a large ungreased cookie sheet on hand.

Mix flour with baking powder, and salt. Set aside.

Cream butter in a large mixing bowl with a strong wooden spoon. Mix in sugar. Mix in egg, milk, vanilla extract, and grated coconut, then mix in flour mixture. Using two greased tablespoons, drop 3-inch-wide mounds of cookie dough on the cookie sheet, 1 inch apart. Flatten them slightly with the back of a spoon. Bake in the upper third of the preheated oven until slightly golden, about 20 to 25 minutes. Cool on the cookie sheet for 3 minutes, then transfer to a rack to cool completely.

Yields about 25 cookies.

Variation

*Be sure that coconut is fresh and does not taste rancid. Before grating the coconut, use a vegetable peeler to remove the thin brown layer that coats it. Canned coconut milk is available in Caribbean, Latin-American, and Asian groceries, and the ethnic section of most supermarkets and groceries.

The following recipe is a variation made with packaged coconut flakes.

1 1/2 cups all-purpose flour
1 1/2 teaspoon double acting baking powder
1/4 teaspoon salt
1/2 cup (1 stick) butter or margarine, at room temperature
1/2 cup granulated sugar

1 large egg, beaten just to mix
3 tablespoons fresh coconut milk or canned coconut milk
1/2 teaspon pure vanilla extract
3 cups package sweetened coconut flakes

Proceed as above then bake in the middle of preheated oven until slightly golden, about 20 minutes. Cool on the cookie sheet for 3 minutes, then transfer to a rack to cool completely.

Moustache (Mousach, Bonbon Amidon)

These cookies are heavenly! They melt in the mouth and are very delicious. Tapioca flour, also called tapioca starch, is the dominant ingredient in *Moustache*. In Haiti, tapioca flour is made by artisans, thus it is still a homemade product with a pure and authentic taste. It is sometimes available at some Haitian groceries, but it is rather difficult to find a good quality product in the U.S.A.

The texture of these cookies is by far finer than the texture of the ones we make in Haiti, and their taste is different. This is because the tapioca flour in the American market is very refined, losing the true taste of the flour. The following recipe gives thus a finer, rather different, but very delicious adaptation of our *Bonbon Amidon*.

Estimated time: 30 minutes.

3/4 cup powdered sugar
1 cup butter or margarine (2 sticks), softened
1/4 teaspoon salt
1 teaspoon pure vanilla extract
1 1/2 cups all-purpose flour
1 1/2 cups tapioca flour*
2 tablespoons water, plus a few more drops if needed

Preheat oven to 350 degrees Fahrenheit. Have a large ungreased cookie sheet on hand.

In a large bowl, using a wooden spoon, mix sugar, butter, salt, and vanilla extract until creamy, 1 to 2 minutes. Mix in flour and tapioca gradually until well combined, transferring the mixture to a smooth surface as soon as it becomes difficult to mix in the bowl. The mixture should resemble a coarse meal. Add water and work with tips of fingers until a smooth dough is formed, about 1 minute. Do not overwork the dough because it will toughen. Form a ball with the dough. Flatten it slightly with the palm of your hand on a lightly floured surface. Roll out the flattened dough with a lightly floured rolling pin into a 1/2 inch thick circle. Cut round shapes with a 2-inch cookie cutter. Using a spatula, carefully transfer cookies onto the ungreased cookie sheet, 1 inch apart. Bake in the middle of preheated oven until slightly golden, about 20 minutes.

Yields 24 cookies.

*Tapioca flour is also called tapioca starch. It is found in the baking section of most supermarkets.

Meringue Sighs

Soupi
Soupirs

Airy, delicious, and easy to make, these meringues will allow you to use any leftover egg whites you may have in your refrigerator, and will fill an empty spot on your dessert table. We always make them pastel. For this recipe, five to six drops of food coloring should be enough if you wish to obtain delicate and ethereal colors. After cooling, *Meringues Sighs* can be dipped in melted chocolate.

Estimated time: 2 hours (including 1 hour 30 minutes baking).

3 large egg whites
pinch of salt
1/4 teaspoon cream of tartar
3/4 cup granulated sugar
1 teaspoon pure vanilla extract
5 to 6 drops of food coloring (a color of your choice)

a large pastry bag, or a large decorating syringe fitted with a large round plain tip (nozzle), or a large round indented tip (1-inch opening will do)

Line a large baking sheet with foil. Preheat oven to 200 degrees Fahrenheit.

Using an electric mixer at high speed, beat egg whites with salt in a large bowl until soft peaks are formed. Beat in cream of tartar until stiff, then gradually beat in sugar. Beat until stiff and glossy peaks are formed. Mix in vanilla extract, and food coloring while beating.

Fill the pastry bag with meringue. Pipe meringue in mounds about 1 1/2-inches in diameter, onto the prepared baking sheet. Bake them in the upper third of preheated oven for 1 hour 30 minutes. Turn oven off and let them stand in oven for one additional hour. Cool completely on a rack. Store meringues in wax bags and keep in airtight container for one week. The recipe can be doubled.

Yields 25 to 30 meringues.

Sweet Potato Pudding I

Pudding de Patate I
Pen Patat I

This sweet dessert, made with dry-flesh sweet potatoes, is very simple, but yet delicious. It can be made days ahead. Be sure to use the dry-flesh sweet potatoes. If coconut milk is used, make sure it is fresh and does not taste rancid.

Estimated active time: 1 hour. Steaming time: 3 hours.

9 cups grated dry-flesh sweet potatoes*
(about 6 pounds of potatoes)
1 1/2 cups whole milk
two 12-ounce cans evaporated milk (3 cups)
or one 12-ounce can evaporated milk plus
1 1/2 cups fresh coconut milk**
1 1/2 teaspoons ground cinnamon
1/2 teaspoon ground nutmeg

1/4 teaspoon salt
1 cup light brown sugar
1 tablespoon pure vanilla extract
1 cup raisins
3 tablespoons mild unsulphured molasses
1 well-ripened banana, finely mashed (optional)
3 tablespoons margarine

Generously grease a 9 x 5-inch loaf pan and set aside.

In a large heavy pan, mix grated potatoes with whole milk and evaporated milk. Mix in cinnamon, nutmeg, and salt, then bring to a boil over medium heat. Cook uncovered for 15 to 20 minutes, scraping bottom of the pan often to prevent potatoes from sticking.

Preheat oven to 400 degrees Fahrenheit.

Add sugar, vanilla, raisins, molasses, banana (if using), and margarine to potato mixture. Continue to cook uncovered over medium heat for about 5 additional minutes, scraping bottom of the pan almost constantly. Mixture should be very thick. Pour in the prepared pan. Cover the pan with aluminum foil, and place it in a large baking dish. Put hot water in the baking dish halfway to the top of the pan and bake in the middle of preheated oven for three hours. Check water level every 30 minutes, and add hot water to the baking dish when necessary. Cool, loosely covered, in the pan at room temperature. Refrigerate to cool completely. To unmold, gently shake the pan to loosen the dessert, and overturn onto a serving dish. *Pen Patat* can be made in a 6-cup pudding mold, or individually in ramekins.

Yields 8 to 10 servings.

*Read about sweet potatoes in the Glossary of this book.

**To make fresh coconut milk for *Sweet Potato Pudding*, triple the recipe given in *Sweet Potato Cake*. You may also use 1 1/2 cups canned coconut milk. Canned coconut milk is available in Caribbean, Latin-American, and Asian markets and groceries, and in some supermarkets.

Sweet Potato Pudding II

Pen Patat II
Puddding de Patate II

This is a modified version of the *Pen patat* recipe, made with the moist variety of sweet potatoes, called yams in the U. S.A. By making a few modifications to the recipe, I gave it the "body" it was lacking, making it possible to have this dessert even when the moist sweet potatoes are the only ones available. If coconut milk is used, make sure it is fresh and does not taste rancid.

Estimated active time: 1 hour 30 minutes. Steaming time: 3 hours.

8 cups grated "dark orange skinned" sweet potatoes* (about 5 pounds)
1 1/2 teaspoons ground cinnamon
1/2 teaspoon ground nutmeg
1/4 teaspoon salt
one 12-ounce can evaporated milk, or 1 cup evaporated plus 1/2 cup fresh coconut milk**
1 cup light brown sugar
1/2 cup granulated sugar
1 tablespoon pure vanilla extract
1 cup raisins
1 tablespoon mild unsulphured molasses
1 well-ripened banana, finely mashed (optional)
3 tablespoons margarine
1 cup *Fresh Bread Crumbs*

Generously grease a 9- x 5-inch loaf pan, and set aside.

Mix grated sweet potatoes with cinnamon, nutmeg, and salt in a heavy pan. Cook covered over medium heat for about 30 minutes, scraping the bottom of the pan often to prevent potatoes from sticking to the pan. Then mix in milk, brown sugar, granulated sugar, vanilla extract, raisins, molasses, banana (if using), and margarine. Combine well. Cook uncovered over medium heat for 30 additional minutes, scraping the bottom of the pan almost constantly.

Meanwhile, preheat oven to 400 degrees Fahrenheit.

Remove potato mixture from heat. Add bread crumbs to potato mixture. Combine well. Pour into the prepared pan. Cover the pan with aluminum foil, and place it in a large baking dish. Put hot water in the baking dish halfway to the top of the pan. Bake in the middle of preheated oven for about 3 hours. Check water level every 30 minutes, and add hot water to the baking dish when necessary. Cool, loosely covered, in the pan at room temperature. Refrigerate to cool completely. To unmold, gently shake the pan to loosen the dessert, and turn onto a serving dish. It can also be made in a 6-cup pudding mold, or individually in ramekins.

Yields 8 to 10 servings.

*Read about sweet potatoes in the Glossary of this book.

**To make fresh coconut milk for *Sweet Potato Pudding II*, use the recipe in *Sweet Potato Cake I*. You may also use 1/2 cup canned coconut milk. Canned coconut milk is available in Caribbean, Latin-American, and Asian groceries, and the ethnic section of most supermarkets.

Sweet Potato Cake I

Gato Patat I
Gateau de Patate I

Sweet Potato Cake is made with mashed boiled sweet potatoes in contrast to *Sweet Potato Pudding,* which is made with grated raw sweet potatoes. This cake is usually made with dry-flesh sweet potatoes. Let the cake cool completely before serving. It is best after cooling for at least 12 hours in the refrigerator. The cake is then set, and the flavors are nicely blended.

Estimated time: 1 hour 45 minutes.

2 pounds sweet potatoes* (yields about 3 cups mashed sweet potatoes)
2 teaspoons double acting baking powder
1/2 teaspoon salt
1 teaspoon ground cinnamon
1 teaspoon ground nutmeg
1 cup light brown sugar

1/2 cup vegetable oil
2 large eggs, lightly beaten
1 teaspoon pure vanilla extract
1 cup raisins
1/2 cup evaporated milk or fresh coconut milk* (or 1/2 cup canned coconut milk)

Lightly grease and flour a 9x 9x 2-inch cake pan. Bring a large pot of unsalted water to a boil over medium high heat. Add potatoes, cover, and boil potatoes until cooked through, about 30 minutes.

Preheat oven to 350 degrees Fahrenheit.

Meanwhile, mix baking powder, salt, cinnamon, and nutmeg in a small bowl. Set aside.

In a large bowl, mix sugar with oil until well blended. With a strong wooden spoon, stir in beaten eggs until creamy, 2 to 3 minutes. Mix in vanilla extract. Set aside.

Finely mash cooked potatoes with a fork, potato ricer, or food mill. Add to egg mixture. Mix in coconut milk and raisins until creamy and homogeneous. Then mix in baking powder mixture. Pour into the prepared cake pan. Bake in the middle of the preheated oven for 1 hour. A thin knife inserted in the middle of the cake will remove a few small moist bits. Cool completely in the refrigerator before serving. Serve cold or at room temperature.

Serves 8.

*Read about sweet potatoes in the glossary of this book.

**To make fresh coconut milk for *Sweet Potato Cake*, put 1/2 cup thinly chopped fresh coconut in a blender with 1/2 cup hot milk. Process on high speed for 2 minutes. Coconut will look as if it has been grated. Press coconut through a fine strainer to collect the milk. Strain again. Make sure that the coconut is fresh and does not taste rancid. Canned coconut milk is available in Caribbean, Latin-American, and Asian markets and groceries, and most supermarkets.

Sweet Potato Cake II

Gato Patat II
Gateau de Patate II

This *Sweet Potato Cake* is a dense and smooth pudding. Its texture is like that of *Sweet Potato Pudding*, but with less moisture. I made it with the moist variety of sweet potatoes. It is best after cooling for at least twelve hours in the refrigerator. The cake is then set, and the flavors are nicely blended. If you are using fresh coconut, make sure that it is fresh and does not taste rancid. To add more interest to the cake, replace 1/4 cup milk with the same amount of Haitian rum.

Estimated time: 2 hours 45 minutes (including 2 hours 30 minutes of cooking and baking).

2 1/2 pounds (3 medium) dark orange sweet potatoes* (yields about 4 cups mashed potatoes)
1 1/2 cups sifted all-purpose flour
1/2 teaspoon salt
1 teaspoon ground cinnamon
1 teaspoon ground nutmeg
4 teaspoons double acting baking powder

2 cups brown sugar
1/2 cup vegetable oil
2 large eggs, lightly beaten
2 teaspoons pure vanilla extract
1 1/2 cups raisins
1 cup fresh coconut milk**, or 1 cup canned coconut milk, or 1 cup evaporated milk

Lightly grease and flour a 13x 9x 2-inch cake pan. Bring a large pot of unsalted water to a boil. Add potatoes, cover, and boil until cooked through, about 45 to 50 minutes. Cool until they are easy to handle and then peel and mash them.

Preheat oven to 350 degrees Fahrenheit.

Mix flour, salt, cinnamon, nutmeg, and baking powder in a medium bowl. Set aside.

In a large bowl, mix sugar with oil until well blended. With a strong wooden spoon, stir in beaten eggs until creamy, 1 to 2 minutes. Mix in vanilla extract, mashed potatoes, raisins, and milk. Then gradually stir in flour mixture until the batter becomes smooth and homogeneous. Pour into the prepared cake pan. Bake in the middle of the preheated oven for 1 hour and 45 minutes. A fine knife inserted in the middle of the cake will remove a few small moist bits. Cool completely in the refrigerator before serving. Serve cold or at room temperature.

Serves 12.

*Read about sweet potatoes in the Glossary of this book.

**To make fresh coconut milk for *Sweet Potato Cake II*, put 1 cup of finely chopped fresh coconut flesh in a blender with 1 cup of hot milk. Process on high speed for 2 minutes. Coconut will look as if it has been grated. Press coconut through a fine strainer to collect the milk. Strain again.

Cornmeal Pudding

Pen Mayi
Pudding de Mais Moulu

This recipe is a sweet version of our traditional pudding called *doukounou* in Haitian Creole. *Doukounou* is neither sweet nor savory. Thus, it is eaten with a sweet sauce or a savory one. Traditionally, each *doukounou*, made with a small portion of a thick mixture of cornmeal, is wrapped in fresh banana leaves, then slowly steamed over a stack of fresh banana leaves. Cornmeal Pudding can be made one day ahead, and stored in the refrigerator. To serve, bring to room temperature.

Preparation: about 1 hour. Steaming time: 2 hours.

1 cup medium yellow cornmeal (not cornmeal flour)
2 cups whole milk
2 cups evaporated milk
1 cup fresh coconut milk*
1 cup granulated sugar

1/4 teaspoon ground cinnamon
1 cup raisins
1 cup whipping cream
1 teaspoon pure vanilla extract
1 large egg, beaten

Generously grease with margarine the inset portion of a 6-cup pudding mold**. Set aside.

Mix cornmeal with whole milk and evaporated milk, coconut milk, sugar, cinnamon, and raisins in a heavy pan. Cook over medium setting, beating constantly with a wooden spoon until thick, about 10 minutes. Reduce heat to medium low, cover tightly and cook for about 30 minutes.

Remove from heat, then add cream and vanilla extract, beating for 1 minute. Cool for 15 to 20 minutes, then mix in beaten egg. Transfer to prepared pudding mold, and steam over medium low heat for 2 hours, adding boiling water whenever necessary. Allow pudding to cool for 2 hours at least before unmolding. Serve at room temperature with *Vanilla-Cinnamon Sauce****. *Pen Mayi* can be steamed in a 9-x 5-inch loaf pan, or individually in ramekins.

Serves 6.

*To make fresh coconut milk for *Pen Mayi*, put 1 cup of finely chopped fresh coconut in a blender with 1 cup of hot milk. Process on high speed for 2 minutes. Coconut will look as if it has been grated. Press coconut through a fine strainer to collect the milk. Strain again. It might yield a little more than 1 cup, but it will not make any difference. You can also grate coconut with a fine grater. Then thoroughly mix in 1 cup of hot milk, and press through a fines trainer as above. Make sure that the coconut is fresh and does not taste rancid.

**Read note about pudding molds in the Glossary of this book.

*** The recipe for this sauce is given in *Bread Pudding with Vanilla-Cinnamon Sauce*.

Cassava Bread Pudding with Vanilla-Cinnamon Sauce

Poudin Kasav ak Siwo Vaniy ak Kanel
Pudding de Cassave avec Sauce à la Vanille et à la Canelle

This recipe is a revised version of our traditional pudding, called *Bonbon Makoue* in Haitian Creole. *Bonbon Makoue*, made with small portions of a cassava mixture, is steamed in fresh banana leaves just like *doukounou* (Read the Introduction to *Cornmeal Pudding*).

Make this delicious dessert at least one day ahead, and store it in the refrigerator. This will allow the flavors to blend nicely, and also allow you to be prepared ahead of time. To serve, bring to room temperature.

Estimated time: 5 hours 30 minutes (including 2 hours soaking, and 3 hours steaming).

3 cups cassava bread pieces* (break cassava bread into small pieces)
two 12-ounces cans evaporated milk
1 1/2 cups whole milk
1/4 cup butter or margarine, melted
1/2 cup granulated sugar
3/4 teaspoon salt

1/2 teaspoon ground cinnamon
1/2 teaspoon freshly grated lime zest
1 tablespoon pure vanilla extract
1 cup raisins
2 eggs, slightly beaten
1/4 cup dark Haitian rum (Rhum Barbancourt)

Generously coat the inset portion of a 6-cup pudding mold** with margarine. Set aside.

In a large bowl, mix cassava bread pieces with evaporated milk and whole milk. Let soak for

2 hours. Then mash with a fork to form a sticky paste (the paste will have tiny bits of soaked cassava). Mix in remaining ingredients until homogeneous. Pour mixture in prepared pan, and steam over medium-low heat for 3 hours, adding boiling water whenever necessary. Uncover and cool in the pan for at least 2 hours before unmolding. To unmold, run a knife between the pudding and the pan, then between the pudding and the tube to ease the unmolding. Turn pan upside down onto a serving plate, and remove the pan. Store pudding covered in the refrigerator. Bring to room temperature before serving. Serve with *Vanilla-Cinnamon Sauce****.

Serves 6.

*Kasav, very popular in Haiti, is the Creole name for a dry and flat preparation made with yucca (cassava), called cassava bread and yucca bread. It is available in Caribbean and Latin-American groceries and markets.

**Read note about pudding molds in the Glossary of this book.

***Prepare the sauce while pudding is steaming. The recipe for the sauce is given in this book in *Bread Pudding with Vanilla-Cinnamon Sauce.*

Bread Pudding with Vanilla-Cinnamon Sauce

Poudin Pen ak Siwo Vaniy ak Kanèl

Pudding de Pain avec Sauce à la Vanille et à la Canelle

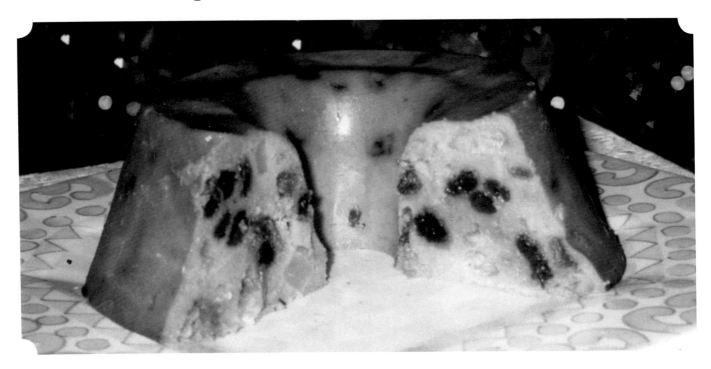

Make this dessert and sauce at least one day ahead, and store it in the refrigerator. This will allow the flavors to blend nicely, and also allow you to be prepared ahead of time. To serve, bring to room temperature. This is my revised version of my mother's recipe.

Estimated time: 2 hours 50 minutes (including 2 hours 30 minutes for steaming)

For pudding:

2 cups *Fresh Bread Crumbs**
one 12-ounce can evaporated milk
one 15-ounce can fruit cocktail in heavy syrup
1 tablespoon pure vanilla extract
2 large eggs, slightly beaten
1/2 cup light brown sugar

1/2 teaspoon ground cinnamon
3/4 cup raisins
1/4 cup (1/2 stick) margarine, melted
1/4 teaspoon salt, or to taste
1/4 cup dark Haitian rum (Rhum Barbancourt)

For vanilla-cinnamon sauce:

1 cup light brown sugar
1 cup water
1/4 cup raisins
2 teaspoons fresh lime juice

1/2 teaspoon ground cinnamon
1 tablespoon pure vanilla extract
1/4 cup dry vermouth

Generously coat the inset portion of a 6-cup pudding mold** with margarine. Set aside.

Pudding

In a large bowl, combine the pudding ingredients until the mixture becomes homogeneous. Pour the mixture into the prepared pan, and steam over medium-low heat for 2 hours and 30 minutes, adding boiling water whenever necessary. Uncover, and cool in the pan for at least 45 minutes before unmolding. To ease unmolding, run a knife between the pudding and the pan, then between the pudding and the tube. Overturn the pan onto a serving plate, shake gently, and remove the pan. Store the pudding covered in the refrigerator. Bring to room temperature before serving. Serve with the sauce.

Sauce

Mix sugar, water, raisins, lime juice, and cinnamon in a heavy 2-quart pan. Bring to a boil. Reduce heat to medium, and boil undisturbed (do not stir or whisk) and uncovered for about 8 to 10 minutes. Remove from heat and add vanilla extract and vermouth. Cool to room temperature before serving. This sauce can be prepared in advance and kept in the refrigerator. Bring to room temperature before serving.

Yields 6 servings.

*See how to make fresh bread crumbs in the *Bread and Pastry* chapter.

**Read note about pudding molds in the Glossary of this book.

Rum Caramel Custard

Flan
Crème Renversée Parfumée au Rhum

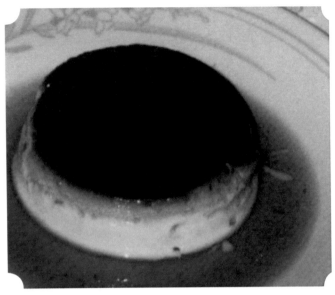

This simple yet elegant and delicious dessert is easily made. All the required ingredients are very common in refrigerators and pantries. This makes it the kind of dessert to think about when you have unexpected guests. You will not have to run to the grocery to buy ingredients.

Be sure to mix milk and eggs delicately otherwise the mixture will bubble and ruin the texture of the custard. Overbaking will also destroy the smooth texture of the custard. Rum can be omitted if the dessert is being made for children. To prevent the dessert from collapsing in the center, it is best to use individual molds, or a pudding mold as described in this book.

Estimated time: 1 hour 30 minutes.

Caramel

1 cup granulated sugar
1/4 cup water
a 1 1/2-quart soufflé mold, or six 8-ounce ramekins*

Custard

3 cups (two 12-ounce cans) evaporated milk
1/2 cup whole milk
3 large eggs
4 large egg yolks
3/4 cup granulated sugar

1 teaspoon pure vanilla extract
2 to 3 tablespoons dark Haitian rum (Rhum Barbancourt)
a large baking dish (a 15 x 10 x 2-inch baking dish will do)

Preheat oven to 350 degrees Fahrenheit.

Caramel

Mix sugar with water in a heavy 2-quart saucepan. Stir over medium setting until sugar is completely dissolved. It takes about 2 to 3 minutes for the sugar to dissolve. Once the sugar is dissolved, stop stirring. Continue to boil until a syrup forms and is a beautiful golden color, about 8 to 10 minutes. Remove from heat. Caramel will continue to darken. Holding mold with kitchen cloths, pour caramel immediately into the mold (or into the ramekins). Swirl caramel all around mold halfway to the top until caramel hardens. Set aside.

Custard

Heat milk in a heavy 2-quart pan over medium setting. As soon as the milk starts bubbling, remove it from heat. Cover and set aside.

Put egg yolks and eggs in a large bowl. Add sugar and whisk gently until creamy. Do not beat. Pour hot milk in a small stream over egg mixture while whisking gently. Do not beat. Add vanilla extract and rum. Strain through a fine strainer. Pour mixture into the prepared mold. Cover with aluminum foil, and put mold in the baking dish. Fill baking dish with very hot water half way to the top of the mold. Bake in the middle of the preheated oven for 1 hour, or until the center is set. Do not overbake. A knife inserted 1/4 of the way into the center of the custard should leave a fine slit when the dessert is done. The center will jiggle slightly when the mold is gently shaken. Chill completely in the refrigerator before unmolding. To unmold, run a knife between the custard and the mold. Cover the mold with a serving dish and turn upside down. Remove the mold.

Serves 6.

*You may also use a 6-cup pudding mold. In this case, there is no need to use a baking dish. Read about pudding molds in the Glossary of this book.

Ramekin Coated with Caramel

Coconut Pudding

Blan Manje I
Blanc-Manger au Coco I

This is one of the most popular and delicious desserts in Haiti. The coconut must be very fresh. Otherwise, the dessert will taste rancid. Crack the coconut one day ahead to avoid a bad surprise. Read *About Coconut* in *The Cook's Techniques* chapter.

1 cup chilled evaporated milk
3 tablespoons unflavored gelatin
1 cup boiling evaporated milk
2 tablespoons granulated sugar
2 1/2 cups fresh coconut milk*, or 2 1/2 cups canned coconut milk** (slightly less than two 14-ounce cans)

one 14-ounce can condensed milk
1 teaspoon pure vanilla extract
1/8 teaspoon salt
two 15-ounce cans fruit cocktail in heavy syrup

Pour chilled milk into a heavy 2-quart saucepan. Sprinkle gelatin over it. Let stand for 2 minutes. Stir in boiling milk and sugar. Then simmer over medium-to-medium-low heat, stirring constantly until gelatin is completely dissolved, about 3 minutes. Remove from heat, then mix in coconut milk, condensed milk, vanilla extract, salt, and fruit cocktail. Transfer into a serving bowl, and chill until set and cold, at least 6 hours. You may make *Coconut Pudding* one day ahead. Serve cold.

Serves 6 to 8.

*To make fresh coconut milk for *Coconut Pudding*, remove the thin brown skin that covers the coconut flesh with a vegetable peeler or a sharp knife, then chop coconut finely to obtain 2 1/2 cups. Put the chopped fresh coconut in a blender with 2 1/2 cups of hot milk. Process on high speed for 2 minutes. Coconut will look as if it has been grated. Press coconut through a fine strainer to collect the milk. Strain again. It might yield a little more than 2 1/2 cups, but it will not make any difference. You can also grate coconut with a fine grater. Then thoroughly mix in 2 1/2 cups of hot milk, and press through a fine strainer as above.

**Canned coconut milk is available in Caribbean, Latin-American, and Asian markets and groceries, and the ethnic section of most supermarkets.

Coconut and Cream Pudding

Blan Manje II
Blanc-Manger au Coco II

This is a sophisticated and more delicious *Blanc-Manger* recipe. You may serve it with a smooth fruit purée, if you wish. The coconut must be very fresh. Otherwise, the dessert will taste rancid. Read *About Coconut* in *The Cook's Techniques* chapter.

two 15-ounce cans fruit cocktail in heavy syrup, chilled
1/4 cup cornstarch
1/2 cup granulated sugar
1/4 teaspoon salt
1 cup evaporated milk
1 cup fresh coconut milk*, or 1 cup canned coconut milk**

1/2 tablespoon unflavored gelatin
1/2 teaspoon pure vanilla extract
1 cup heavy whipping cream (keep refrigerated until ready to use)
1/4 cup powdered sugar

Chill a 2-quart bowl, a spatula, and the beaters of an electric hand mixer in the freezer. Strain fruit cocktail and reserve the syrup. Keep the fruit refrigerated until ready to use.

Mix cornstarch, sugar, and salt in a heavy 3-quart pan. Stir in milk, coconut milk, syrup from the fruit cocktail, and gelatin. Whisk continuously over medium heat until soft and silky, 5 to 6 minutes. Remove from heat. Mix in vanilla extract. Transfer to a large heat-resistant bowl, cover with plastic wrap, and refrigerate until completely cold, about 1 hour.

Put the cream in the chilled bowl, and whip with an electric hand mixer at medium speed until stiff peaks are formed, adding the powdered sugar gradually. With the same mixer at high speed, beat the cornstarch preparation until soft, then beat in the whipped cream until the mixture becomes soft and creamy. With the chilled spatula, fold in the fruit cocktail. Transfer to a serving dish. Cover with plastic wrap and refrigerate until ready to serve.

Serves 6.

*To make fresh coconut milk for *Coconut and Cream Pudding*, remove the thin brown skin that covers the coconut with a vegetable peeler or a sharp knife, then chop coconut finely to obtain 1 cup. Put the chopped fresh coconut in a blender with 1 cup of hot milk. Process on high speed for 2 minutes. Coconut will look as if it has been grated. Press coconut through a fine strainer to collect milk. Strain again. It might yield a little more than 1 cup, but it will not make any difference. You can also grate coconut with a fine grater. Then thoroughly mix in 1 cup of hot milk, and press through a fine strainer as above.

**Canned coconut milk is available in Caribbean, Latin-American, and Asian markets and groceries, and the ethnic section of most supermarkets and groceries.

Rice Pudding

Diri Olè
Riz au Lait

Estimated time: 45 minutes.

1 cup medium or short grain white rice
3 cups (two 12-ounce cans) evaporated milk
2 cups whole milk
1/4 teaspoon salt
2 teaspoons pure vanilla extract
1/8 teaspoon ground cinnamon, or 1 cinnamon stick

3/4 cup raisins
1 strip of lime zest
1/2 cup granulated sugar
2 tablespoons butter or margarine

Wash rice with fresh water 3 to 4 times, or until water runs clear. Drain carefully. Mix rice, evaporated milk, whole milk, salt, vanilla extract, cinnamon, raisins, and lime zest in a heavy 5-quart pan. Bring slowly to a boil over medium heat. Then reduce heat to medium low, cover tightly, and simmer for about 25 minutes, stirring often. Mix in sugar at the last minute. Discard lime zest. The pudding should be thick and creamy, and the rice should be tender. Mix in the butter. Transfer the pudding to a serving bowl. Cover with plastic wrap and chill in the refrigerator until ready to serve. This recipe can be doubled.

Serves 6.

Fruit Salad

Salad Fwi
Salade de Fruits (Macédoine de Fruit)

2 passion fruit
3 cups 1/2-inch fresh pineapple cubes or
1-inch balls
3 tablespoons granulated sugar
1/2 cup fresh orange juice
1 tablespoon fresh lime juice

2 1/4 cups 1/2-inch watermelon cubes or 1- inch balls
2 1/4 cups 1/2-inch cantaloupe cubes or
1-inch balls
one 15-ounce can mixed fruit cocktail
1/4 cup grenadine (*Pomegranate Syrup*)

Cut passion fruit in half and spoon the moist pulp in a large bowl. Discard shells. Mix in 1 cup pineapple cubes, and sugar. Cover and let stand for 15 minutes in the refrigerator.

With a blender, purée passion fruit and pineapple mixture at low speed for about 1 minute or so, without water. Strain through a fine strainer. Discard the residue. In a large bowl, mix juice with remaining pineapple pieces, orange juice, lime juice, watermelon pieces, cantaloupe pieces, fruit cocktail, and grenadine. Transfer to a serving bowl. Cover and chill until ready to serve.

Yields 6 servings.

Flamed Bananas

Fig Mi Flanbe
Bananes Flambées

If you have unexpected guests, *Flamed Bananas* is the kind of dessert to think about. It is delicious and, most of all, easy and quick. Serve it with one or two scoops of vanilla ice cream if you wish.

Estimated time: 15 minutes.

1/2 cup fresh orange juice
2 tablespoons fresh lime juice
1/3 cup granulated sugar
1/2 cup dark raisins
1 teaspoon ground cinnamon

6 ripe bananas, still firm
6 tablespoons butter, or margarine
1/3 cup dark Haitian rum (Rhum Barbancourt)

Mix orange juice, lime juice, sugar, raisins, and cinnamon in a small saucepan. Stir over medium heat until sugar dissolves. Stop stirring, and boil down for a few minutes until a light syrup is formed.

Meanwhile, peel and slice bananas in half lengthwise. Heat butter over medium setting in a large skillet. Add banana slices and sauté for 2 to 3 minutes. Drizzle with the fruit syrup. Continue to cook for 1 minute. Remove from heat. Carefully, slide banana slices and cooking sauce into a heat resistant serving dish, drizzle with rum, and ignite with a lighted match. Serve immediately, while flaming.

Serves 6.

Cream Puffs

Bouche
Choux à la Crème

30 small choux (follow the recipe for *Choux Pastry*)
1/2 recipe of *Pastry Cream* (add 2 tablespoons of sugar to the recipe)
1 cup heavy whipping cream
A small chilled bowl, or a chilled 2-cup measuring cup
A large pastry bag fitted with a large tip

Cover *Pastry Cream* with plastic wrap and put it in the refrigerator until completely cold. Chill the beaters of an electric hand mixer. Put whipping cream in the chilled bowl, and whip at medium speed until stiff peaks are formed, 1 to 2 minutes. Then fold it into the *Pastry Cream*.

Cut off the top 1/3 of the choux. Remove and discard the moist dough inside each of them. Fill the pastry bag with *Pastry Cream* and pipe into the choux just before serving. Cover with the tops. Serve immediately.

Yields 30 Cream Puffs.

Variation. *Pastry Cream* may be flavored with a fruit syrup, or with dark Haitian rum. See variation of *Pastry Cream* in the *Bread and Pastry* chapter.

Sweet and Soft Banana Fritters

Beniyè (Benyen)

Beignets de Bananes (Beignets de Carnaval)

These beignets remind me of Carnaval (Mardi-Gras) and good times. In Haiti during the Carnaval, families, relatives, and friends gather together to enjoy the festivities and this delectable casual dessert made with bananas.

Estimated time: 30 minutes

1 cup all-purpose flour
1/4 teaspoon baking soda
pinch of ground cinnamon (optional)
1/4 teaspoon salt
1 cup mashed bananas (2 to 3 medium well-ripened bananas)
1/4 cup whole milk (or 2 tablespoons whole milk plus 2 tablespoons dark Haitian rum)
1/2 cup granulated sugar
vegetable oil for deep-frying
granulated or powdered sugar for dusting

Mix flour with baking soda, cinnamon, and salt. Set aside.

In a large bowl, mix mashed bananas with milk and sugar until smooth. Combine with flour mixture and stir until smooth.

Heat oil in a medium pan over medium high setting. Drop the batter by tablespoons in hot oil. Do not overload. Fry until golden, about 1 minute for each side. Use a slotted spoon to remove them from the pan. Squeeze the oil out by gently pressing them on the slotted spoon with the back of a tablespoon. Drain on paper towels. Dust with granulated sugar or powdered sugar. Serve warm.

Yields 25 to 30 beignets.

Note. This recipe does not include eggs. Eggs toughen beignets which are supposed to be soft and moist.

ICE CREAMS AND DRINKS

Krèm ak Bwason
Les Crèmes Glacées et les Boissons

Papaya-Lime Juice

Mango Ice Cream

Krèm Mango
Glace à la Mangue

This ice cream is a true tropical delight! The mangos must be very ripe and very sweet. The mango purée should be made just before making the ice cream. Otherwise, it may not taste fresh. *Mangue Madame Francisque* is by far the best for making this ice cream. Substitute 1 cup soursop juice for the mango purée to make *Soursop Ice Cream*.

Estimated time: 1 hour (cooling time not included).

4 egg yolks
pinch of salt
3/4 cup powdered sugar
1 3/4 cups whole milk

2 very ripe mangos, peeled, pitted, and chopped
(gives about 1 1/4 cups mango purée)
1 1/2 cups heavy whipping cream

Whisk egg yolks, salt, and sugar together in a large bowl until creamy. Set aside.

Heat milk over medium heat until just beginning to bubble. Gradually pour hot milk on egg mixture, whisking continuously. Transfer to the top of a double-boiler* and cook over medium low heat, stirring continuously with a wooden spoon until the sauce coats the spoon, about 15 minutes**. The sauce should not boil because it will curdle. Remove from heat. Cool completely, then cover with plastic wrap and cool in the refrigerator for at least 2 hours.

Meanwhile, purée mango gradually in a blender at high speed until smooth. Strain through a fine strainer, and discard the residue. Keep mango purée in the refrigerator until ready to use.

Mix the cream with the cold sauce. At this point, you can refrigerate the preparation up to one day before use. Process in ice cream maker according to the manufacturer's instructions. Mix in 1 cup of mango purée halfway through the freezing process. Serve immediately or transfer ice cream to a covered container and put in the freezer until ready to use. Thaw in refrigerator for 30 to 45 minutes before serving. Serve with a caramel sauce or a sauce of your choice, and garnish as desired.

Yields about four 1-cup servings.

Snow cones. Called **fresco** in Haiti, and sold on the streets, they are made of grated ice saturated with all kinds of fruit syrup. They are delicious, and refreshing, but not as elaborate as ice cream.

*If you do not have a double-boiler, then make egg mixture in a heat resistant 3-quart bowl. Bring 1 1/2 cups of water to a boil in a heavy 3-quart round pan. Reduce heat to medium. Set the bowl on the pan, and cook sauce stirring constantly. The bottom of the bowl should not touch the water. The sauce may take a little longer, about 20 minutes.

**A good way to know if sauce is ready is to draw a clean finger across back of the wooden spoon coated with the sauce. Sauce is ready when your finger leaves a neat trace on the spoon.

Coconut Ice Cream

Krèm Kokoye
Glace au Lait de Coco

Another true tropical delight! Coconut purée can be made one day ahead, and kept in the refrigerator. Make sure that the coconut is fresh and does not taste rancid.

Estimated time: 1 hour (cooling time not included).

4 large egg yolks
pinch of salt
1 cup powdered sugar
1 cup finely chopped fresh young coconut
(See the Glossary and *The Cook's Techniques*), or 1 cup canned coconut milk*
(keep refrigerated)

2 1/4 cups hot whole milk
2 teaspoons pure vanilla extract
1 1/2 cups heavy whipping cream

Whisk egg yolks, salt, and 3/4 cup powdered sugar together in a large bowl until creamy. Set aside.

Put half of the chopped coconut in a blender with 1/2 cup of hot milk. Purée on medium speed for about 1 minute. Add remaining powdered sugar and remaining coconut, then purée on medium speed until creamy, about 1 minute. Strain through a fine strainer. You should not have any residue and should have a creamy coconut purée. Mix in the vanilla extract. Keep coconut purée in the refrigerator until ready to use.

Heat remaining milk over medium heat until just beginning to bubble. Gradually pour hot milk on the egg mixture, whisking continuously. Transfer to the top of a double-boiler** and cook over medium low heat, stirring continuously with a wooden spoon until the sauce coats the spoon, about 15 minutes***. The sauce should not boil because it will curdle. Remove from heat. Cool completely, then cover with plastic wrap and cool in the refrigerator for at least 2 hours. Mix in the heavy cream. At this point, you can refrigerate the preparation up to one day before use. Process in ice cream maker according to the manufacturer's instructions. Mix in 1 cup of coconut purée halfway through the freezing process. Serve immediately or transfer ice cream to a covered container and put in the freezer until ready to serve. Thaw in refrigerator for 30 to 45 minutes before serving. Serve with a creamy chocolate sauce or a sauce of your choice, and garnish as desired.

Yields about four 1-cup servings.

---

*Canned coconut milk is available in Caribbean, Latin-American, and Asian markets and groceries, and the ethnic section of most supermarkets and groceries. If canned coconut milk is used, reduce the amount of milk to 1 3/4 cups.

**If you do not have a double-boiler, then make the egg mixture in a heat resistant 3-quart bowl. Bring 1 1/2 cups of water to a boil in a heavy 3-quart round pan. Reduce heat to medium. Set the bowl on the pan, and cook the sauce stirring constantly.

The bottom of the bowl should not touch the water. The sauce may take a little longer, about 20 minutes.

***A good way to know if sauce is ready is to draw a clean finger across back of the wooden spoon coated with the sauce. Sauce is ready when your finger leaves a neat trace on the spoon.

Pineapple Ice Cream

Krèm Anana
Glace à l'Ananas

Again another true tropical delight! Serve it with a ginger-flavored sauce, a butterscotch sauce, or a sauce of your choice. Pineapple syrup can be prepared one day ahead, and kept in the refrigerator.

Estimated time: 1 hour (cooling time not included).

2 cups finely chopped fresh pineapple, or one 20-ounce can sliced pineapple in juice
1/4 cup granulated sugar
4 large egg yolks
1/4 teaspoon salt
3/4 cup powdered sugar
1 3/4 cups whole milk
1 1/2 cups heavy whipping cream

Put pineapple in a blender with 1/2 cup of water (if you chose to use a canned pineapple, use juice in the can instead of water). Process on medium speed for about 15 seconds. Strain twice through a fine strainer. Discard the residue. Pour the pineapple juice in a heavy pan, mix in granulated sugar, and reduce uncovered, over medium heat, until a light syrup forms, about 10 minutes. Cool in the refrigerator until ready to use.

Whisk egg yolks, salt, and powdered sugar together in a large bowl until creamy. Set aside.

Heat milk over medium heat until just beginning to bubble. Gradually pour hot milk on egg mixture, whisking continuously. Transfer to the top of a double-boiler* and cook over medium low heat, stirring continuously with a wooden spoon until the sauce coats the spoon, about 15 minutes**. The sauce should not boil because it will curdle. Remove from heat. Cool completely, then cover with plastic wrap and cool in the refrigerator for at least 2 hours. Mix in heavy cream. At this point, you can refrigerate the preparation up to one day before use. Process in ice cream maker according to the manufacturer's instructions. Mix in 1 cup of pineapple syrup halfway through the freezing process. Serve immediately or transfer ice cream to a covered container and put in the freezer until ready to serve. Thaw in refrigerator for 30 to 45 minutes before serving. Serve it with a ginger-flavored sauce or a butterscotch sauce, and garnish as you wish.

Yields about four 1-cup servings.

*If you do not have a double-boiler, then make the egg mixture in a heat resistant 3-quart bowl. Bring 1 1/2 cups of water to a boil in a heavy 3-quart round pan. Reduce heat to medium. Set the bowl on the pan, and cook the sauce stirring constantly. The bottom of the bowl should not touch the water. The sauce may take a little longer, about 20 minutes.

**A good way to know if sauce is ready is to draw a clean finger across back of the wooden spoon coated with the sauce. Sauce is ready when your finger leaves a neat trace on the spoon.

AKASAN (AK 100)

Akasan, made from very ripe corn kernels, or broken dry corn kernels, is a delicious drink that can be served warm or cold. It is very often part of a Haitian breakfast. If *Akasan* is made with dry kernels, they are soaked overnight in water, then drained and rinsed, then boiled, puréed, and strained. *AK 100* is a creamy drink.

Estimated time: 2 hours 30 minutes.

1 cup yellow broken hominy (samp)*	two 12-ounce cans evaporated milk
3 cinnamon sticks, or 1 /8 teaspoon ground cinnamon	1/2 cup fresh coconut milk**
	3/4 cup granulated sugar
3 star anise	2 teaspoons pure vanilla extract
2 cups whole milk	1/2 teaspoon salt

Put hominy in a bowl, cover it with 3 inches of water. Allow to soak overnight in a cool place.

Drain hominy, then rinse with fresh running water. Mix hominy and 14 cups of water in a large pot, add cinnamon, then bring to a boil. Cover (leaving lid slightly ajar), and cook over medium heat for 1 hour 30 minutes. At this point, hominy should be very mushy and the cooking liquid very thick. Allow to cool down until easy to handle. Remove cinnamon sticks if used, and anise. Purée corn mixture with whole milk in a blender, then strain three times, using a very fine strainer at the last time. Add evaporated milk, coconut milk, sugar, vanilla extract, and salt. *AK 100* should be thick and creamy, but drinkable. If *AK 100* is grainy, just blend it at high speed until smooth. Serve warm, or chill in the refrigerator before serving.

Serves 8 to 10.

Note. *AK 100* tends to become very thick when cold. To thin it out, simply mix in a small amount of cold milk, a small pinch of salt, and additional sugar if necessary.

Variation. For a quick and still delicious version of *AK 100*, boil 1 cup of medium yellow cornmeal with 8 cups of water, over medium heat for 30 to 40 minutes. Then proceed as above. It will be ready in about 45 to 50 minutes.

---

*Broken hominy is made from dry corn kernels that have been hulled, degerminated, and broken. It is available at Caribbean and Latin-American groceries and supermarkets, and health stores. There is a yellow corn flour, called Acassan, available in some ethnic groceries. If you use it, you still have to blend it for a short while until smooth.

**To make fresh coconut milk for *Akasan*, put 1/2 cup of finely chopped fresh coconut in a blender with 1/2 cup of hot milk. Process on high speed for 2 minutes. Coconut will look as if it has been grated. Press coconut through a fine strainer to collect the milk. Strain again. It might yield a little more than 1/2 cup, but it will not make any difference. Make sure that the coconut is fresh and does not taste rancid.

Foskawo I

Foskawo is a creamy chocolate drink made with unrefined Haitian cocoa, chokola peyi. That tells how authentic and how delicious it is. It can be made with bittersweet or semisweet chocolate morsels, which taste like the unrefined cocoa we have in Haiti. *Foskawo* can be enjoyed hot or cold, but is usually served very cold. I provided two *Foskawo* recipes in this book.

½ cup very cold whole milk
5 tablespoons corn starch
Two 12-ounce cans evaporated milk
3 cups whole milk
3 cinnamon sticks, or a pinch of ground cinnamon

2 star anise, or 1/8 teaspoon anise seeds
1/4 cup semisweet chocolate morsels, or chokola-peyi if available*
1/4 cup granulated sugar
Pinch of salt
1 teaspoon pure vanilla extract

Mix ½ cup very cold milk and cornstarch in a small bowl until well blended. Set aside.

Mix evaporated milk, 3 cups whole milk, cinnamon, and star anise in a 2-quart heavy pan. Heat over medium setting until it just starts bubbling. Keep hot.

Slowly melt chocolate in a heavy 4-quart saucepan over medium-low heat, stirring constantly. Using a wire whisk, stir in sugar, salt, and then gradually stir in the hot milk with the spices. Mix in the cornstarch mixture, and whisk over medium heat until thick and creamy, about 2 to 3 minutes. Remove from heat, and mix in vanilla extract. Mix in additional sugar if desired. Remove the cinnamon sticks and the star anise before serving.

Foskawo should be thick and creamy, but drinkable. Serve hot or chill in the refrigerator before serving.

Serves 6 (yields about 6 cups).

Variation. Make a richer *Foskawo* by replacing 1/2 cup of milk with 1/2 cup of heavy whipping cream.

Note. If anise seeds and/or chokola peyi are used, *Foskawo* must be strained.

*The local Haitian cocoa is shaped into small sticks or small balls. It is best to break it into smaller pieces when using. If you are using it, add it after the milk.

Foskawo II

Foskawo is a creamy chocolate drink made with unrefined Haitian cocoa, *chokola peyi*. That tells how authentic and how delicious it is. It can be made with bittersweet or semisweet chocolate morsels, which taste like the unrefined cocoa we have in Haiti. *Foskawo* can be enjoyed hot or cold, but is usually served very cold.

Two 12-ounce cans evaporated milk
3 1/2 cups whole milk
3 cinnamon sticks, or a pinch of ground cinnamon
2 star anise, or 1/8 teaspoon anise seeds
2 tablespoons butter or margarine

3 tablespoons all-purpose flour
1/4 cup semisweet chocolate morsels, or *chokola peyi* if available*
1/4 cup granulated sugar
pinch of salt
1 teaspoon pure vanilla extract

Mix evaporated milk, whole milk, cinnamon, and star anise in a 2-quart heavy pan. Heat over medium setting until it just starts bubbling. Keep hot.

Heat butter in a 3-quart heavy pan over medium setting. Add flour and cook for 1 to 2 minutes stirring constantly. Reduce heat to medium low, add chocolate morsels, and stir until chocolate melts. Gradually, stir in hot milk with the spices using a wire whisk, then stir in the sugar and the salt. Increase heat to medium, and reduce *Foskawo* for 8 to 10 minutes, whisking often. Remove from heat, and mix in vanilla extract. Mix in additional sugar if desired. Remove the cinnamon sticks and the star anise before serving. *Foskawo* should be thick and creamy, but drinkable. Serve hot or chill in the refrigerator before serving. *Foskawo* tends to become very thick when cold. To thin it out, simply mix in a small amount of cold milk, a small pinch of salt, and additional sugar if necessary.

Serves 6 (yields about 6 cups).

Variation. Make a richer *Foskawo* by replacing 1/2 cup of milk with 1/2 cup of heavy whipping cream.

Note. If anise seeds and/or chokola peyi are used, *Foskawo* must be strained.

*The local Haitian cocoa is shaped into small sticks or small balls. It is best to break it into smaller pieces when using. If you are using it, add it after the milk.

Chocolate Milk

Chokola Olè
Chocolat au Lait

Chocolate milk made with unrefined Haitian cocoa (*chokola peyi*) is a true delight. It can be made with bittersweet or semisweet chocolate morsels, which taste like the unrefined cocoa we have in Haiti.

1 cup semisweet chocolate morsels, or 1/4 cup *chokola peyi* if available*
1/2 cup granulated sugar
8 cups hot milk
2 cups fresh coconut milk, or canned coconut milk at room temperature**

4 star anise, or 1/4 teaspoon anise seeds
3 cinnamon sticks or 1/2 teaspoon ground cinnamon
pinch of salt
1 teaspoon pure vanilla extract

Slowly melt chocolate in a heavy 4-quart saucepan over medium low heat, stirring constantly. Mix in sugar, hot milk, and coconut milk. Add anise, cinnamon, and salt. Bring to a boil. Remove from heat. Mix in vanilla extract. Remove anise star and cinnamon sticks. Strain through a fine strainer, pressing on the residue if any. Serve hot or cold.

Serves 10 (yields 10 cups).

*If you are using it, add 1/2 cup milk to the recipe, mix all the ingredients and boil for 5 minutes over medium to medium low heat. Wisk often and make sure it does not stick to the bottom of the saucepan. Then proceed as above.

**To make fresh coconut milk for *Chocolate Milk*, put 2 cups of finely chopped fresh coconut in a blender with 2 cups of hot milk. Process on high speed for 3 minutes. Coconut will look as if it has been grated. Press coconut through a fine strainer to collect the milk. Strain again. It might yield a little more than 2 cups, but it will not make any difference. You can also grate coconut with a fine grater. Then thoroughly mix in 2 cups of hot milk, and press through a fine strainer as above. Make sure that the coconut is fresh and does not taste rancid. Canned coconut milk is available in Caribbean, Latin-American, and Asian markets and groceries, and the ethnic section of most supermarkets and groceries.

Eggnog

Ponch Ze
Punch aux Oeufs (Lait de Poule)

A hot drink in Haiti, *Eggnog* is considered a breakfast drink when very little rum is added. Without alcohol it is considered a tonic for growing children. Often duck eggs are used instead of chicken eggs and because of that, the drink is considered even more restorative.

Estimated time: 15 minutes.

4 large egg whites
4 large egg yolks
1/2 cup granulated sugar
2 cups whole milk
2 cups evaporated milk

1 cinnamon stick, or 1/4 teaspoon ground cinnamon
1/4 teaspoon ground nutmeg
1/4 cup dark Haitian rum (Rhum Barbancourt)
ground nutmeg, to garnish

With an electric mixer at high speed, beat egg whites in a large bowl until stiff.

With a wire whisk, mix egg yolks with sugar in another large bowl until creamy.

Mix whole milk, evaporated milk, cinnamon, and nutmeg in a 3-quart pan, and bring to a full boil. Remove cinnamon stick, if used.

Pour beaten whites into the yolk-sugar mixture, and beat at high speed. Pour hot milk on egg mixture while beating at high speed. Add rum, still beating. *Eggnog* should be very foamy. Pour in tall glasses. Sprinkle with ground nutmeg. Serve immediately.

Serves 6.

Banana

In Haiti we call *Banana* a smooth drink made with grated unpeeled green plantains. It is a delicious and drinkable plantain purée, often served at breakfast with toasted bread and butter. It is among the breakfast favorites of Haitian children.

Estimated time: 45 minutes.

two medium green plantains, about 1 pound (yields about 2 cups grated plantain)
7 cups water
2 cinnamon sticks, or 1/2 teaspoon ground cinnamon

4 cups whole milk
1 1/2 teaspoons pure vanilla extract
1 cup granulated sugar
1/2 teaspoon salt
one 12-ounce can evaporated milk

Carefully brush plantains under fresh water. Trim and discard both ends. Do not peel. Chop* plantains and purée plantain pieces with 3 cups of water in a blender at high speed for about 30 seconds. Mix purée with remaining water in a 5-quart heavy pan. Add cinnamon, and boil covered over medium heat for 20 minutes, with lid ajar. Stir and scrape the bottom of the pan occasionally. Mixture should be fairly thick. Remove from heat. Remove and reserve cinnamon sticks for another use. Strain purée twice, forcing the residue through a fine strainer. The residue should be less than 1/2 cup.

Rinse the same pan with fresh water to remove any residue stuck to the bottom. Transfer plantain purée to the pan. Mix in whole milk, vanilla extract, sugar, and salt. Boil over medium heat for 10 minutes, stirring and scraping the bottom of the pan often. Remove from heat, and mix in evaporated milk. *Banana* should be thick and creamy, but drinkable. Serve at room temperature or cold, with toasted bread.

Serves 8.

Note. *Banana* tends to become very thick when cold. To thin it out, simply mix in a small amount of cold milk, a small pinch of salt, and additional sugar if necessary. Sometime the purée is served thick, and is eaten with a spoon. It is then a porridge called *Bouillie de Banane* or *Labouyi Bannann* in Haiti.

*Plantain can also be finely grated, then mixed with 7 cups of water to boil.

Wheat "Akasan"

Akasan Ble
Akasan de Blé

In Haiti we do not produce wheat. The wheat sold in the open-air markets comes from the USA. The Haitian people have been very innovative in regard to this grain. This recipe is one reflection of our creativity.

Delicious and easy, just like the preceding recipes, this wheat drink is very similar to *Akasan*, and in fact we call it *Akasan de Ble* (*Akasan Ble*). It does not take a long time to prepare.

Estimated time: 1 hour 10 minutes (including soaking time).

2/3 cup wheat (cracked or whole)	2 1/2 cups whole milk
4 cups water	2 cups evaporated milk
1 cinnamon stick, or 1/4 teaspoon ground cinnamon	1/2 cup fresh coconut milk* (optional)
	1/2 cup sugar
3 star anise	1 teaspoon pure vanilla extract

Soak wheat in the water in a 3-quart pan for 45 minutes. Then add cinnamon, anise, and bring to a boil over high heat. Reduce heat to medium and cook covered for 15 minutes, with lid slightly ajar. Water should be almost completely evaporated. Remove from heat. Remove cinnamon stick and star anise. Mix in whole milk, then purée in a blender at high speed until creamy, 1 to 2 minutes. Strain twice through a fine strainer. Discard the residue. Mix in evaporated milk, coconut milk, sugar, and vanilla extract. *Akasan Ble* should be thick and creamy, but drinkable. Serve in tall glasses, at room temperature or cold. The recipe can be doubled.

Serves 6.

Note. *Akasan Ble* tends to become very thick when cold. To thin it out, simply mix in a small amount of cold milk, a small pinch of salt, and additional sugar if necessary.

*To make fresh coconut milk for *Akasan Ble*, put 1/2 cup of finely chopped fresh coconut in a blender with 1/2 cup of hot milk. Process on high speed for 2 minutes. Coconut will look as if it has been grated. Press coconut through a fine strainer to collect the milk. Strain again. It might yield a little more than 1/2 cup, but it will not make any difference. You can also grate coconut with a fine grater. Then thoroughly mix in 1/2 cup of hot milk, and press through a fine strainer as above. Make sure that the coconut is fresh and does not taste rancid.

Creamy Sweet Potato Drink

Ji Patat lan Lèt
Purée de Patate au Lait

Patate au Lait is a popular children's dish in Haiti. Traditionally, sweet potatoes are peeled, cubed, then boiled with spices (cinnamon, vanilla, etc. . .) in milk. Puréed, it becomes a smooth and delicious drink, with the same great taste, that can be enjoyed by adults as well.

Estimated time: 50 minutes.

1 1/2 pounds sweet potatoes (any variety)
2 cups evaporated milk
1 1/2 cups whole milk
1 1/2 teaspoons ground cinnamon

2 teaspoons pure vanilla extract
1/8 teaspoon salt
1/2 cup granulated sugar

Brush potatoes under fresh running water. Put them in a large pot. Cover them with 3 inches of water. Cover the pot and bring to a boil over high heat. Reduce heat to medium, and boil with lid ajar, until potatoes are very tender, about 40 minutes. Drain and let stand until they are cool enough to be handled.

Peel and dice potatoes. Put diced potatoes in a blender with evaporated milk, whole milk, cinnamon, vanilla, salt, and sugar. Purée at high speed until smooth, about 1 minute. Chill in the refrigerator. Serve cold in tall glasses.

Yields 6 cups.

Note. Make a very delicious *Creamy Breadfruit Drink* by substituting breadfruit for the potatoes. Breadfruit must be ripe and green but not ripened and sweet. You will need a little less breadfruit, or a little more milk for this drink.

Papaya Smoothie

Ji Papay Olè
Jus de Papaye au Lait

4 cups cubed papaya* (well ripened)
1 1/2 cups (one 12-ounce can) very cold evaporated milk
1/4 cup granulated sugar, or to taste
1 cup crushed ice

Put papaya, milk, sugar, and ice in a blender. Process on high speed until smooth, 1 to 2 minutes. Serve immediately. The recipe can be doubled or tripled.

Yields 4 servings.

Note. To make *Watermelon Smoothie* and *French Melon Smoothie*, use 4 cups of chopped watermelon or 4 cups of chopped French melon instead of the papaya. The fruits must be very ripe.

*Peel, seed, and cube papaya. Discard skin and seeds. If papaya is not very ripe, it tastes bitter, and the smoothie will be grainy. Papaya also tends to become bitter shortly after it has been cut, thus it must be eaten promptly. If you use only part of a papaya, wrap any remaining, uncut, in plastic wrap and store it in the refrigerator for up to one day. Before using, cut around the edges and discard the trimmings to reduce the risk of bitterness. Cubed papaya or papaya juice should always be kept in the refrigerator, and no longer than one hour; otherwise they can become bitter. However, perfectly ripe papaya can be stored peeled and cubed in the freezer for a very long time. This can only be used to make smoothie or juice.

Papaya-Lime Juice

Ji Papay ak Sitwon
Jus de Papaye au Citron

This is a very delicious and refreshing juice. It is easy to make, and is ready in minutes.

3 cups cubed papaya* (well ripened)
Juice of 2 Persian limes (about 1/2 cup of fresh juice)
1/2 cup granulated sugar
1 1/2 cups very cold water
1 1/2 cups crushed ice

Put papaya, lime juice, sugar, water, and crushed ice in a blender. Process on high speed until smooth, 1 to 2 minutes. Serve immediately. The recipe can be doubled or tripled.

Yields 4 servings.

*Peel, seed, and cube papaya. Discard skin and seeds. If papaya is not very ripe, it tastes bitter, and the juice will be grainy. Papaya also tends to become bitter shortly after it has been cut, thus it must be eaten promptly. If you use only part of a papaya, wrap any remaining, uncut, in plastic wrap and store it in the refrigerator for up to one day. Before using, cut around the edges and discard the trimmings to reduce the risk of bitterness. Cubed papaya or papaya juice should always be kept in the refrigerator, and no longer than one hour; otherwise, they can become bitter. However, perfectly ripe papaya can be stored peeled and cubed in the freezer for a very long time. This can only be used to make smoothie and juice.

Passion Fruit Juice

Ji Grenadia
Jus de Fruit de la Passion

This is as delicious and refreshing as the preceding juice. It is also very easy to make, and ready in minutes.

4 passion fruit
2 cups very cold water
1/4 cup granulated sugar, or to taste

Halve passion fruit and spoon the pulp in a blender. Add water, and process at low speed, on and off, for a few seconds. Drain carefully through a fine strainer. Discard the residue. Mix in sugar. Serve over ice cubes. The juice can be prepared in advance and kept in the refrigerator, then stirred before serving. The recipe can be doubled, or tripled.

Yields 2 servings.

West Indies Cherry Juice

Ji Seriz
Jus de Cerise

This juice is as refreshing, as delicious, and as easy to make as the preceding ones. Information about West Indies cherries is given in the Glossary of this book.

6 cups West Indies cherries
3 cups very cold water
1/2 cup of granulated sugar, or to taste
Ice cubes

Wash the fruit carefully under fresh running water. Remove and discard stems if any. Place fruit in a blender, add water, and process at medium speed for 2 minutes. Drain carefully through a very fine strainer. Discard the residue. Mix in sugar. Serve over ice cubes. The recipe can be doubled, or tripled.

Yields 4 to 6 servings.

Note. To make fresh *Pineapple Juice*, use 6 cups cut pineapple, then proceed as above.

Soursop Juice

Ji Kowosòl
Jus de Corossol

One soursop (guanabana), well ripened
1 1/2 cups (one 12-ounce can) evaporated milk
1/3 cup granulated sugar, or to taste
Ice cubes

Peel soursop, and discard skin. Cut the fruit in two. Remove and discard the core. Place the juicy pulp in a large bowl, and mash it with a strong fork so it becomes very mushy*. Using a fine strainer, strain the mashed fruit into a large bowl, working and pressing well on the residue. Mix one cup of water with residue, and mash again. Strain through the fine strainer into the juice in the bowl. Discard the residue. Stir in milk and sugar. Stir in additional sugar if desired. Transfer juice to a pitcher. Cool in the refrigerator for a few hours before serving. Serve over ice cubes.

Serves 3 to 4.

Note. We make also a delicious sweet mash called *Boubouille (Boubouy)* with soursop. Peel and core the fruit. Put pulp in a large shallow dish, and mash it with a fork. Remove and discard the seeds. Mix in 1/2 cup of evaporated milk, and sugar to taste. Transfer to a serving bowl and refrigerate until chilled. Just before serving, mix in 1/2 cup of crushed ice. Serve in ice cream cups.

Make a delicious and fresh *Custard Apple Juice* following the same recipe. Just use custard apples instead of the soursop. One custard apple yields juice for one or two persons.

* Never use the blender to make soursop juice. See the entry for soursop in the Glossary.

Fruit Punch

Ji Fwi
Jus de Fruits Frais

This is one of the many delicious fruit punches we make in Haiti.

2 cups fresh pineapple juice
1 cup fresh orange juice
1 cup fresh watermelon juice*
1/4 cup fresh lime juice

1 cup fresh West Indies cherry juice**
1/3 cup granulated sugar, or to taste
1 cup fresh *Passion Fruit Juice*
ice cubes

Mix all the fruit juices and the sugar in a large pitcher. Serve over ice cubes.

Serves 6.

*To make fresh *Watermelon Juice*: Remove and discard melon seeds and skin, then cut the melon flesh into small pieces. Purée part of the fruit in a blender at high speed for a few seconds, then gradually add the remaining fruit pieces. Strain through a very fine strainer. Discard the residue.

**If West Indies cherries are not available, replace the juice with the same amount of fresh pineapple or orange juice.

Goudrin

Goudrin is an amber drink produced by the fermentation of pineapple peels. It is surprisingly delicious, very refreshing, and slightly alcoholic. The fruits must be very ripe, very sweet, and ready to be eaten; otherwise the peels will rot instead of inducing the process of fermentation. Use any part you remove from the pineapple with the exception of the top and the bottom. The signs of fermentation, detectable by the existence of little bubbles in the pitcher, are present as early as the first day. By the second day, the top of the water will be covered with a grayish white coat. Remove it carefully and discard it before straining the *Goudrin*.

An alternative is given in case mature pineapples are not available. See the note below.

Peels of two very ripe and very sweet large pineapples
4 cups of water
1 tablespoon granulated sugar

Pack the peels in a 2-quart glass pitcher. Mix the sugar with the water, and pour over the peels. Do not cover the pitcher. Place the pitcher on the kitchen counter, and let steep for 3 to 4 days. Strain through a very fine strainer into a pitcher. Discard pineapple peels. Chill in the refrigerator until ready to serve. To serve, sweeten to taste, and pour over ice cubes in tall glasses.

Serves 3.

Note. Clean the pineapples before peeling them. If pineapples are slightly underripe, cover the pitcher and allow the peels to steep in the refrigerator for 4 to 5 days. Then strain, and serve.

Rum Punch

Wonm Ponch
Rhum Punch

1 tablespoon fresh lime juice
1/4 cup fresh orange juice
1/4 cup fresh West Indies cherry juice*
1/4 cup fresh pineapple juice
1 tablespoon grenadine (*Pomegranate Syrup*)
1/4 cup sugar syrup (recipe given in the *Preserves* and *Confectionery* chapter)

1/4 cup dark Haitian rum (Rhum Barbancourt)
crushed ice or small ice cubes
4 maraschino cherries
2 lime slices

Mix fruit juices with grenadine, sugar syrup, and rum. Pour on ice in two tall glasses. Garnish with maraschino cherries and lime slices. Serve immediately.

Serves 2.

Note. *Rhum-Coca* is an easy drink served at parties. It is a blend of dark rum and coca-cola on ice.

*Use as little water as possible to make the pineapple juice and the cherry juice. If West Indies cherries are not available, replace the juice with the same amount of fresh pineapple juice.

Pineapple Rum Punch

Wonm Ponch Anana
Rhum Punch à l'Ananas

2 tablespoons fresh lime juice
1 cup fresh pineapple juice*
5 tablespoons sugar syrup**
1/4 cup dark Haitian rum (Rhum Barbancourt)

crushed ice or small ice cubes
4 maraschino cherries to garnish
pineapple wedges to garnish

Mix fruit juices with sugar syrup, and rum. Pour on ice in two glasses. Garnish with maraschino cherries and pineapple wedges. Serve immediately.

Serves 2.

*Use as little water as possible to make the pineapple juice.

**Recipe is given in the *Preserves and Confectionery Chapter.*

Crémas (Kremas)

Crémas is one of the favorite Christmas season drinks in Haiti. This quick version takes only a few minutes to prepare. It will taste better if you allow the flavors to blend for a few days, in the refrigerator. You may also keep the essential ingredients in the refrigerator. This way, you will have them ready in case you need to serve the drink at once.

2 cups sweetened cream of coconut*
2 tablespoons pure vanilla extract
2 cups condensed milk
2 teaspoons ground nutmeg

2 cups dark Haitian rum (Rhum Barban-court)
4 teaspoons fresh lime juice
small ice cubes

Mix all the ingredients, and serve over the ice cubes. This can be prepared ahead and stored in bottles in the refrigerator. Shake well before serving.

Yields about 6 cups.

*Cream of coconut is usually found in the drink section of groceries and supermarkets. Do not use the coconut cream made for pie filling.

Pa Regrèt

Pa Regrèt and *Crémas* are very similar. The difference is that *Crémas* contains coconut whereas *Pa Regrèt* does not. Both are delicious.

4 cups condensed milk
2 teaspoons ground nutmeg
1 1/3 to 1 1/2 cups dark Haitian rum (Rhum Barbancourt)

1 teaspoon fresh lime juice
1 tablespoon pure vanilla extract
small ice cubes

Mix all the ingredients, and serve over the ice cubes. *Pa Regrèt* can be prepared ahead and stored in bottles in the refrigerator. Shake well before serving.

You may also keep the necessary ingredients in the refrigerator, just as you would for *Crémas*. This way, you will have them ready in case you need to serve the drink at once.

Yields about 6 cups.

Liqueurs

Ti Pike (Tranpe)
Liqueurs

There are different kinds of *Ti Pike*. They vary depending on the fruit used. Very popular drinks in Haiti, they are the products of steeping fruit in sugar and alcohol. Traditionally, people use *clairin*, a popular alcohol produced during the distillation of sugar cane juice, sometimes referred to as white rum.

1 pound fresh fruit (West Indies cherries, peaches, pineapple chunks, ginep)
1 pound granulated sugar
1 quart dark Haitian rum (Rhum Barbancourt), about 4 cups
A clean, large preserving jar, or a large, tightly covered glass jar

You may use one kind or an assortment of fruits. Wash cherries and/or peaches under fresh running water. Pat dry with a kitchen towel. Peel ginep, and discard the peels. Pierce the fruit several times with a fork, then drop them into the jar. Cover the fruit with sugar and fill the jar with rum. Screw the lid tightly, and let steep in the refrigerator for 3 to 12 months. Strain through a fine cheesecloth. Transfer into a clean bottle. Keep refrigerated. Serve over small ice cubes.

Yields about 1 1/2 quarts.

Variation. *Asowosi* (*asosi*) is *Ti Pike* made with a plant called *asowosi* (*asosi*) in Haitian Creole.

Herbal Teas

Te
Infusions

In Haiti, we are coffee and *Herbal Tea* lovers. We drink tea for various reasons; we drink it for the pleasure of it (which is my concern in this book), and because some herbs are believed to possess curative properties. We make infusions with leaves, tree barks, and roots. We use the freshest and tenderest leaves since almost everybody in our country has a corner reserved for growing herbs in the yard. These herbs are also sold in open-air markets. The most popular plants used for *Herbal Teas* are basil, lemon grass (citronella), lemon balm, mint, lime, cinnamon, and ginger. Serve tea alone, or with *Moustaches*, *Sugar Cookies*, *Konparèt*, or an enriched bread along with a fruit preserve.

For two cups of tea, use any of the following herbs.

2 cups of water
Two fresh basil buds, four sprigs of fresh lemon grass, or two fresh mint buds*
Granulated sugar or sugar cubes, to taste
2 lime wedges (optional)

Bring water to a boil in a tea kettle or in a small saucepan used solely for this purpose. Add the herb of your choice. Remove from heat. Cover, and allow to steep for 3 to 5 minutes. The infusion should be green. Remove the herb. Serve hot with sugar, and lime wedges if desired.

Serves 2.

*Use buds and tender leaves that form just below the buds. Fresh herbs are available in the vegetable section of most supermarkets and at farmers' markets.

Chilled Infusions

Rafrechi (Tizàn Glase)
Tisanes Glacées

Rafrechi is always served chilled. It is thus a hot day drink, contrary to herbal tea. One could compare it to iced tea. The plants used to make *Rafrechi* are largely different from those used in herbal teas. Lettuce leaves, hibiscus flowers, okra pods, and *mabi** are some of the most popular plants used for this purpose. *Mabi* is usually sweetened with brown sugar.

10 to 12 lettuce leaves
10 to 12 cups water
Sugar to taste
Ice cubes

Carefully wash the lettuce leave under fresh running water. Bring the water to a full boil, in a large and very clean pot, over high heat. Add the leaves, cover, and boil for 1 minute. Remove from heat, and allow to steep for 1 hour. Strain and discard the leaves**. Sweeten the infusion to taste. Chill before serving over ice cubes.

Yields about 10 to 12 cups.

*The bark of the *mabi* tree is boiled with cinnamon, ginger, and anise star. This is also called *mabi*.

**Very often the leaves are allowed to steep longer; the infusion is then chilled with the leaves. These may be removed just before serving.

PRESERVES AND CONFECTIONERY

Konfiti, Siwo, Tablèt, ak Dous
Les Confitures et la Confiserie

Pineapple Preserves

Grapefruit Trimmed for Preserves

Guava Preserve and Papaya Preserve

Konfiti Gwayav ak Konfiti Papay
Confiture de Goyave et Confiture de Papaille

3 pounds guavas, ripe but still firm
4 cups water
3 cups granulated sugar
3 cinnamon sticks
4 star anise
2 tablespoons fresh lime juice

Clean a 3-cup preserving jar. Set aside.

Wash guavas carefully under fresh running water. Peel and reserve the peels*. Cut guavas in halves. Spoon out and reserve the moist seedy center pulps*. Put guavas with water in a 3-quart heavy pan and cook over medium heat for 20 minutes. Add sugar, cinnamon sticks, stars anise, and lime juice. Boil for 1 hour 45 minutes, removing froth often. Guavas should become soft and tender but they should remain intact. Remove from heat and cool before filling the prepared jar.

Yields about 2 1/4 cups of preserve.

To make *Papaya Preserve*, use a 3-pound ripe and firm papaya. Peel and seed it, then slice it. Discard peels and seeds. Cook as above, using 1/4 cup of fresh lime juice instead of 2 tablespoons.

*Reserve the peels and the center pulps to make *Guava Jelly* (the recipe follows).

Guava Jelly

Jele Gwayav
Gelée de Goyave

Estimated time: 1 hour 30 minutes.

2 1/2 cups chopped guava peels and seedy
center pulp (from 3 pounds of guavas)
3 cups water
2 cups granulated sugar
2 cinnamon sticks
2 star anise
1 tablespoon fresh lime juice

Clean a 2-cup preserving jar. Set aside.

Put guava peels and pulp with water in a heavy 3-quart pan. Boil for 35 minutes. Strain through a fine strainer. Discard the residue. Add sugar, spices, and lime juice. Boil for 45 minutes, removing the froth often. Remove from heat and cool before filling the prepared jar.

Yields about 1 1/2 cups.

Note. Overripe and mushy guavas can be used to make the jelly, since the fruits will be too soft to use for preserves.

Pineapple Preserves

Konfiti Anana
Confiture d'Ananas

Estimated time: 45 minutes.

One 4 pound pineapple
1 cup water
1 1/2 cups granulated sugar

Clean a 3-cup preserving jar. Set aside.

Brush pineapple carefully under fresh running water. Peel the fruit, and slice it crosswise into 1/4- inch slices. Core the slices. Collect any juice that comes from the pineapple. Use slices as they are or quarter them. Put pineapple pieces and juice with water in a 2-quart heavy pan and cook uncovered over medium heat for 15 minutes. Mix in sugar. Reduce until a thick syrup is formed, about 15 minutes. Pineapple pieces should not disintegrate. Cool before filling the prepared jar.

Yields about 2 1/2 cups

Note. Here is a good way to have some pineapple syrup and pineapple preserve at the same time: If you need a small amount of syrup, as in *Baba au Rhum*, you can collect some syrup after the first 10 minutes of reducing. You may use the pineapple peels to make *Goudrin*.

Grapefruit Preserves

Konfiti Chadèk
Confiture de Chadèque

These preserves are made with the grapefruit pith which is the soft, bitter, sponge-like substance between the zest and the pulp. The pith must be boiled and soaked to drain out bitterness. Pummelo is preferred because of the thickness of its pith, but other varieties of grapefruit may be used as well. The pummelo is also known as shaddock and Chinese grapefruit

Estimated time: 1 hour 30 minutes.

3 large pummelo (grapefruit)
4 cups granulated sugar
1 cup of fresh grapefruit juice
3 star anise
3 cinnamon sticks

Clean a large preserving jar. Set aside.

Peel and discard zest from grapefruit. With a sharp knife and starting at one end, cut the pith lengthwise around the pulp (without cutting into the pulp) to make four sections. Lift one of the ends of each section with the tip of the knife, then detach the pith from the pulp by sliding your thumb underneath it. It should come off easily. See photograph on page 390.

Put the grapefruit piths in a large pot with 8 quarts of fresh water. Cover and bring to a boil. Cook for 25 minutes. Drain. The pith should be semi-transparent. Add 8 quarts of cold water. Drain. Add 8 quarts of cold water again. Drain again. Making sure the pith is cool enough to be handled, press it between the palms of your hands to express the excess water, being careful not to tear it. Repeat the soaking-pressing twice. Bring 8 quarts of water to boil, add pith, remove from heat. Let stand for 5 minutes. Drain, add cold water, and repeat the soaking-pressing once again. At this point, the pith will have lost all its bitterness. Cut each pith section, diagonally or crosswise, into 3 pieces, or leave it as it is.

Dilute sugar in 2 cups of water in a heavy 5-quart pan. Add grapefruit juice, star anise, cinnamon sticks, and cooked pith. Boil uncovered over medium heat until a syrup is formed, about 40 to 45 minutes. Pith should appear translucent. Remove from heat and cool before filling the prepared jar.

Yields 6 cups.

Sugar Syrup

Siwo Sik
Sirop de Sucre

Estimated time: 10 minutes.

1 cup granulated sugar
1 cup water

Mix sugar and water in a heavy 2-quart pan, and stir until sugar is completely dissolved. Boil over medium high heat for 6 to 7 minutes. Remove from heat. Cool at room temperature.

Yields about 1 1/2 cups.

Fresh Fruit Syrup

Siwo Fwi
Sirop de Fruits Frais

Excellent on ice cream, cakes, puddings, and pancakes, these fruit syrups are worthwhile to make. They can also be added to fruit salads, and to rum cocktails. They can be combined for a richer flavor.

Pineapple syrup and Pomegranate syrup (grenadine)

2 1/2 cups finely chopped fresh pineapple, or 3 cups fresh pomegranate seeds
1 cup water
1 cup granulated sugar

Pineapple syrup. Put pineapple in a blender with 1/2 cup of water (you may also use a 20-ounce can of pineapple in juice; use the juice instead of water). Process on medium speed for about 15 seconds. Strain twice through a fine strainer. Discard the residue.

Pomegranate syrup. Put the seeds in a blender with 1/2 cup of water. Process on medium speed for about 15 seconds. Strain twice through a fine strainer, pressing well on the residue. Discard residue.

Pour the fruit juice of your choice in a heavy 2-quart pan, stir in granulated sugar. Reduce uncovered, over medium heat, until syrup forms, about 5 minutes. Refrigerate until ready to use. After cooling, if syrup is too thick, mix in a small amount of water.

Yields about 2 cups.

Orange syrup, lime syrup, and passion fruit syrup

1 cup granulated sugar
1 cup water
1/4 cup strained fresh lime juice, or 1/3 cup strained fresh orange juice, or 1/3 cup fresh passion fruit juice*

Stir the sugar in the water to dissolve it completely. Boil over medium high heat for 10 minutes without stirring. Cool to room temperature. Mix in the fruit juice of your choice. Refrigerate until ready to use. After cooling, if syrup is too thick, mix in a small amount of juice.

Yields about 2 cups.

Orange-Ginger Syrup

1 cup granulated sugar
1 cup water
Zest of one orange, freshly peeled (be sure to take only the zest, not the pith)
3/4 to 1 teaspoon ground ginger
1/4 cup strained undiluted fresh orange juice

Make the sugar syrup as above. Remove from heat, add the zest and let steep until cool. Then discard the zest. Stir in the ginger and the orange juice. Refrigerate until ready to use.

Yields about 2 cups.

*To make fresh passion fruit juice, cut the fruit in half, spoon the pulp into a fine strainer over a bowl. Then strain, pressing well on the residue with the back of a spoon to express the juice.

Grated Coconut Candy

Tablèt Kòk Graje
Tablettes de Noix de Coco Râpée

Estimated time: 45 minutes (time to grate coconut not included).

2 cups granulated sugar
1 cup evaporated milk
One 14-ounce can sweetened condensed milk
Pinch of salt
1 cinnamon stick, or pinch of ground cinnamon
2 cups packed freshly grated coconut*

Lightly grease a large baking sheet. Set aside.

Mix sugar and evaporated milk in a heavy 3-quart saucepan. Mix in condensed milk, salt, cinnamon, and grated coconut. Bring to a boil over high heat. Reduce heat to medium and cook for 40 minutes, stirring and scraping the bottom of the pan often during the first 25 minutes, then constantly during the last 15 minutes to prevent scorching. The mixture should be very thick, and should turn a beautiful ivory color. Do not let it caramelize. Remove from heat. Drop by tablespoons on prepared baking sheet. Cool at room temperature. Will keep one week in an airtight container.

Yields about 30 Tablèt Kòk Graje.

Variation. The following quick version made with packaged coconut flakes takes only 20 minutes to prepare, and is also delicious.

2 cups granulated sugar
One 14-ounce can sweetened condensed milk

Pinch of salt
1 cinnamon stick, or pinch of ground cinnamon
3 cups packaged sweetened coconut flakes

Lightly grease a large baking sheet. Set aside. Mix sugar, condensed milk, salt, cinnamon, and coconut flakes in a heavy 2-quart saucepan, then boil over medium heat for 12 minutes, stirring and scraping the bottom of the pan constantly with a wooden spoon to prevent scorching. Mixture should be very thick, and should turn a beautiful ivory color. Do not let it caramelize. Remove from heat. Drop by tablespoons on prepared sheets. Cool at room temperature. Will keep one week in an airtight container.

Yields about 30 Tablèt Kòk Graje.

Variation. Use brown sugar instead to obtain golden candies.

*Make sure that the coconut is fresh and does not taste rancid. Use a vegetable peeler to remove the brown thin coat on the coconut.

Coconut Milk Candy

Dous Kokoye
Fondants au Lait de Coco

2 cups evaporated milk
2 cups sweetened cream of coconut*
2 cups granulated sugar
pinch of salt

Grease an 8 x 8 x 2-inch heat resistant dish. Set aside.

Mix all ingredients in a heavy 3-quart saucepan. Bring to a boil. Cook on medium heat for 35 to 40 minutes, stirring often, and stirring constantly toward the end. Remove from heat and pour immediately in the prepared dish. Cool for 20 minutes at room temperature. Cut into small squares or small irregular pieces. Will keep one week in an airtight container.

Yields about 25 to 30 pieces.

Note. To cut into regular shapes, allow the mixture to cool down a little, then use a greased sharp knife to cut while still warm.

*Cream of coconut is usually found in the drink section of groceries and supermarkets. Do not use the coconut cream made for pie filling. You may also use unsweetened cream of coconut.

Candied Coconut Slices

Tablèt Kokoy (Tablèt Gran Fèy)
Tablettes de Noix de Coco en Lamelles

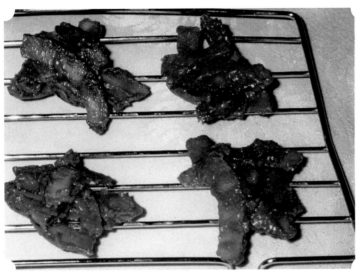

Estimated time: 1 hour 50 minutes.

1 coconut, thinly sliced (yields about 3 cups
  of thin slices)
1/2 cup fresh coconut milk (read *About
  Coconut* in *The Cook's Techniques* chapter)*
1 cup milk
1 1/2 cups brown sugar
1/4 cup (4 tablespoons) mild unsulphured
  molasses

Lightly grease a large baking sheet. Set
aside.

Put coconut with 10 cups of water in a heavy 5-quart pan. Bring to a boil. Reduce heat to medium and boil, covered, for 1 hour. Drain. Discard water.

Mix coconut milk, milk, sugar, and molasses in the same pan. Add coconut. Boil over high heat for 10 minutes, stirring occasionally. Coconut slices should be coated with a thick layer of syrup. Reduce heat to medium low. Stirring often with a wooden spoon, cook until the mixture becomes very sticky and coconut slices clump together, about 15 minutes. Drop by small portions on the prepared baking sheet. Cool at room temperature. When completely cool, the coconut slices should stick together to form a "tablet." Will keep one week in an airtight container.

Yields 10 Tablèt Kòkòy.

*Make sure that the coconut is fresh and does not taste rancid.

Pan Roasted Grated Coconut

Kòk Griye
Noix de Coco Grillée

This is another popular snack in Haiti. It is usually sold in small paper cones. It can also be used to garnish ice cream, or other desserts.

3 cups freshly grated coconut
3 cups water
3 cups brown sugar

Mix coconut and water in a 5-quart heavy pan. Boil over high heat for 8 minutes. Add sugar. Reduce heat to medium and cook for 30 minutes, stirring occasionally with a wooden spoon. At this point coconut should be caramelized; it should be sticky and should clump together. Continue to cook for about 10 additional minutes, stirring continuously and watching closely to avoid scorching. Coconut will gradually loose its stickiness and the flakes will separate. Remove from heat, and spread coconut on a large baking sheet to cool completely.

Yields about 3 1/2 cups.

Cashew Candy

Tablèt Nwa
Tablettes de Noix de Cajou

Traditionally, at least in the south of Haiti, each *Tablèt Nwa* and *Tablèt Pistach* are individually wrapped in pieces of dry banana leaves or dry plantain leaves. This prevents them from sticking to one another, and also prevents them from drying out. This is a home-style recipe.

Estimated time: 15 minutes.

1/2 cup evaporated milk
1/2 cup coconut milk
1 cup mild unsulphured molasses
1/4 cup brown sugar
3 cups unsalted roasted cashew nuts

Grease a cookie sheet. Set aside.

Mix milk, coconut milk, molasses, and sugar in a heavy 3-quart sauce pan. Boil over medium heat for 3 minutes, stirring often. Add nuts, and continue to cook for 10 additional minutes, stirring constantly. Remove from heat. The mixture should be very sticky. Immediately drop by tablespoons on the prepared sheet. Cool at room temperature. Wrap individually in small plastic bag. Will keep one week in an airtight container.

Yields about 20 Tablèt Nwa.

Peanut Candy

Tablèt Pistach
Tablettes de Cacahuètes (Tablettes d'Arachides)

Roast and peel peanuts days ahead, and store in a wax bag to keep them fresh. This is a home-style recipe.

Estimated time: 15 minutes (without roasting time).

3 cups shelled raw peanuts
1/2 cup evaporated milk
1/2 cup coconut milk
1 cup mild unsulphured molasses
1/4 cup brown sugar

Preheat oven to 325 degrees Fahrenheit. Arrange peanuts in a single layer on cookie sheet, and bake for 10 minutes. Cool them at room temperature, then shell. Discard the shells.

Grease a large cookie sheet, and set aside.

Mix milk, coconut milk, molasses, and sugar in a heavy 3-quart sauce pan. Boil over medium heat for 3 minutes, stirring often. Add nuts, and continue to cook for 10 additional minutes, stirring constantly. The mixture should be very sticky. Remove from heat. Immediately drop by tablespoons on prepared sheet. Cool at room temperature. Wrap individually in small plastic bags. Will keep one week in an airtight container.

Yields about 20 tablèts.

Caramelized Popcorn Balls

Bougonnen Mayi (Breton Mayi)
Boules de Maïs Soufflé Caramelisé

The addition of caramels to these popcorn balls makes them very appealing and delicious. They are a joy to children.

7 cups freshly popped popcorn	1/8 teaspoon salt
1 cup light brown sugar	1 cup water
1 1/2 tablespoons mild molasses	1/2 pound caramel cubes (about 30 pieces)

Place popped corn in a large heat-resistant bowl. Set aside. Lightly grease nine 12 x 10-inch sheets of waxed paper. Set aside.

Mix sugar, molasses, salt, and water in a heavy 2-quart pan. Boil over medium high setting for 5 minutes. Then reduce heat to medium. Stirring continuously, add caramels, and continue to boil syrup until caramels are melted, 3 minutes. Reduce heat to medium low, and continue to boil for 10 additional minutes, stirring frequently. Remove from heat and pour immediately over popped corn. Mix well to coat. Using a large greased spoon and a small greased spoon, put a small pile of caramelized popcorn in the middle of each waxed paper sheet. Bring the ends of each pieces of paper together and twist to shape into a small ball about 3 inches in diameter. Cool completely at room temperature before serving. The recipe can be doubled.

Yields about 9 popcorn balls.

MENUS

Tossed Salad

Following are more than thirty menus given as examples. There are numerous other ways to combine dishes to create other Haitian menus. You will find four menus for breakfast, a Haitian popular meal, one "Plat de Friture" menu, one menu for midnight supper, one menu for Holy Week, and twenty-eight menus for simple everyday dinners as well. Desserts are your choice. Very often, we conclude our dinner with a demi-tasse of the excellent Haitian coffee.

The very few dishes marked with an asterisk (*) are not included in this book.

Breakfast Menus

Stuffed Omelette, or Fried Eggs
Toasted bread and butter
Cantaloupe Salad*, or other fresh fruit
Akasan (AK 100)
Coffee

***

Scrambled Eggs, or Poached Eggs
Toasted bread and butter
Guava Preserve or Guava Jelly
Milk
Fresh fruit salad or a banana
Coffee

***

Creole Breakfast

Smoked Red Herring in Creole Sauce
Boiled Eggs (sliced), Avocado slices
Bread or boiled plantain
Fresh fruit juice (lime juice, papaya-lime juice, or orange juice)

***

New Year's Day or Sunday Breakfast

Pumpkin Soup
Toasted bread and butter
Milk
Fresh fruit or fresh fruit salad
Coffee

Haitian Popular Meal and "Plat de Friture"
Haitian Popular Meal

Potato, Beet, and Carrot Salad
Griyo with Sauce Ti Malice and Pikliz
Twice Fried Pressed Plantains
Rice and Beans (our national dish)
Dessert

***

Plat de Friture

A "Plat de Friture" (*Plat fritay* in Haitian Creole) is a fried food medley usually served at the beach, or anywhere when having a good time with friends and family. The following "Plat de Friture" is a lavish menu. A more frugal one often has only one kind of meat, frequently *Griyo*, may not include *Fried Breadfruit*, French fries, or *Fried Flat Bread*. *Plat de Friture* is usually served with avocado slices, and *Pikliz*. For this particular menu, I would suggest ice-cream for dessert, or *Rum-Caramel Custard*, or even a trifle.

Griyo, Tasso, Fried Fish
Twice Fried Pressed Plantains, Fried Sweet Potatoes, Fried Breadfruit, French Fries*
Meat Fritters, Malanga Croquettes, Fried Flat Bread
Sauce Ti Malice and Pikliz

Midnight Supper

In Haiti, there are two traditional midnight suppers, one on Christmas Eve and one on New Year's Eve. They usually last until dawn. The following is an example of menu served during those celebrations. They can be formal family suppers, but they are very often buffets for family and close friends. Throughout the event, consomme and/or stew is served. Before the end of the party, early in the morning, *Pumpkin Soup* is served, along with coffee and croissants or savory turnovers, or simply with coffee and toasted bread. The dinner on Christmas Day or New Year Day follows a similar but more rigid menu, and is a very formal family dinner.

***

Cocktail Hour

Rum Punch, Crémas, Ti Pike, aperitif, and sometimes Champagne
Vegetable Consommé,
and/or Vegetable stew
Akra, and/or Meat Fritters
Canapé and/or Choux with Seafood Filling

***

Main Menu

Table wine, Champagne
Vegetable Consommé, and/or Vegetable stew
Onion Quiche, and/or Seafood Quiche, and/or Quiche Lorraine*
Fish "Gwo Sèl" with
Twice Fried Pressed Plantains
Roast Turkey, Honey-Rum Glazed Ham with Pineapple, and Chicken in Creole Sauce
Tossed Salad* and Vinaigrette
Potato, Beet, and Carrot Salad, or Potato Salad
Macaroni au Gratin, and Creamy Corn au Gratin
Black Haitian Rice Ring, and/or Rice with Seafood Ring,
and Rice and Beans
Coconut and Cream Pudding
Christmas Log (for Christmas Eve), a layer cake, a charlotte*,
or a trifle* (New Year's Eve)
Coffee and Liqueurs

Holy Week Menu

More than ninety percent of Haitians are Catholics. In Haiti, Lent and Easter meals are unique, and are as special as Christmas and New Year's meals. Not only do we eat fish every Friday of Lent, but also we consume lots of vegetables and roots, and fish (mostly dried salt fish) during the Holy Week; everything is generously drizzled with olive oil. The following is an example of a menu usually served during the Holy Week.

Holy Week Salad
Boiled White Name Root
Boiled Plantains
Holy Week Cod, and/or Salt Fish, or Fish "Gwo Sèl"
Olive oil

Sometimes a dish of rice is added to the dinner. It can be White Rice served with a bean purée, Rice with Cod and Carrots, or Rice with Cod and Okra.

The habit of consuming fish on Fridays during Lent is so anchored in our tradition that many Haitian dinner tables display a dish of fish every Friday all year long.

We consider Easter Sunday a celebration as important as Christmas; the dinner menu is likewise close to the Christmas menu, with a table as abundant as possible.

Simple Dinner Menus

Trifle

Braised Spinach
Fish au Gratin
Boiled Plantains
Rice with Cod and Carrots
Dessert

***

Tossed Salad
Chicken with Green Peas
White Rice
Kidney Bean Purée
Dessert

***

Steamed Broccoli with Hollandaise Sauce
Avocado Slices
Salt Beef
Boiled Plantains, or Boiled Name Root
White Rice
Bean Purée
Dessert

***

Braised Greens with Pork and Crab
White Rice
Bean Purée (optional)
Dessert

***

Braised Chayote Squash with Pork
Boiled Plantains or Boiled Name Root
White Rice
Bean Purée (optional)
Dessert

***

Green crisp salad
Tasso
Twice Fried Pressed Plantains
Rice and Beans
Dessert

***

Watercress
Boiled Name Root
Avocado Salad
Tomato slices
Salt Fish
Rice with Green Peas
Dessert

***

Tomato Slices
Avocado Slices
Fish "Gwo Sel"
Twice Fried Pressed Plantains
Rice and Beans
Dessert

***

Tossed Salad
Chicken with Cashew Nuts
Twice Fried Pressed Plantains
Creamy Corn au Gratin
Rice with Green Peas and Carrots
Dessert

***

Lettuce and Tomato Salad
Conch in Creole Sauce
Creamy Cabbage au Gratin
Black Haitian Rice
Dessert

***

Green Crisp Salad
Pepper Steak
Scalloped Potatoes
Rice with Mixed Vegetables
Dessert

***

Lettuce Salad
Chicken in Creole Sauce
Boiled Plantains
White Rice
Kidney Bean Purée
Dessert

***

Potato Salad on Lettuce
Fish in Creole Court-Bouillon
White Rice
Kidney Bean Purée
Dessert

***

Tossed Salad
Roast Chicken
Mashed Potatoes Au Gratin
Black Haitian Rice
Dessert

***

Avocado Salad with Shrimp and Crab
Grilled lobster
Twice Fried Pressed Plantain
Black Haitian Rice
Dessert

***

Lettuce Salad
Chayote au Gratin
Chicken in Creole Sauce
White Rice
Green Pea Purée
Dessert

***

Tomato and Lettuce Salad
Roast Chicken
Creamy Corn au Gratin
Rice and Beans
Dessert

***

Tossed Salad
Sautéed Beef Tenderloin
Potatoes Sautéed with Butter and Garlic
Rice with Green Peas
Dessert

***

Crisp Green Salad
Fried Chicken
Twice Fried Pressed Plantain
Rice with Green Peas and Carrots
Dessert

***

Tomato and Lettuce Salad
Hen in Creole Sauce
Mashed Potatoes au Gratin
Rice and Beans
Dessert

***

Chicken with Vegetables
White Rice
Red Bean Purée
Macaroni au Gratin
Dessert

***

Green Salad
Turkey Drumsticks in Creole Sauce
White Rice
Kidney Bean Purée
Dessert

Avocado Salad
Cod with Potatoes in Creole Sauce
Rice with Seafood
Dessert

***

Tomato and Lettuce Salad
Pork Ragout
Boiled Name Root
White Rice
Bean Purée
Dessert

***

Creamy Spinach au Gratin
Conch in Creole Sauce
Boiled Name root
Rice with Cod and Carrots
Dessert

***

Tomato and Lettuce Salad
Pork in Creole Sauce
Creamy Carrots au Gratin
Rice with Green Peas
Dessert

***

Avocado Salad
Grilled Sardines with Hot Sauce
Twice Fried Pressed Plantains
Rice and Beans
Dessert

***

Green Salad
Beef Tongue in Creole Sauce
Scalloped Potatoes
Black Haitian Rice
Dessert

Tomato Slices
Avocado Slices
Fish "Gwo Sel"
Twice Fried Pressed Plantains
Rice and Beans
Dessert

***

Tossed Salad
Chicken with Cashew Nuts
Twice Fried Pressed Plantains
Creamy Corn au Gratin
Rice with Green Peas and Carrots
Dessert

***

Lettuce and Tomato Salad
Conch in Creole Sauce
Creamy Cabbage au Gratin
Black Haitian Rice
Dessert

***

GLOSSARY AND TIPS

Glosè ak Konsèy
Glossaire et Conseils

The vast majority of the products listed below are available worldwide. Nowadays, many supermarkets and groceries carry an array of fresh exotic products, and feature an ethnic section. A few specific products are found mainly in large ethnic communities (Caribbean, African, or Latin-American communities); for more information, check the Yellow Pages of cosmopolitan cities such as NYC, Miami, Chicago, Boston, Los Angeles, ... etc. In addition, some websites offer an extensive variety of exotic and ethnic products. The peak season is provided for every fruit and vegetable entry. Expensive out-of-season produce is often available in groceries. All entries are in English, Haitian Creole, and French, and in alphabetical order.

Avocado - Zaboka - Avocat

Called *zaboka* in Haitian Creole, avocado is a fruit that varies in size, color, shape, and looks. It can be round or oblong. It can be green to dark purplish brown. Its skin can be thick to thin, and smooth and shiny to bark-like. An avocado contains one seed, and can be easily peeled when ripe. Its flesh is yellow with an external yellowish green layer covered by a green to greenish brown coat depending on the color of its skin. It has nutty flavor with a hint of sweetness and a smooth texture. To use, cut all the slices lengthwise around the seed, detach them, then peel them. You may also cut the fruit in half lengthwise around the seed, and pull on one avocado half to remove it. The seed will stay attached to one of the halves. Firmly pierce the seed with a heavy sharp knife, then twist gently and pull the seed up. Slice avocado and peel the slices. To peel avocado slices, pinch the skin at one of the ends between the thumb and the tip of a blunt knife, and pull down on the skin. If the avocado is ready to be eaten, it will peel easily. The slices can then be cubed if desired. Once cut, avocado tends to discolor. To avoid that, sprinkle it with lime juice, or cut avocado just before using. When buying, choose those that are heavy, firm, unblemished, and can withstand gentle finger pressure. Usually they are still hard when displayed in the vegetable section of most supermarkets and groceries. Keep at room temperature for up to 3 days, depending on the stage of ripeness. Placing them in a brown paper bag hastens ripening. Avocado is found in most supermarkets, year-round.

Baste - Wouze - Arroser

To baste is to moisten periodically with a liquid while cooking. This is generally done when roasting meat. This can be done with a spoon, a brush, or a baster.

Blanch - Chode - Blanchir

To blanch is to immerse food briefly in boiling water.

Blend - Brase (mele, melanje) - Mélanger

To blend is to mix food together to form a uniform mixture. This can be done with a fork, a spoon, a whisk, an electric blender, ... etc.

Braise - Toufe - Braiser

To braise is to brown in fat and then cook in a small quantity of liquid in a tightly covered pan over medium-low heat. It can be a long process.

Breadfruit - Veritab (labveritab, lam) - Véritable

Breadfruit, called *veritab*, *labveritab*, or *lam* in Haitian Creole, is a large spherical, green, hard, and very fleshy fruit with rough patterned skin. It varies from 8 to 10 inches in diameter. It is very perishable and must be cooked the day of purchase. Otherwise, it becomes soft and unpleasantly sweet. Breadfruit can be immersed in a large container of cold water for one day if not to be used the day of purchase. Its flesh is cream-colored and contains many tiny seeds near the core. Cut in wedges with a strong knife, then core and peel. Like potatoes, it can be boiled, baked, mashed, fried, and grilled. When buying, choose those that are hard, heavy, unblemished, fully ripe but without a sweet smell. Breadfruit is found in Caribbean and Latin-American groceries. It is also available canned. Additional information is provided in *The Cook's Techniques*.

Cassava (yucca, tapioca) - Manyòk - Manioc

This tuber, called *manyòk* in Haitian Creole, has a tough, bright brown, and shiny skin. It is about 6 to 12 inches in length and 2 to 3 inches in diameter. Its flesh is white and crisp, and has a slightly fibrous core that is removed after cooking. There are two main varieties of cassava: sweet cassava and bitter cassava. Sweet cassava is cooked and eaten just like yams and potatoes. When boiled, cassava becomes somewhat crunchy and pale yellowish beige. Peel, and cut crosswise into 2 to 3 pieces if it is long. It can be an alternative to name root. The bitter cassava is used to make cassava flour (also called tapioca flour), cassava bread, and cassava meal. Because of its toxicity, the juice must be squeezed out of the bitter cassava before using. When buying, choose those that are hard, unblemished, and bright. Sweet cassava is displayed in the vegetable section of Caribbean and Latin-American groceries and markets, and some supermarkets, year round. Store in a cool, dark place for up to 7 days.

Chayote squash - Militon - Mirliton

This member of the gourd family, called *militon* in Haitian Creole, is pear-shaped and light green, dark green, or white. Its flesh is very pale and watery. It has a small whitish seed. Choose squash that are heavy, firm and bright without blemishes. Chayote squash are found in most supermarkets, year-round. Store in the refrigerator for up to 7 days.

Cherry, West Indies (acerola, Barbados cherry, Puerto Rican cherry) - Seriz - Cerise

Called *seriz* in Haitian Creole, these small fruits vary from 1/2 to 3/4 inch in diameter on average. When ripe, they are bright red, juicy, sweet with a hint of sourness, and they have a very refreshing taste. They can be very acidic, and in this case they are used only to make juice or preserves. They have a soft core. Wash to eat fresh, to make juice or preserve. They are very common in the Caribbean, and are also found in Florida. When buying, choose those that are firm without soft spots. They are usually available from May to November. Store in plastic bags in the refrigerator for up to 3 days.

Chestnut - Labapen - Marron (chataigne)

Chestnuts are called *labapen* in Haitian Creole. There are many varieties of chestnuts. In Haiti, the nuts are enclosed in a large fruit, also called labapen, that looks very much like breadfruit but with prickly skin. The fruit is filled with lots of brown nuts embedded in a cream-colored flesh. The ripened fruit is opened to pick the nuts out by hand. The nuts are boiled, then peeled. The peeled nuts are cream-colored and deliciously firm. They are eaten as a snack or added to meat dishes. The chestnuts found in Haiti are not available on the U.S. market. The chestnuts in the U.S. do not withstand boiling, and are somewhat powdery when roasted. Thus, they are not good substitutions for Haitian chesnuts.

Chile, habanero (habanero pepper, habanero chili) - Piman bouk - Piment

Called *piman bouk* or *piman pike*, or sometimes simply *piman* in Haitian Creole, this lantern-shaped chile is a member of the pepper family, and is among the hottest. Its size varies from 1 1/2 to 2 inches in length and 1 1/4 to 1 3/4 in diameter, on average. In Haiti, color usually varies from pale green to orange. Habanero chile is closely related to Scotch bonnet pepper and to Jamaican hot pepper. Choose peppers with their stems attached, that are shiny, smooth and firm without blemishes and soft spots. They are found in most supermarkets, year-round. Store for up to 7 to 10 days in the refrigerator, or in the freezer almost indefinitely. They become soft when thawed, but will not lose any flavor or hotness. Cut while still frozen. Additional information about habanero chile is provided in *The Cook's Techniques*. Also used in the traditional Haitian cooking is the fiery bird pepper, called *piman zwazo* in Haitian Creole. It is a very small finger-shaped pepper that is deep red when ripe.

Chop-Rache-Hacher

To chop is to cut an ingredient into small pieces with a heavy sharp tool.

Clove-Jiwòf-Girofle

Called *jiwòf* in Haitian Creole, this pungent spice is very common in Haitian cuisine. It is the dried, nail-shaped, unopened, dark reddish-brown flower bud of an evergreen tree. Available whole or ground, this aromatic spice is used sparingly because of its sharpness and its overwhelming flavor. If used correctly, it blends beautifully with other spices and herbs. Usually one whole clove mashed with other spices, or just a pinch of ground cloves is enough. Contrary to peppercorns, cloves do not seem to loose any flavor when ground in advance. Clove is available in the spice section of groceries and supermarkets.

Coconut - Kokoye (kòk) - Noix de coco

Called *kokoye* or *kòk* in Haitian Creole. The thick, dry, and fibrous husk has been removed from the coconut on store shelves, where it appears with a very hard, hairy, dark brown shell. Coconut is filled with a refreshing "coconut water." The flesh of the mature fruit is hard, white, sweet, and tightly coated with a thin brown layer. Coconut is found in most groceries and supermarkets, year-round. Although there is no obvious sign indicating that the coconut has gone bad, choose

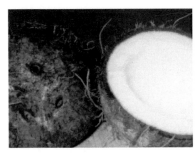

those that are heavy for their size, full of liquid, and whose "eyes" are not moldy. Young coconut, called *kòk ole* or *kokoye ole* in Haitian Creole, is available in some Asian, Caribbean, and Latin-American groceries, and via some websites. Its shell is flexible and its flesh is tender, making it easy to handle. The flesh of the youngest coconut is gelatinous; it may be eaten with a spoon right out of the shell or used in drinks. Additional information is provided in *The Cook's Techniques.*

Cod, salt - Mori (lanmori) - Morue salée

Called *mori* or *lanmori* in Haitian Creole, salt cod has been soaked in a solution of salted water, then dried. It must be soaked in fresh water before using. Salt cod is found in Caribbean and Latin-American groceries, and also in some specialty Italian import stores. It is also called bacalao in Spanish, and baccala in Italian. A very simple and good salt cod recipe is given in the *Special Condiments* chapter, and a method of soaking is given in *The Cook's Techniques* chapter.

Conch - Lambi - Conque

Called *lambi* in Haitian Creole, conch is a tropical marine mollusk living in a pinkish, pearly, spiral shell. It tastes like clams and has about the same consistency. In Haiti, it is never prepared with lime which is believed to toughen the flesh. It is instead prepared with bitter orange. Lime juice is added only when conch is cooked and already tender. Conch flesh is tough; it must be tenderized by butterflying and by pounding with a meat hammer before cooking. Conch is available fresh or frozen. Choose fresh conch that are firm and have a fresh smell. Buy them frozen if you do not have the choice. Conch is found in specialty fish stores, and is quite expensive. Conch can also be ordered via some websites.

Custard apple (sugar apple) - Kachiman - Cahiman

This delicious tropical fruit is called *kachiman* in Haitian Creole. The fruit is creamy and delicious with numerous shiny dark seeds. There are two varieties of custard apples in Haiti. One, *kachiman kè bèf* in Creole, is the size of a large apple, with a tan patterned skin. It can be eaten out of the skin with a spoon, and is also used to make juice. The other, called *kachiman bouton* because it has very bumpy skin, is green and smaller. This variety is eaten as is. Custard apples are available in supermarkets and groceries usually from November to May. The ripe fruit can be stored in the refrigerator for up to 3 days.

Deep-fry. Fri lan anpil gres. Grande friture

To deep-fry a food is to cook it by immersing in a deep pan of hot fat or oil.

Deglaze - Dekrase - Dégalcer

To deglaze is to remove all the cooking juice that remains in the pan after food (generally meat) has been cooked, using a small amount of liquid. Pour the liquid (water, wine, broth, stock, or juice) into the pan, simmer shortly over low heat stirring frequently.

Devein - Wete venn - Enlever les boyaux

To devein a shrimp is to remove the grayish black vein from the back of the shrimp. This can be done with the tip of a pointed knife. The grayish black vein is the intestine.

Dice - Rache piti - Couper en petits dés

To dice is to cut food into small cubes or squares, usually 1/8 to 1/4 inch. Dicing gives more uniform pieces than chopping or mincing, but diced food is not as fine as minced food. To dice, cut the ingredients into regular strips, then cut the strips crosswise.

Eggplant (garden egg) - Berejenn - Aubergine

Called *berejenn* in Haitian Creole, the most common eggplant is a large purple, drop-like fruit that has a thin, shiny, and smooth skin, and contains lots of tiny seeds. Its flesh is cream-colored. Skin, flesh, and seeds are edible. Choose eggplants that are heavy, shiny, firm, and without blemishes. Eggplant is very perishable. Store in refrigerator up to 5 days. Although a fruit, it is eaten as a vegetable, and found in the vegetable section of most groceries and supermarkets, year-round.

Fish, salt - Pwason sale (pwason seche) - Poisson salé

Called *pwason sale* or *pwason seche* in Haitian Creole, salt fish is any kind of fish that has been salted, then dried. Salt fish must be soaked in water before using. It is found in Caribbean, African, and Latin-American groceries. Generally, when we refer to salt fish in Haiti, we do not include either salt cod or smoked herring, which are instead referred to by their specific names.

Fold - Vlope - Incorporer en pliant

To fold is to combine ingredients by turning gently one ingredient over another, mixing them in the process.

Ginep (mamoncillo, Spanish lime, genip, honey berry) - Kenèp - Quenèpe

These delicious fruits are called *kenèp* in Haitian Creole. They are spherical, sometimes slightly oblong, about the size of a large grape. They grow in clusters just like grapes. Their shell-like skins are olive-green. When very ripe and ready to use, their skin may show a few light brown spots. Their semitransparent flesh is juicy, soft, peach-colored, sweet, with a hint of sourness. They contain one round seed that is big for the size of the fruit. In Haiti, they are eaten fresh or used to make *Ti Pike*. To eat, wash, crack the skin between your teeth, discard the skin, then suck on the fruit to detach the pulp. Discard the round seed. Do not give *ginep* to small children, because they can choke on the seed.

Guava - Gwayav - Goyave

Called *gwayav* in Haitian Creole, these fruits are generally round or oblong, and vary in size from of a lemon to the size of a small apple. They have a thin edible skin that is pale green or yellow when the fruit is ripe. Flesh is pale yellow, pink, or white with a fine grainy texture. They contain lots of tiny, ivory seeds in a smooth core. Choose unblemished, firm, and delicately fragrant fruit. Let ripen completely at room temperature. Once ripe, they are very fragrant. They are found in Caribbean, African, and Latin-American groceries and markets, usually from April to December. Store ripe guava in the refrigerator for up to 4 days.

Herring, smoked red - Aran sò - Hareng saur

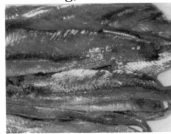

Called *aran sò* in Haitian Creole, smoked red herring is a saltwater fish that has been salted, smoked, and dried. It has a very distinctive smell and taste. It is found, whole or in filets, in Caribbean and Latin-American groceries and markets. Additional information is provided in *The Cook's Techniques*.

Lobster, spiny (Caribbean Lobster, Rock Lobster) - Woma - Langouste

Commonly referred to as rock lobster, spiny lobster is called *woma* in Haitian Creole, and is the only lobster available in Haiti. Like other lobsters, this expensive member of the crustacean family has an articulated body but it has no claws. It is available in fish stores and some groceries and supermarkets. If not available, use another kind of lobster available in the USA. Additional information is provided in *The Cook's Techniques*.

Malanga (yautia, tannia) and taro root - Malanga ak mazoumbel - Malanga et mazoumbelle

Also called *malanga* in Haitian Creole, malanga is smaller than name root, about the size of a large potato. It has a yellowish brown, fuzzy-looking skin crossed by lighter circles. Flesh is white and slippery when raw, but when cooked, it has a delicious creamy texture and a nutty flavor. Malanga is sometimes confused with taro root.

Taro root, also known as *dasheen*, is called *mazoumbèl* in Haitian Creole, and looks like *malanga*. However, taro can vary from 6 to more than 12 inches long and can be very broad. When cooked it has a delicious nutty flavor, and there is a variety of taro root that becomes pale grayish purple after cooking. The edible taro leaves, called *fèy mazoumbèl* or *kenlenbe* in Haitian Creole, and *callaloo* in other parts of the Caribbean, are used as spinach.

When choosing malanga or taro, look for those that are very firm and unblemished. They are found in the vegetable section of Caribbean, and Latin-American groceries and markets, and some supermarkets, year-round. Store malanga and taro in a cool dark place for up to 7 days. Additional information is provided in *The Cook's Techniques*.

Mango - Mango (mang) - Mangue

Called *mango* or *mang* in Haitian Creole, this delicious tropical fruit has a smooth thin skin that is usually yellow, sometimes with shades of red, when ripe. It has a juicy, sweet, yellow flesh with sometimes a soupçon of tartness. Among others, Mangue Madame Francisque (*mango madan fransik, mango fransik*), Mangue Baptiste (*mango batis*), and *mango kòn* are three varieties that deserve to be mentioned. *Mango blan* is a variety of mango which stays green even when ripened. To use, peel, then slice and discard seed and skin. There are countless varieties of mangos. Some of them, excessively juicy like mango kòn, cannot withstand slicing and have to be eaten as is. Choose *mangos* that are firm, smooth, and unblemished. They are found in the fruit section of groceries and supermarkets, usually from May to September. Store in the refrigerator for up to 5 days.

Mince - Rache piti-piti - Hacher menu (émincer)

To mince is to cut an ingredient into very small pieces.

Mushroom, Haitian - Djondjon - Champignon haïtien

This variety of small sun-dried mushrooms, called *djondjon* in Haitian Creole, is dark brown and very fragrant. It gives foods with which it is cooked a surprising black color, and a delicious flavor and aroma. They are worth a trip to the grocery. Choose mushrooms that are dry and have a fresh smell. They are expensive. They may need sorting and trimming but do not wash them; boil them for 20 minutes over medium heat in a covered pan with lid slightly ajar, then let them steep for at least 20 minutes. Strain and use the black liquid. Store the mushrooms in a cool and dry place. They will stay fresh for a very long time if they are put in a wax bag, then placed in an airtight container and refrigerated.

Name root (yam) - Yanm - Igname

Called *yanm* in Haitian Creole, this tuber has a rough brown skin. There are several varieties of yams; one of the Haitians' favorites is the *yanm franse blan*. Size can vary from less than 4 inches to more than 12 inches long. Flesh is slippery and white or cream-colored, not sweet at all (as opposed to sweet potatoes). To use, peel and rub with lime, then rinse under fresh running water. Place in a bowl of water mixed with fresh lime juice until ready to use. When cooked, texture can vary from firm and compact to powdery, depending on the variety. Name root has a nutty flavor but not as pronounced as malanga. Choose roots that are firm and unblemished. Name root is found in the vegetable section of Caribbean and Latin-American groceries, and in some supermarkets, year-round. Store in a cool and dark place for up to 7 days. More information is given in *The Cook's Techniques*.

Okra - Kalalou - Gombo (Gumbo)

Also known as Lady's Finger, okra called *kalalou* in Haitian Creole, is a small, oblong, and

bright green pod divided lengthwise by small ridges and covered by tiny soft hairs. Okra is filled with rows of tiny beige seeds. When cooked, it produces a very thick liquid. Okra is used to make stews, and sometimes used to make an infusion called *tizàn* or *rafrechi* in Haitian Creole. Choose pods that are firm, without blemishes, and less than 4 inches long. Okra is found fresh in most supermarkets, year-round. It is also available canned or frozen. Store in the refrigerator for up to 2 days.

Orange, bitter (sour orange, Seville orange) - Zoranj si - Orange amère

This variety of orange called *zoranj si* in Haitian Creole is used in Haiti whenever red meat is prepared. It has a thick and sometimes bumpy skin with a strong zest, and a bitter-sour taste. It must be peeled and seeded before using because of its strong tasting zest. Choose heavy and firm fruits without blemishes just as for other varieties of oranges. It is found in Caribbean and Latin-American groceries and supermarkets. If bitter orange is not available, lemon is a good alternative (not lime); it must be peeled and seeded too.

Papaya (paw-paw) - Papay - Papaille

This fleshy yellow fruit is called *papay* in Haitian Creole. It is oblong with thin skin, thick smooth and delicious yellow or reddish yellow flesh, and lots of little black seeds. It can vary from 7 to more than 12 inches long. When using, peel the fruit and discard the skin. Then cut papaya in half, and scoop out and discard the seeds. If papaya is not well ripened, it tastes bitter. Choose fruits with smooth skin that are yellow and firm. Papaya is found in the fruit section of most supermarkets and groceries, year-round. Refrigerate for up to 4 days.

Passion fruit - Grenadia - Fruit de la passion

This tropical fruit, called *grenadia* in Haiti, has shell-like skin and is filled with small seeds that have black cores embedded in bright yellow, succulent, and sweet-sour pulp. There are a yellow variety (found in Haiti) and a purple one. Both have a yellow pulp and the same delicious taste reminiscent of guava, pineapple, and lime, with guava being strongest flavor. When ripe, their skins are wrinkled. To use, cut in half and spoon the moist pulp out of the shell. Choose fruits that are wrinkled and unblemished. Passion fruits are found in the fruit section of most groceries and supermarkets, usually from January to July. Store in a refrigerator for a few days.

Pea, Congo (Pigeon Pea, No-eyed Pea) - Pwa Kongo - Pois Congo

Called *Pwa Kongo* in Haitian Creole, this variety is about the size of a green pea but not as round or green. It is greyish green and greyish beige with occasionally a few reddish brown spots. It is available dried and split in many supermarkets and often fresh and frozen in Latin-American and Indian markets. It can also be found canned (poor alternative).

Pineapple - Anana - Ananas

Called *anana* in Haitian Creole, this very fragrant and delicious fruit looks like a huge pine cone, thus its name. Its bumpy and diamond-patterned skin is usually bright golden yellow, or golden orange. There is a variety of pineapple with green skin even when ripe, the sugar loaf (*anana penn sic* in Haitian Creole). Pineapple flesh is somewhat fibrous, very juicy, sweet with a soupçon of sourness. To use, brush carefully under fresh running water, then peel the fruit whole. Remove the "eyes" with a sharp pointed knife, then slice crosswise, and core each slice separate separately with a 1-inch cookie cutter. You may use a pineapple slicer as well, or quarter the whole fruit, then core and peel by section. The handling technique depends on the utilization. Choose fruits that are very fragrant, bright in color, unblemished, and with deep green and stiff leaves. To store, refrigerate ripe pineapple in a plastic bag for up to 3 days. Pineapple is available fresh year-round in the fruit section of most supermarkets; it is also available canned.

Pinch - Priz - Pincée
A pinch is the amount that can be held between the tips of the thumb and the tip of the forefinger.

Plantain - Bannann fran (bon bannann, bannann konn bèf) - Banane platain

Plantain, called *bannann fran, bon bannann, bannann konn bèf*, or *bannann miske* (the smaller one) in Haitian Creole, looks a lot like a large banana. It is sometimes referred to as cooking plantain. There is more than one variety of plantain. Generally, plantains have thick ridged green skin and pinkish yellow starchy flesh with tiny dark seeds along the core. Skin becomes dark yellow when ripe. If you are making a recipe with sweet plantains, buy them as ripe as possible (you may need to place them in a paper bag for 1 to 2 days), or buy green ripe plantains, and place them in a paper bag for 5 to 6 days. Check often to avoid over-ripeness. Chose green plantains that are firm. Although a fruit, plantains is eaten as a vegetable and found in the vegetable section of most groceries and supermarkets, year-round. Additional information is provided in *The Cook's Techniques*.

Plantain press - Pèz bannann - Presse-banane

This utensil called *Pèz bannann* in Haitian Creole, is the key tool in making *Bannann Peze*. It is made out of two pieces of wood attached with two hinges. Each piece of wood is about the size of an adult hand. *Pèz bannann* is found in Caribbean and Latin-American groceries. A tortilla press is a good alternative to a plantain press.

Pomegranate - Grenad - Grenade

Called *grenad* in Haitian Creole, this is a round fruit with a distal end topped with a crown-like extension. It is about the size of a small orange and its skin is thin and leatherlike. When ripe, it is red filled with a myriad of glassy red seeds, or pinkish yellow with a myriad of glassy pink seeds. The yellow variety is available in Haiti. The edible parts of the fruit are the glassy seeds, which have an ivory and crunchy core, set in sections divided by bitter pale yellow membranes. Cut in half and remove the seeds. In Haiti, pomegranate is eaten fresh or used to make grenadine. Choose fruits that are firm, heavy, bright, and free of blemishes. Pomegranates are available from October through November and can be stored in the refrigerator for 1 to 2 months.

Potato, sweet - Patat (patat dous) - Patate

Sweet potatoes are called *patat* or *patat dous* in Haitian Creole. There is more than one variety and the Haitians' favorite is the "white sweet potato," also called *boniato*, and sometimes referred to as "dry-flesh sweet potato." Its thin skin is reddish purple and its flesh is very pale green, or white. Flesh is dry, crumbly, almost powdery, and smooth when cooked. It can be cooked with or without its skin, depending on its use. This variety is found mostly in Caribbean and Latin-American groceries, usually from April to December-January. It can be stored in a cool dry place for a few days.There is a very moist variety of sweet potato, called yam in the U. S.A., with dark orange skin and orange flesh. In fact, this variety is not related to the yam plant. It is widely found in groceries and supermarkets, year-round. In Haiti this variety is called *patat jonn* and is much smaller than the one found in the U.S.A. When buying any kind of sweet potato, choose small to medium tubers that are hard and unwrinkled.

Pudding mold - Moul poudin - Moule à pudding

This 3-piece utensil is in fact a double-boiler with a fitted inset shaped like a tube pan. If you do not have a pudding mold, you can create your own. Use a tube pan that fits into a tightly covered pot. Grease and fill the tube pan with the pudding mixture as indicated in the recipe. Cover the pan with aluminum foil. Fasten the foil with kitchen thread. Place a steamer basket in the pot. Put water in the pot almost touching the steamer basket, then place the tube pan on the steamer basket, and cover the pot. Then steam as directed in the recipe, checking water level every hour or so. In this book, a 6-cup pudding pan is used when this utensil is required.

Pummelo (pomelo, shaddock, Chinese grapefruit) - Chadèk - Chadèque (pamplemousse)

Called *chadèk* in Haitian Creole, pomelo is one of the largest citrus fruits, if not the largest. It is also referred to as Adam's apple. This pear-shaped or round fruit has a fairly thick, green or yellow zest over a very thick whitish and bitter pith. It is eaten fresh or used to make juice and preserves. Chose heavy, firm, and unblemished fruits. Available usually from November through March in the fruit section of supermarkets. Keep at room temperature for up to one week, or store in the refrigerator for up to 2 weeks.

Pumpkin, West Indian (calabaza squash) - Jouwoumou (joumou) - Giraumon

Called *jouwoumou* or *joumou* in Haitian Creole, this round squash ranges from green to cream to light orange in color. It can be as small as a cantaloupe, or as large as a watermelon. It is extremely popular throughout the Caribbean. In Haiti we use it to make *Pumpkin Soup*, to make a dish called *Jouwoumounad*, and sometimes, we add it to *Congo Pea Purée*. Its skin is hard, and in Haiti people peel it before cooking, but it can be cooked unpeeled. Just like other squash, it contains lots of small seeds. Flesh is firm, bright orange, with a sweet butternut-like flavor. Pumkin can be baked, boiled, or steamed just like acorn squash. Choose heavy unblemished pumkins with their stems still attached. West Indian pumpkins are found in the vegetable section of Caribbean, African, and Latin-American groceries and markets, and are usually available year-round. They can also be found pre-cut in chunks. Store whole pumpkins in a cool place for up to 15 days, and cut pumpkin in plastic wrap and refrigerate for up to 7 days.

Purée - Moulen (kraze) - Purer

To purée is to transform solid food into a thick and pulpy liquid. This can be done with a blender, a mortar, or by forcing food through a mill or a strainer. Purée can be thinned by the addition of liquid.

Reduce - Seche - Réduire

To reduce is to concentrate liquid by boiling, thus thickening and intensifying flavor.

Saute - Sote (Fri lan you ti grès) - Sauter

To saute is to fry food quickly in a small amount of very hot (not smoking) fat.

Sorrel - Lozèy - Oseille

Called *lozèy* in Haitian Creole, and mainly used in Pumpkin Soup, sorrel is a perennial herb with leaves like those of spinach in the USA. There are many variety of sorrel, each having a certain degree of sourness. One of the more sour varieties is garden sorrel, also called Belleville sorrel, sourdock, and sourgrass. Choose sorrel with bright green fresh leaves. Very perishable, sorrel is found in some supermarkets, in limited supply.

Soursop (guanabana) - Kowosòl - Corossol

 This oblong fruit, called *kowosòl* in Haitian Creole, has a thin, dark olive skin covered with soft spines. When ripe, it feels slightly soft when pressed. It is delicious, exceedingly juicy, and sweet with a touch of sourness. The fibrous pulp and thick juice are white. About two or three times the size of a small papaya, the fruit contains lots of black and shiny seeds that are believed to be toxic, and in a white, moist edible membrane. Soursop is used to make juice and ice cream, or is eaten fresh as it is. To make juice, peel and discard the skin and the core, then press the pulp through a large strainer to express as much juice as possible. Mix a small amount of water with the residue, and work again through the strainer. To make juice for ice cream, use the undiluted soursop juice (do not add water).

Stir-fry - Fri lan you ti grès pandan w ap brase - Faire revenir dans de l'huile

To stir-fry is to fry quickly in a small amount of oil while stirring continuously.

Taro root (dasheen) - Mazoumbèl - Mazoumbelle

See Malanga.

Truss - Mare (bride) - Trousser (brider)

To truss a fowl is to attach its wings and legs to the body before cooking so it keeps its shape during cooking (roasting). Trussing a fowl makes it neater and more presentable. There is more than one way to truss a bird, but here is an easy way: Tie the tips of the legs together with a piece of kitchen thread. Twist the tips of the wings under the back of the fowl, then attach the skin of the neck to the back with a skewer. Et voila! The bird is now ready to be roasted. When ready to serve, remove the thread and the skewer.

MORE TIPS

Recipe

Recipe names are in English, Haitian Creole, and French. However a few recipes have only Creole names (*Papita, Kabich, Konparèt, Griyo, Moustache*, . . . etc.). Recipes should be read entirely before using.

Timing

In this book the cooking times are calculated for an electric oven. For other types of ovens, times may vary slightly. Sometimes the time varies slightly from oven brand to oven brand. Cooking time varies also with the condition of the dripping pans under the burners. It also depends on the type and quality of the cooking ustensil you use. Always check the dish you are cooking, especially toward the end of the cooking time.

Sizes and measures

Pot and pan sizes are given. It is usually acceptable if they are slightly bigger, except for desserts and confections. All measures are level, if not otherwise specified.

Substitutions

Because of the availability of exotic and ethnic products on the American market, substitutions are rarely needed. However, when it is necessary and when possible, I indicate the potential substitute in the recipe. Also take advantage of the comprehensive Glossary included.

Salt

I used table salt in all the recipes because of its availability. Haitian traditional cooking uses sea salt. You may use sea salt, or kosher salt. They are excellent substitutions available in most supermarkets and groceries. Keep in mind that sea salt is saltier than table salt and kosher salt.

Garlic

Use regular garlic, not "elephant garlic". Because garlic cloves vary so much in size, one garlic clove yields one teaspoon of crushed garlic in this book. For example, if a recipe asks for 3 garlic cloves, you may use 3 teaspoons of crushed garlic instead. Garlic is called *lay* in Haitian Creole and *ail* in French.

Lime

Although key limes (West Indian lime) are used in Haiti, I use Persian limes which are bigger, less sour, and easier to handle. You may use key limes, but keep in mind that they are more sour than Persian limes. Lime is called *sitwon* in Haitian Creole and *citron vert* in French.

Bitter orange

If bitter orange is not available, lemon is a good alternative (not lime).

Chives

Chives cultivated in Haiti are wild variety called *siv* in Haitian Creole that is not available in U.S.A.. I substitute the chives carried by most groceries, or use scallions.

Cheese

The cheese commonly used to make gratins in Haiti is very aged Dutch cheese, Edam 40+, popularly called *Fromage Tete de Maure* and *fwomaj tèt mò*. It is hard, delicious, and extremely sharp. Because aged Edam cheese is not usually available in U.S., I use a mixture of Parmesan and extra sharp cheddar. Both cheeses are available at any grocery and supermarket. If using the Edam 40+, you will not need as much as the Parmesan-cheddar mixture.

Rum

The excellent dark Haitian rum (Rhum Barbancourt), highly praised by connoisseurs is used in this book. If it is not readily available, you may substitute any good dark rum or a good brandy or cognac.

Onion shavings

Remove and discard the papery onion skin, then cut off the top. Use a sharp knife to cut very thin slices of onion crosswise. The semi-transparent thin slices are the shavings.

INDEX

Since the table of contents is very detailed, I have enclosed in this index only the variations of certain recipes and other recipes that do not appear in the table of contents. The index will help you locate them easily, and will also allow you to locate other useful hints.